CW00433674

My So-Called

PUNK

My So-Called PUNK

Green Day, Fall Out Boy, the Distillers, Bad Religion—
How Neo-Punk Stage-Dived into the Mainstream

MATT DIEHL

 ST. MARTIN'S GRIFFIN ✺ NEW YORK

For my "punk family": my mother, Carol Diehl, who turned me
on to punk in the first place; my punk godfather, Ric Addy; and
Greg Dulli, who's proven to be the most punk ever—
maybe by not being "punk" at all . . .

MY SO-CALLED PUNK. Copyright © 2007 by Matt Diehl. All rights reserved. Printed in
the United States of America. No part of this book may be used or reproduced in any
manner whatsoever without written permission except in the case of brief quotations
embodied in critical articles or reviews. For information, address St. Martin's Press,
175 Fifth Avenue, New York, N.Y. 10010.

www.stmartins.com

Design by Phil Mazzone

Library of Congress Cataloging-in-Publication Data

Diehl, Matt.
    My so-called punk : Green Day, Fall Out Boy, the Distillers, Bad Religion : how
neo-punk stage-dived into the mainstream / Matt Diehl. — 1st ed.
        p. cm.
    Includes bibliographical references (p. 243)
    ISBN-13: 978-0-312-33781-0
    ISBN-10: 0-312-33781-7
    1. Punk rock music—History and criticism. 2. Green Day (Musical group).
3. Fall Out Boy (Musical group). 4. Distillers (Musical group). 5. Bad Religion
(Musical group). I. Title.

ML3534.D54 2007
781.66—dc22

                                                              2006051074

First Edition: April 2007

10 9 8 7 6 5 4 3 2 1

CONTENTS

Contents

Acknowledgments

First and foremost, I'd like to thank the bands that agreed to be interviewed for this book. In particular, I want to thank Brody Dalle and Tony Bevilacqua for truly opening up throughout this process—and Ian MacKaye for fulfilling a long-held dream. From the execs (a word I never thought I'd type in conjunction with "punk") I can't appreciate enough the time that Kevin Lyman, Brett Gurewitz, Lawrence Livermore, and Chris Appelgren gave to this project. Others who made invaluable contributions and to whom thanks are due: Hector Martinez, Hilary Villa, Alexis Henry, and Sue Lucarelli at Epitaph Records; Vanessa and Fat Mike at Fat Wreck; Karen Wiessen at Island/Def Jam; Kristine Ashton-Magnuson and Libby Henry at MSO PR; Sue Marcus at Stunt Company; Brian Bumbery at Warner Bros.; Lisbeth Cassaday and Amy DeRouen at Lava/Atlantic; my brilliant counsel, Jamie Feldman and Jonathan Shikora; Jed Weitzman and Sanctuary; Jeffrey Light of Myman, Abell, Fineman, Greenspan & Light; Arthur Spivak; Matthew Guma/Guma Agency; Mike Brillstein and Adam Lublin; my family (especially my father, Lawrence Diehl); Wendy Yao; Rich Green and Gregory McKnight from CAA; the HAPPY diaspora; Jennifer Vogelmann at mPRm Public Relations; Missy Suicide and the SGs; Virgin Records' publicity department; Rose Hilliard, Abbye Simkowitz, and the Internet geniuses at St. Martin's; Todd Roberts and family; David J. Prince and Ariel Borow; Anthony Bozza; Susan Golomb, Casey, Corey and all at Susan Golomb Agency; Derrick Parker; Eddie Rehfeldt and family; Steve Nalepa; Ray Rogers; Steve Garbarino; Stephen Mooallem;

Bill Vourvoulias, Ingrid Sischy; Brad Goldfarb; Adam Shore; Serena Kim and family; Anthony DeCurtis; Sophia Nardin; Tony Chan; Jason Fine, Joe Levy, Nathan Brackett, Jonathan Ringen, and all at *Rolling Stone*... The list goes on and on: If I forgot you, I apologize—you're in here somewhere...

My So-Called
PUNK

Meet the new punk.

Same as the old punk?

This was the question rattling through my head as I interviewed Lars Frederiksen backstage at the 1997 Tibetan Freedom Concert. Lars Frederiksen is the guitarist and vocalist for Rancid. Rancid is not the biggest of the first wave of neo-punk bands to stage-dive into the pop music mainstream in the mid-1990s; that distinction would belong to Green Day and The Offspring. But Rancid may be neo-punk's most important voice: since its inception, the band has always served as current punk's heart and soul, its conscience—the torchbearers for *real* punk today.

Indeed, while Rancid has sold hundreds of thousands of records and are worldwide stars—their breakthrough, 1995's . . . *And Out Come the Wolves* has sold over a million copies—they've maintained a raggedy persona, as if they've just rolled out of the gutter circa 1983. As such, in between questions about how rock stars can help end Chinese repression of Tibetan Buddhism, I mention to Lars that he's dressed just as I might have a decade and a half earlier during my mid-'80s punk heyday.

In fact, with his "liberty-spiked" hair (shellacked into vertical points that resemble those of the Statue of Liberty's tiara), studded belts, drainpipe-straight black trousers, and thick-soled "creeper" shoes, he's dressed just as I used to. In fact, I note to him that I even owned the same stringy neon-colored mohair sweater and U.K. Subs badge back in the day. At this, Lars visibly rolls his eyes.

"Yeah," he responds with disdain, "but *I'm* still wearing 'em."

Silence.

Immediately, I knew what Lars is saying. Between the lines, he's implying, basically, that *I* sold out—that I haven't kept the flame of punk alive, *maaaan* . . . I don't mention that *he's* the rock star, the one playing to a sold-out crowd—tens of thousands of people at Downing Stadium on New York's Randall's Island (although admittedly for a cause). When I was a punk, there were no stadium-filling punk bands. Such a thing didn't exist.

Funny how times change. And how some things stay the same.

When I first got into punk rock back in the day, it wasn't yet big business like it is now; it wasn't on the *radio*. Green Day hadn't won a Grammy yet; The Offspring hadn't sold tens of millions of albums; the Warped tour wasn't the most successful, longest-running package tour in music-industry history. They didn't sell punk clothes at mall stores like Hot Topic, or on the Internet. There was no Internet. You certainly didn't see pop-punk bands constantly on MTV; in fact, MTV didn't even *exist* yet.

"We didn't start playing music to win trophies or anything," Green Day drummer Tré Cool told *Entertainment Weekly*, with appropriate "core" punk modesty. "But it feels really fuckin' good to be appreciated." But is "being appreciated" to the tune of a gazillion records sold mean selling out? It's a question that's plagued punk rock for decades—at least as long as I've been into punk, which is, yes, decades. When it comes to punk rock's beginnings, *I* was sorta there. And I was there when punk rock went big business, too. Ever since, I've been trying to piece together how this all came about, which has led to this book: perhaps seeing the origins of the punk era through my eyes—and the subjects of this book—will go some length to showing just where we've landed today in punk rock history.

I first got into punk in 1977, at the age of 9. My mother, having divorced my father around that time, had moved to New York City to pursue a career as an artist. The New York art and punk worlds were symbiotic at that time, and my mom did her share of hanging around early punk venues like CBGB, Mudd Club, and Peppermint Lounge.

On one early visit, she gave me the Sex Pistols' *Never Mind the Bollocks* and the first Suicide album; I was never quite the same after that. But it was when my mom took me in 1979 to see Johnny Thunders and the Heartbreakers at Club 57 that everything changed. Punk rock had entered, and permanently altered, my life.

Johnny Thunders was the guitarist for the proto-punk greats the New York Dolls, and was venerated by the early punks as a major influence. Thunders's chunky, confrontational barre-chord rhythm guitar style would be borrowed wholesale by the Sex Pistols. Later, his junkie outlaw persona and classicist fondness for early, rough-and-tumble rock and roll would be appropriated by the likes of Social Distortion, among others.

As an awkward adolescent, however, I found Thunders's don't-give-a-fuck abandon exhilarating: he made as much noise as he wanted, looked weird, and everyone loved him. Slinging his guitar like a machine gun, stumbling around the stage and slurring his words while singing heroin anthems like "Chinese Rocks," Thunders was dangerous—freedom personified. To me, Thunders made it okay to be a freak; in fact, he made it *cool* to be a freak. The very next day, I purchased a Johnny Rotten T-shirt at Trash and Vaudeville on New York's "punk street," St. Mark's Place. I was now officially a punk. I returned home to Chicago—actually, the city's North Shore suburb Evanston—and began my punk life in earnest.

I began scouring record stores like Wax Trax! and Vintage Vinyl for rare, imported punk singles and albums. I spiked my hair, then shaved it off. I wrote for fanzines like *Last Rites* and *Matter*. I joined a variety of bands: I played bass for Chicago's first "Oi!" group, who opened for punk heroes like The Exploited and The Damned. When that band broke up in 1983, I started my own, Nadsat Rebel, playing guitar and shouting backup vocals alongside my suburban pal bandmates who all hung out at Record Exchange, the *High Fidelity*–style record store I worked at after school.

"Nadsat" meant "teenage" in the Slavic-inspired language Anthony Burgess invented for his dystopian novel *A Clockwork Orange*, which was seen by most punks as a clairvoyant view into an inevitable punk future. Nadsat Rebel forged a hybrid of the "leather, bristles, studs, and acne" style of metallic street punk favored by British bands like GBH and Discharge with the more "American" leanings of Minor Threat, topped off with a *soupçon* of proto-industrial favorites Killing Joke. In deference to the fashion of the day, I sported a "liberty spikes" hairstyle along with leather belts and clothing covered in all manner of metal studs. The lapels of my *de rigueur* motorcycle jacket were covered in badges advertising my favorite bands, the back painted with the U.K. Subs' stenciled logo and the three-skull graphic associated with the band Discharge. In other words, in 1983 I pretty much looked like a member of Rancid today.

Nadsat Rebel went fairly far on the local punk scene, but stopped short of making it into the history books. We played shows with simpatico local groups like Naked Raygun, the Effigies, and Big Black, as well as every notable band that came through town—GBH, Hüsker Dü, The Dicks, Die Kreuzen, Jody Foster's Army, and Samhain—Glenn Danzig's first band after quitting The Misfits.

Our demo tapes were recorded by Big Black's Steve Albini, who would go on to become a studio guru for underground rock, recording well-known artists like Nirvana, the Pixies, and PJ Harvey as well as more obscure heroes such as Slint. Nadsat Rebel songs appeared on indie compilations of local bands, and got played on local college radio stations like WNUR and WZRD. It was the perfect perch to watch the birth of the American punk movement.

Or its death.

At least, its first death . . . Like a cat, punk rock has something along the lines of nine lives: some time after it's proclaimed over, punk rock eventually resurfaces, transformed in some new way that reflects the society at large. I felt that when I first discovered Green Day: I was twenty-three years old when Green Day's debut *Kerplunk!* was released, and twenty-five when the band put out *Dookie*, the success of which changed, and in some ways created, a new generation of punks far larger than I ever imagined the cult would grow. I was young enough to be part of *Dookie*'s target audience and old enough to bring some perspective to its rampant pop-cultural triumph. After that, I was fascinated to watch the process of punk rock stage-diving into the mainstream. Like many a stage dive, where punk would land—if it was to split its head on the mainstream's cement floor (or ceiling)—nobody knew. Like many, punk had given my suspicious logic a place to land and focus: a healthily cynical lens with which to view the world. Through this prism, how would punk's latest evolution end up looking after all?

There have been many a compelling, comprehensive analysis of punk rock's glory days (daze?). In fact, numerous amazing histories and analyses of the early punk movement already exist, thank you very much. There's *Please Kill Me: The Uncensored Oral History of Punk* by Legs McNeil and Gillian McCain, the ultimate you-are-there document, a *Rashomon* journey through the nascent mid-'70s punk culture via the words of American punk originators like the Ramones. (McNeil supposedly helped first coin the term "punk" as an editor/founder of *Punk* magazine). Meanwhile, *England's Dreaming: Anarchy, Sex Pistols, Punk Rock, and Beyond* by Jon Savage brilliantly traces the birth of the English punk movement through the rise and fall of the Sex Pistols, following how 1977-era bands like the Clash and the Buzzcocks sprung up in the wake of the Pistols' sound and fury. Greil Marcus's classic *Lipstick Traces: A Secret History of the Twentieth Century* also assesses the sprawling impact of the Pistols, tackling larger questions about punk's place in art, history, and culture (as well as a bird's-eye view of the Pistols' tragic final gig at San Francisco's Winterland in January 1978).

In the cinematic realm, Penelope Spheeris's landmark *Decline of Western Civilization* series, especially the first edition, centering on Los Angeles' punk/hardcore golden age (Black Flag, X, Fear, Circle Jerks et al,), was a key document of American punk. And recent efforts, from Stephen Blush's *American Hardcore: A Tribal History* to Andy Greenwald's *Nothing Feels Good: Punk Rock, Teenagers and Emo*, have tackled admirably and thrillingly vital subsets of the already subcultural punk experience. Still, I wanted to know more. What happened to the genre's original values when punk rock became a global-business concern? What do the words "punk rock" even signify anymore, even to those who use it to describe their own life? Would punk today be able to withstand the heat of the Clash's trusty "bullshit detector"? What part of punk's original vitality survived the transition to major success? Did the neo-punk generation prove a shock to the system, or did the system win in the end?

Punk rock: it's all about life or death, death or glory. But this time around, punk was not the same old story. Or was it? This was not my so-called punk anymore. In its stead, success had created something both far more simple and far more complicated.

1

A BRIEF HISTORY OF PUNK ... BUT FIRST, GREEN DAY WINS A GRAMMY!

It makes me extremely proud to make punk rock the biggest music in the world right now.

—Green Day bassist Mike Dirnt,
quoted in a September 21, 2005,
article in the *East Bay Express*

In 2005, Green Day won the Grammy award for "Best Rock Album" for their 2004 release *American Idiot*. In fact, *American Idiot* wasn't the band's first Grammy—Green Day received the 1994 Grammy for Best Alternative Music Performance, too. But Green Day's triumph at the 2005 ceremony felt . . . different. For one, the 2005 Grammy Awards proved something of an upset: Ray Charles's *Genius Loves Company*, the sentimental favorite, took the honors for "Album of the Year," but many felt that *American Idiot* was the better, more relevant effort.

As "Album of the Year," *American Idiot* certainly carried all the elements the award should commemorate. For one, *American Idiot* was both the most critically acclaimed album of the year and (most important to the Grammy voters) a massive commercial success. It also felt thrillingly relevant, as the title track and other songs pointedly commented on the declining state of our world. *American Idiot* sounded more than anything like an expression of life midway through the first millennium: as exuberant and passionate as it is cynical and jaded, it struck a universal (barre) chord with many.

Also, *American Idiot* represented a comeback on two fronts. Green Day had been on a stylistic wane for some time, and had never been a critical

7

favorite; the same could've been said for their chosen genre, "pop punk." *American Idiot*'s transcendent success changed all that. Green Day's Grammy was the most significant embrace from the music-business mainstream of music descended from punk rock yet: in years previous, the music biz was always happy to make money off punk rock, but always reluctant to give it any respect. "Ten years ago, a lot of people [wrote us off]," Green Day bassist Mike Dirnt exclaimed to *Entertainment Weekly*. " 'That's just a snotty little band from the Bay Area.' " But Green Day's Grammy moment showed that punk, after years of growth, just might be ready for prime time. Punk was now "classic." The outsiders had won. Right?

In fact, the peers and followers of Green Day in the punk world they had exploded out of had varying reactions to *American Idiot*'s Grammy win. "I think it's amazing," exclaims Chuck Comeau, drummer for the popular pop punk band Simple Plan. "I'm absolutely stoked and happy for them. It's amazing that this kind of music is so anti-establishment but goes on to win a Grammy from the most stuck-up organization in the music world. It's amazing how far it's traveled, how far we came from being totally underground to being recognized as important, viable, and serious. Lots of people don't take it seriously, but a lot of the pop-punk songs are really important—they're fucking great, amazing pop songs. It's amazing they're being recognized. It gives us a lot of hope that our music will get to that level. Winning a Grammy is nothing to be embarrassed about; it's definitely a goal of ours."

At the same time, Comeau sees Green Day's Grammy win as a beacon pointing the way out of the pop-punk ghetto. "We don't want to stop at being a punk band, but here's the thing, though: we don't see ourselves as a 'punk' band, and at this point I'm not sure Green Day wants to be limited to being a punk band, either," Comeau says. "We just want to be a *band*—not a pop-punk band, not a punk band, just Simple Plan. Take No Doubt: No Doubt came from the Southern California ska scene, and they're so beyond that now. Every record they pushed the boundaries, and they became just . . . *No Doubt*. Same with U2 and Weezer—they came from scenes but are now just considered on their own merits. Weezer is just . . . Weezer, U2 is just U2. Those are the models for us now."

That punk has moved from a cult obsession for insiders to mainstream phenomenon still rankles some purists, however. "As soon as Green Day hit the Grammy awards this year," Greg Attonitoi, front man for long-running, stalwart indie pop-punkers Bouncing Souls, grumbles with vitriol, "I had to be hospitalized."

Attonitoi's anticonformist brio has always been a punk rock mainstay, regardless of its commercial virility. When punk first pogoed its way onto the radar of the 1970s mainstream music scene, Grammy Awards seemed like the last thing on its amphetamine-addled collective consciousness. Still, punk's Molotov-cocktail immediacy made it seem like it just might be the next big thing. Punk was so assaultive, so trenchant and colorful, so circa *now* even then, that its success somehow seemed inevitable. And it was, give or take seventeen or so years . . .

Punk's notorious beginnings have become such a part of mainstream pop music legend, in fact, that going over them seems redundant. Punk is now part of the fabric of the greater culture, a "type" that's wordless lingua franca shorthand across numerous cultures for a specific kind of person and music.

Punk rock as it's thought of today began in New York City during the mid to late 1970s, spawning itself in Manhattan dive bars like the now-infamous CBGB—its name an acronym for "Country, bluegrass, and blues," chosen well before anyone knew it would become punk's Mecca.

In such appropriately ramshackle, almost improvised environments, bands like the Ramones, Blondie, and Richard Hell and the Voidoids cannibalized everything rebellious, trashy, and authentic (and often *trashily authentic*) from pop music history. These young rebels were hellbent on creating a new formal language of rock music out of their stylistic clusterfuck collage. They succeeded all too brilliantly, resulting in one of the twentieth century's most important art movements—although one whose legacy just may have been to self-destruct. That it might destroy itself under the weight of so many platinum plaques, well . . . no one saw that one coming.

If anything, early punk influences read like a history of defiance in pop music up to that point. Many of the first wave of New York punk bands looked to the stripped-down strum and leather-jacketed switchblade style of 1950s rock and roll, perceiving a minimalist immediacy in the raw rave-ups of Chuck Berry and Elvis. They soaked up the amphetamined, black-nail-polished androgynous sexuality of glam-rock à la the New York Dolls and Bowie along with the brassy, torn-fishnet cattiness of 1960s girl-group pop. Most of all, the punks emulated the feedback-drenched debauchery of the Velvet Underground, which was the art-school educated big-city cousin to another punk trope, the stomping, simpleton sneer of 1960s garage rock like the Stooges, who featured a key proto-punk icon in its frontman, a young Iggy Pop. "I didn't know much about what was happening at CBGB's, and all of that," Pop explains in *Please Kill Me*. "I mean, I thought there must be two or three bands in the universe that weren't complete dicks, but I never thought, Oh, punk is happening, it's taking over and gonna be big and huge."

New York's proto-punk fringe contained enough artsy types to keep a balance of improvisational experimentation and a social critique of *moderne* society going. Some, of course, just wanted to be obnoxious and loud, but punk was the twain where all forms of irreverence could meet and hang out. Punk was indeed one of the first moments in pop music where a youth culture movement self-consciously critiqued not just society, but the *style* of music and art movements within that society. And despite punk's media image of hooliganism—thanks to the Ramones' street-gang persona and ironic, taboo-threatening humor that evoked underground comics of the time—the early New York scene was surprisingly diverse.

The Ramones' self-titled 1976 debut album was primal three-chord monte, reducing rock and roll to its barest, fastest essentials. Its monochrome guitars, village-idiot yelling, and sheer velocity set the tone—song titles like "Blitzkrieg Bop" and "Chain Saw" served as truth in advertising manifestos, perfectly capturing the band's sound in words. In reality, The Ramones were just one facet of the early New York punk scene, of the CBGB's era. Coexisting alongside them were bands that vitally reflected different influences.

There was the arch retro pop of Blondie, given a heavy dose of Y-chromosome postfeminist kick courtesy of sex symbol front woman Debbie Harry, who made a career out of blonde ice-queen charisma. Then there were "New Wave" synth-pop forerunners Suicide, who juxtaposed violent, reverbed-out scenarios over raw soundscapes of primitive, thumping electronics; without Suicide, the template for bands like Depeche Mode would never have existed.

Then there were the bohemian punks, leather-bound poetic *artistes* like Patti Smith, Richard Hell, and Tom Verlaine, the iconic, reedlike frontman/co-guitarist for Television. Fronting her self-named band, Patti Smith outrageously reinvented the androgynous cock-rock sex symbol epitomized by Mick Jagger and Jim Morrison in her own tragic-romantic persona that reeked of Rimbaud. Likewise, Television's Verlaine was like a downtown, Soho art-scene makeover of a "beat" poet. As such, Television were arguably the most virtuoso musicians of the scene, their angular, twisty songs built on lyrical, epic guitar solos that evoked jammy, San Francisco-style counterculture rock of the '60s more than more stereotypical punk influences. Between these already young archetypes lay the intentionally awkward art-schoolers the Talking Heads. The Heads' paranoid-android honky funk would find itself ubiquitous by the mid-2000s, landing in both the formal ambition of Radiohead (who took their name from a Talking Heads song) and the akimbo body music of '80s-redux bands like Franz Ferdinand. "In New York, there were bands like Blondie, Talking Heads, Patti Smith, the Ramones, all that shit," says Tony Bevilacqua, guitarist for the Distillers, one of the most vital bands to evolve out of today's contemporary punk movement. "They were all different. They all looked different. They all *played* different. *That* was punk rock. That was *rad*."

Punk's greatest impact, however, was to show how decrepit and out of touch popular music had become. By the late 1970s, the heyday of the Rolling Stones and the Beatles was over; those artists had already become "classic rock," a genre stratified into an FM radio format. Soft rock and manufactured disco made up the Top 40 sound of the day. Epic, prog-rock (Yes, Emerson, Lake and Palmer, Jethro Tull, Genesis, Pink Floyd) was the rock sound of choice—bloated, conceptual, navel-gazing. Too many rock bands released what could be called concept albums or rock operas—state-of-the-art symphonic and overdubbed within an inch of their lives.

"It's easy to forget that just a little over a year ago there was *only one thing*: the first Ramones album," iconoclast rock critic Lester Bangs wrote in his brilliant 1977 essay "The Clash" for *Creem* magazine, reprinted in the anthology *Psychotic Reactions and Carburetor Dung*. "Better Slaughter and the Dogs at what price wretchedness than *one more* mewly-mouthed simper-wimper from Linda Ronstadt. Buying records became fun again, and one reason it did was all these groups embodied the who-gives-a-damn-let's-just-slam-it-at-'em spirit of great rock' 'n' roll." It's no surprise, then, that when punk erupted out of England in the form of the Sex Pistols, Pistols frontman Johnny Rotten caused controversy by wearing a homemade "I Hate Pink Floyd" shirt.

"In the '70s, punk was about taking back rock and roll from what it had become—the bloated machine of twenty-minute solos and introverted-musician crap like the Eagles," explains Matt Kelly, drummer for Boston's Dropkick Murphys. Yet for some, it's all come back around again: one man's punk, it seems, is another man's dinosaur. "It seems to me like today's 'punk' has a lot of parallels with the dinosaur rock of the '70s," Kelly adds. "Now it's harder than ever to do something interesting and original because of the popularity 'punk' holds in mainstream music," says Matt Skiba of neo-punk combo Alkaline Trio.

These feelings aren't new, but rooted in punk's dadaist tradition of destroying tradition, which inevitably resulted in a Phoenix-like rebirth. In *Lipstick Traces*, Greil Marcus describes how refreshing it was the way "punk immediately discredited the music that preceded it; punk denied the legitimacy of anyone who'd ever had a hit, or played as if he knew how to play. Destroying one tradition, punk revealed a new one."

London's Calling . . . And the World Picks Up the Phone

As far as punk rock goes, the English punk movement was really the shot heard 'round the world. The U.K.'s embrace of this new sound and style was the moment when punk became a known concept in the popular consciousness, a suitably colorful subject for tourist postcards featuring Day-Glo mohawked punks on London's Kings Road.

Still, punk remained anything but a mass-market phenomenon in terms of real record sales for many years following its first wave. The Sex Pistols' debut album, 1977's *Never Mind the Bollocks*, has only recently achieved platinum status (over one million units shipped), in 2004, over two and half decades after its release. "Mass movements are always so unhip," Legs McNeil wrote in *Please Kill Me*. "That's what was so great about punk. It was antimovement, because there was knowledge there from the very beginning that with mass appeal comes all those tedious folks who need to be told what to think. Hip can never be a mass movement."

Regardless, punk exploded in England when the Brits got their first dank whiff of the Ramones' proletarian shabby chic, all DIY (do it your-self) attitude and speedy two-minute songs packed full of urban alien-ation they could relate to. The moment the Ramones descended upon cool Britannia's shores, it was over. "Our first show in England was July 4, 1976, the weekend of [the United States'] Bicentennial, which I thought was metaphorically appropriate," Ramones manager Danny Fields said in *Please Kill Me*. "Here it was the two hundreth anniversary of our freedom from Great Britain, and we were bringing Great Britain this gift that was going to forever disrupt their sensibilities." "When we went to England, things happened so fast, it was unbelievable," Ramones bassist Dee Dee Ramone added. "I thought I was a huge rock star."

Meet the new rock, definitely not the same as ye olde rock. In the wake of the Ramones, writing album-side-length songs about, say, Hob-bits and Middle Earth (à la Led Zeppelin) and prancing around the stage in Renaissance Faire tights while playing flute (per Jethro Tull) seemed dangerously out of touch. In then-prime minister Maggie Thatcher's iron rule of England, dole lines were long and the youth were angry. Enter the Sex Pistols, stage left. The Sex Pistols' first single declared "Anarchy in the U.K.," and it proved a call to arms for the disenfranchised. "The Sex Pistols came around like a political movement," says Brody Dalle, singer, songwriter, and guitarist for the Distillers. "There was political unrest and depression in England. No money, no jobs, factories; just a gray and drab life. They were fighting against something—and Steve Winwood wasn't exactly going to tell you what was going on in the world."

Musically, *Never Mind the Bollocks* was as subtle as an air raid alarm, about as loud and no less frightening: its walls of distortion guitar, anti-establishment lyrics taking on everything from S&M to the beloved Queen, and most of all Johnny Rotten's defiantly atonal caterwaul, all felt so dif-ferent, so fresh, so ahead of its time. It still shocks today. "It remains new because rock and roll has not caught up with it," Greil Marcus writes in *Lipstick Traces*. "Nothing like it had been heard in rock and roll before, and nothing has been heard since—though, for a time, once heard, that voice seemed available to anyone with the nerve to use it." "If I had to choose one record to listen to, it would be *Never Mind the Bollocks*," wrote Fat Mike, bassist/vocalist for NOFX, one of the leaders of today's neo-punk movement, on the Web site for his record label Fat Wreck Chords. "That record changed my life."

England's punk cavalry rode in quickly behind the Pistols—the Damned, the Buzzcocks, the Stranglers, and so on—creating what smelled to the outside world like a visible movement. One of the greatest rock bands ever, the Clash, erupted out of this first wave of British punk; showing even greater musical range, intelligence, and political bite than the Pistols, the Clash released records of such vitality, they remain as classic and timeless as anything by, say, the Who or the Stones.

Yet punk was gaining international notoriety for its antics more than for its music. The Sex Pistols swore on television. They wore swastikas on T-shirts (designed, with willful paradox, by their Jewish Svengali manager, genius punk mastermind Malcolm McClaren). True to their self-destructive nature, the Pistols flamed out spectacularly, playing their last-ever show in 1978 at a tour stop at San Francisco's Winterland Theater. Soon after, Pistols bassist Sid Vicious made headlines by seemingly committing suicide after he was arrested for killing girlfriend Nancy Spungen.

Around the time U.K. punk made itself heard, the arguments about what really *is* punk began in earnest, and would continue to percolate for years after. Check the Internet—"what is punk?" remains still the number-one issue of discussion central to punk culture today. Punk's "sellout" epitaph was begun seconds after it started, and it's still being written. "It's funny, but now 'punk' was being used to describe something the world thought of as English . . . ," Legs McNeil writes in *Please Kill Me*. "Four years earlier, we had pasted the Bowery with bumper stickers that said 'WATCH OUT! PUNK IS COMING!' Now that it was here, I didn't want to have anything to do with it."

Back in the U.S.A. . . .

It would take nearly two decades for punk to take over mainstream pop music and become truly "big and huge," as Iggy Pop once never thought. But the seeds for that moment were already being sown across the pond Stateside. Just ask Brett Gurewitz, one of the founding fathers of the current punk movement, who remains one of its most vital, visible players as the head of Epitaph Records, for years the preeminent label documenting the current punk moment. Gurewitz is the one of co-founders of Bad Religion, the band that proved to be the catalyst, the true linchpin, for the current punk movement. If American neo-punk has a Sex Pistols, it's Bad Religion. "I'd say by far one of the most important bands was Bad Religion," says Lawrence Livermore. "They created styles of music that bands are still trying to copy today. Also, they showed that you can sell lots of records *and* have a huge cultural impact, all while remaining on an independent label and working on an essentially DIY basis."

Meanwhile, Epitaph remains probably the most commercially successful punk label in the world, and one of the biggest independent labels thanks to hit albums with bands like the Offspring, Rancid, and NOFX. Those commercial triumphs changed not just how punk did business, but challenged how the music industry traditionally works as well. And the thing that brought Gurewitz to this point was the Ramones' first album.

In the mid to late 1970s, Gurewitz, now in his midforties, was a lot like any other rock-obsessed teenager of the "Me Decade." Growing up in Woodland Hills, a northern suburb of Los Angeles in the San Fernando Valley, Gurewitz dug "all kinds of stuff." The Beatles. The Stones. Alice Cooper. David Bowie. T. Rex. Even wanky symphonic prog-rock like early Genesis and Emerson, Lake and Palmer appealed to the young Gurewitz. "I even listened to [jazz-fusion musicians like] Return to Forever and Weather Report," he recalls. "I liked Parliament/Funkadelic, the Ohio Players, Stevie Wonder—I was really super into music."

When Gurewitz discovered the first Ramones album at a record store called Moby Disc a couple suburbs over in Canoga Park, his life and outlook changed forever. "The Ramones were like Pied Pipers to me," Gurewitz explains. "They brought punk into my neighborhood." Radicalized by the album's strange, aggressive sounds, so unlike anything he was listening to, Gurewitz became a punk convert. Soon he'd be part of the movement, putting his own spin on it. "I can remember newly opening that record," Gurewitz says, "It felt very exciting when I first put it on. The first few times I heard it, it really opened my eyes. To me, the Ramones signified rebellion. Jimi Hendrix belonged to the big kids, but punk was anti-authoritarian and anti-establishment in a way that belonged to *me*. I was like, 'Oh my God, I can do this.'"

Indeed, Gurewitz found enough inspiration in the Ramones' DIY aesthetic to start a band. In 1989, at the age of eighteen, he formed Bad Religion with high school friends, including singer Greg Graffin, who remains the only other original member of the group aside from Gurewitz. He started Epitaph, meanwhile, as a vehicle to release Bad Religion's first seven-inch vinyl single.

"Me and the guys from Bad Religion, we were the first punks in our school," Gurewitz says today. "It just felt like punk rock was rock music where I had a chance. Part of the appeal of punk rock, and one of its defining characteristics, is its populist nature. Punk is music for anybody—anybody can do it. You don't have to be a virtuoso, you don't have to know music theory, you don't have to be fucking skinny like Jimmy Page, you don't have to have cheekbones like Mick Jagger. All you have to do is have a lot of heart and put yourself out there. It's inclusive."

Gurewitz wasn't alone in starting his own scene. In an era before the Internet's viral omnipotence, a new punk crept through America, leaving small, vibrant scenes in its wake. By 1980, Gurewitz, in fact, had actually arrived late to the party in terms of being part of punk's second wave in America.

Down the highway a ways from Gurewitz in Hermosa Beach, California, a young guitarist named Greg Ginn also found inspiration in the Ramones following an early Los Angeles appearance by the New York punk forebears in 1976.* Ginn went on to start Black Flag, a band whose sheer influence makes them probably one of the most significant American rock bands ever, regardless of genre. Black Flag—a later incarnation of which included future alternative rock celebrity Henry Rollins—took the Ramones' speedy rifferama and transformed it in its own image. Black Flag made punk that was even faster, more raw, more brutal, more jazzily experimental, resulting in a subgenre known as "hardcore."

Black Flag epitomized punk's DIY spirit. The band's motley collective criss-crossed America numerous times on low-budget tours, playing wherever for whatever pay they could scrounge, sleeping on the floors in kind strangers' homes instead of hotel rooms. In the process, they created a nationwide touring circuit and model for underground bands that exists to this day. Ginn formed an independent record label, SST, to release Black Flag's recorded debut, "Nervous Breakdown," a four-song vinyl seven-inch EP released in 1978; SST would go on to release seminal recordings from bands like the Minutemen, Saccharine Trust, and others. Another Los Angeles label, Slash—originally started as a fanzine to document L.A.'s nascent punk scene—focused on the intense self-destructive aggression of bands like the Germs, Fear, and X.

Between SST and Slash, Los Angeles seemed like the center of the American punk universe, which it may have been, but vital scenes were

---

*Jay Babcock, "Their War, or Black Flag: 1977–1981, or Black Flag: The First Five Years, or The Making of Hardcore: The Problem Child of Punk Rock," *Mojo*, December 2001.

popping up all over the United States, each reflecting its own regional flavor. The Dead Kennedys ruled the roost in San Francisco's Bay Area, also home to the American punk movement's staunchest chronicler, the fanzine *Maximum Rocknroll*, and Alternative Tentacles, the vital independent punk label formed by radical Dead Kennedys frontman Jello Biafra. But by the early '80s, next in line to Los Angeles in terms of stature and influence was probably Washington, D.C., where punk/hardcore bands like Bad Brains, Minor Threat, and Government Issue, along with local labels like Dischord, were causing excitement on the underground with their ultraquick tempos and politicized lyrics.

In songs like "Straight Edge" and "Out of Step," Minor Threat also defined the "straight edge" movement. "Don't drink, don't smoke—at least I can fucking think," went "Out of Step"'s refrain: that was "straight edge"'s dictum, a reaction to the moronic "party down" attitudes of the 1970s. Straight edge demanded total awareness undiluted by intoxicants and meaningless sex, an allegiance that was symbolized by a black "X" scrawled on the wrist. Straight edge continues to exist as a movement—including its surprising appropriation by latter-day Christian punks, whose religious beliefs dovetailed with straight edge's call for celibacy and sobriety.

My hometown, Chicago, Illinois, meanwhile, featured one of the most interesting punk scenes: local bands like the Effigies, Naked Raygun, and Big Black took inspiration from angular, artier British punks like Gang of Four and Wire, while others like Articles of Faith offered up an ersatz Midwestern spin on what they thought SST bands like Hüsker Dü were up to. Myself, I came out somewhere in the middle of all the influences percolating through the Chicago scene, which made itself felt on later generations.

"I think like any punk rock scene anywhere in the world, it's the sense of belonging that's important to a lot of the kids involved," says Matt Skiba, guitarist and singer for Chicago pop punk stars the Alkaline Trio. "I think that the bands in Chicago at the time—Naked Raygun, Effigies, Pegboy, 8 Bark—were some of the best to date, and amazing influences to grow up around. I'm proud to say that I was there."

Is Punk Dead?

In 1981, the Exploited, a scrappy second-wave British punk band, released an album called *Punks* [sic] *Not Dead*. It proved a telling title: usually, when someone has to insist something isn't dead, it's actually fully on its way to the morgue. That said, if punk wasn't in full rigor mortis by the mid-to-late 1980s in America, it certainly wasn't the vital force it had been.

By then, the great second-wave American punk bands like Black Flag, Bad Religion, and Minor Threat had all disbanded. Major labels had gambled on punk bands like the Clash, the Ramones, and the Sex Pistols—and lost; with few hits coming out of punk's originator groups, corporate interest in the genre soured. When the Clash later broke up in 1986, it was a death knell of sorts for the spirit of the original 1977 era. One of the best and most influential second-wave punk bands, Minneapolis, Minnesota's Hüsker Dü, were also accused of "selling out" the scene when they ditched Black Flag's SST label in 1986 for Warner Bros. Alas, the band didn't survive the move, imploding after their two major label albums made disappointing returns. Punk quickly returned to its original cult status—which, despite the initial hype, it never really transcended in the first place. "See, to the major labels, punk was a fad—it was supposed to be the next big thing in '77," Brad Gurewitz explains. "It didn't happen. Warners spent two bucks on the Ramones. Even with the Clash on CBS, the fad didn't happen. The major labels couldn't be bothered, so they moved on to the next thing."

As punk seemed to wither on the mainstream's vine, music business interest diverted elsewhere as such to the "next thing," which had a metallic sheen. Indeed, the "hair metal" era—Warrant, Winger, Trixter, Skid Row, Bon Jovi, Poison, Mötley Crüe, Ratt, Guns N' Roses—had begun.

Even major punk indies like SST moved away from the sound that originally put them on the map: SST began concentrating on more "college rock"-oriented bands like Dinosaur Jr., Sonic Youth, Screaming Trees, and Soundgarden, prefiguring the next "next big things" that would eventually overtake hair metal: grunge and alternative rock. Indeed, by the late 1980s, a little label in Seattle, Washington, called Sub Pop, was making noise on the indie scene with some local groups called Mudhoney and Nirvana.

Both grunge and even aspects of hair metal owed a debt to punk's legacy. Not for nothing did members of Guns N' Roses wear T.S.O.L. and CBGB's T-shirts in music videos—Guns guitarist Izzy Stradlin even knocked off Johnny Thunder's style down to a "T." Guns N' Roses understood punk's power: connecting to its legacy gave them a legitimacy, making what they did stand out and seem more relevant, even more defiant (Guns N' Roses bassist Duff McKagan was, in fact, previously a veteran of numerous Northwest punk outfits like the Fartz and Ten Minute Warning).

As well, Seattle grunge owed no uncertain amount to punk in its distortion and aggression, especially Black Flag's more dirgey "slow" period. However, grunge amped up the metal quotient and the melody, and replaced punk's menacing, shaven-headed front man with more conventionally rock-star-attractive icons like Kurt Cobain and Soundgarden's Chris Cornell.

For the moment, metal and grunge had overtaken punk for pop culture supremacy, but punk wasn't ready to be counted out yet. Instead, punk stayed on simmer, waiting for the right moment to boil back into public consciousness.

Soon enough, punk would come back to the future. As punk grew and mutated outside the mainstream from the late 1980s into the '90s, a retro-revivalist element grew within it, dedicating to preserving the ideals and sonic aesthetics of the "old school." This slavish dedication to punk's past could be seen in the fashion choices sported by the "gutter punks" haunting thoroughfares in Berkeley or lining the curbsides on St. Mark's Place in New York City.

There were few innovations in the visual persona of the urban punk. By 1990, the dominant gutter style was an anachronistic caricature of punk circa 1982: all straight-leg bondage trousers, safety pins, liberty spikes, Doc Martens and, most tellingly, leather jackets nostalgically emblazoned with names of punk bands of previous eras five, ten, fifteen years earlier. Seeing these anarcho-ragamuffin outsiders beg for change, offer up blow jobs for five bucks to strangers, and scrounge through garbage cans for discarded-yet-still edible foodstuffs, one would never guess that punk's mainstream acceptance was around the corner. But it was.

Punk was soon given a leg up into commercial success by the grunge movement. Just three years later, the one-two punch of Green Day's *Dookie* and the Offspring's *Smash* would leave the pop culture mainstream punk drunk. Green Day hailed from Northern California, representing the San Francisco area's Gilman Street scene centered in the East Bay; the Offspring, meanwhile, called Southern California's suburban Orange County home. Southern and Northern California represented twin tentpoles of punkdom, yet with each representing another state of mind.

"Part of it was just cultural geography: Southern and Northern California are vastly different places, and that's reflected both in their styles of music and the way each was packaged and promoted," opines Lawrence "Larry" Livermore, the founder of Lookout! Records and the individual who can most lay claim to having "discovered" Green Day. "Southern California being the entertainment capital of America, if not the world, there's much less baggage attached to a band or a label being professional, or even overtly commercial, in their approach, whereas in Northern California, you almost had to pretend you don't want to sell records or make money if you wanted to be accepted by the hardcore punk rockers." Hailing from the Golden State's disparate yet related factions, Green

Day and the Offspring would spark off a new era for California punk. Separately but together, each created a sound that soon would serve as the gold standard for moving units.

Punk Sells: Stranger Than Fiction?

Grunge proved the bridge, the gateway drug, for punk's initial commercial acceptance. When Nirvana's "Smell's Like Teen Spirit" exploded as an across-the-board hit in 1991, it created new levels of acceptance for sonic dissonance in the ears of music fans, as well as radio and MTV programmers. By 1994, pop-music audiences weren't necessarily attuned to the stylistic nuances distinguishing the grunge of Nirvana from the punk of Green Day or Offspring. To the undiscerning listener, it was all loud, catchy, noisy, raw, melodic fun—good music to pump one's fist to as it blared out of radio stations like Los Angeles' influential KROQ. Yet each carried street cred from California's underground punk scene.

Green Day had released albums like *Kerplunk!* on the tiny Bay Area imprint Lookout before signing with Warner Bros. for *Dookie*; the Offspring, meanwhile, had released *Smash* on indie label Epitaph after three barely noticed previous independent releases. They'd put in years touring punk's underground circuit of basements, rented veteran's halls, and dive clubs first paved during the Black Flag era of yore. Due to such grassroots, DIY effort, punk had trickled quietly all across the country, building a substantial cult audience off of which a mass-market phenomenon would surprisingly be springboarded.

Dookie and *Smash* came out within spitting distance of each other in 1994, and their impact was immediate. Critics initially dismissed both as derivative of golden-era punk, but it didn't matter; even the little girls understood. Green Day connected immediately with mainstream alternative music fans, who heard in *Dookie*'s hits like "Longview" and "Basket Case" the combination of sensitive singer-songwriter idealism and fist-pumping guitar crunch that Kurt Cobain mastered, but imbued with new hope. And after a few years of grunge hysteria saturation, Green Day's classic punk moves sounded fresh in comparison.

Meanwhile, on *Smash*'s surprise hit "Come Out and Play," the Offspring combined the stop-start, loud-soft dynamics of "Smells Like Teen Spirit" with wacky punk vocal grandstanding and kitschy Indo-surf guitars into an irresistible novelty hit. To the indiscriminate ear, "Come Out and Play" was grunge without angst, heavy hooks without the heavy emotions. It was *fun*.

Green Day and the Offspring carried some charge of nostalgic appeal as well. Nary a review of *Dookie* passed without Green Day singer Billie Joe Armstrong's voice being compared to the Clash's Joe Strummer, down to Armstrong's patently ersatz Cockneyisms, or the band being compared to the Buzzcocks. The Offspring, meanwhile, were classic O.C. punk all the way with their multitracked singalong choruses. In a way, the self-consciously retro sonics represented by Green Day and Offspring made perfect sense.

I have a theory that an era's collective nostalgia tends to drift toward the period roughly twenty years earlier than the present, which explains Green Day and the Offspring's nostalgic appeal at this moment in time. For example, in the complicated, dissolute 1970s, popular nostalgia tended toward the uncomplicated 1950s, represented by Sha Na Na, *American Graffiti,* and *Happy Days.* During the go-go '80s, bands like the young R.E.M. gravitated to the idealistic psychedelia of '60s groups like the Byrds. In the businesslike 1990s, the kitschily bell-bottomed party vibes of '70s funk felt like nothing but the real thing, baby—dizzyingly authentic: think of how powerful Kool and the Gang's "Jungle Boogie" sounded at the opening of *Pulp Fiction*, and you'll know what I mean.

Classic punk aesthetics had the same effect. The '90s saw leaders like then-president Bill Clinton compromised in their ethics due to various scandals. No one was what they seemed; everything was relative to something—from all sides, there was always a convenient political excuse for misbehavior, which only fostered more distrust. In this environment, newfangled old school punk via Green Day and Offspring sounded virtuous, pure, direct, *real.* Soon, however, "real" was the new fake.

God Save the Punk: An Idiot Saves the Day . . .

Somewhere around the time history segued into the mid-2000s, punk rock lost its footing as the music of contemporary revolution. The competition for that title suddenly became fierce. In recent years, music that fell under the mainstream punk umbrella seemed particularly weak. For some insiders, punk's descent into *fromage* has been a slow, hard decline. "By 1998 or 1999, Green Day and the Offspring weren't in the limelight anymore, and the headaches seemed to go away," says Bouncing Souls' Greg Attonitoi. "Now there's more music out there than ever before, so there is just a lot more of everything: a lot more junk and a lot more interesting stuff." Punk's originators also began ringing the genre's death knell in earnest. Sex Pistols' guitarist (and current Los Angeles radio personality) Steve Jones has slagged mass-appeal neo-punk à la Good Charlotte in magazines like *Blender*, while Steve Diggle of pop-punk innovators the Buzzcocks disowns his musical stepchildren as well. "If you listen to our lyrics, there's a lot more wisdom than the Green Day kids are writing about, you know?" Diggle states in a pitchforkmedia.com interview.

"Everyone hates change. Everyone hates bigger fish," responds Fall Out Boy bassist/leader Pete Wentz. "We can only understand things in relation to ourselves. I like the Sex Pistols, X, the Ramones, [but] I don't think Fall Out Boy has much of a connection to that era at all—other than in the way it influences us as human beings in the way everything we have done growing up has."

Arguments aside, punk's true values had been appropriated all too well by bands not as stylistically bound. What's more punk than multicultural bands like Bloc Party and TV on the Radio out-Radioheading Radiohead, making challenging, experimental, yet indelibly soulful rock that follows no plan other than their own desire to be innovative? As well, hip-hop often seems more punk and truly populist in values than much of what's considered punk these days. How punk, for example, was Kanye West taking George W. Bush to task after Hurricane Katrina on national TV? And hey, I'd rather hear Li'l Jon at his most wretched and raw than *one more* mewly-mouthed simper-wimper from another Dashboard Confessional wannabe. And it's not just American hip-hop that's stunning: the stripped-down, homemade beats of British hip-hop influenced artists like Dizzee Rascal and The Streets (some of which were made on Playstations) along with their vibrant lyrics drawing on the harsh reality of everyday life, carry a "right now!" urgency associated with the best punk.

Even some of the most crass commercial rap features elements borrowed from punk to high effect; it's not a coincidence that "crunk" rhymes easily with "punk." The self-aware inanity of Li'l Jon—all easily yelled slogans, grotesque grimaces, and simplistic, pounding beats—shares more than a little in common with the knowing, teenage-lobotomized fury of the Ramones; the King of Crunk has even compared the mosh-pit fury of his performances to punk shows. Both Li'l Jon and the Ramones are sophisticated pretend clowns getting their message across in the most essential, sonically reduced means. And really, what's more punk irreverent and politically charged than a dreadlocked Southern black man like Li'l Jon draping himself in a Confederate flag onstage, as he's wont to do? The comparison has some basis in fact: before he was a hip-hop superstar, Li'l Jon was a suburban skate punk who favored bands like Public Image Limited and Fishbone.

That the most innovative hip-hop of today carries the adrenaline-inducing excitement and creativity once associated with punk isn't lost even on a punk stalwart like Brett Gurewitz, either. "That's why I'm signing hip-hop artists to Epitaph," Gurewitz says. "A lot of rappers these days, people like Sage Francis and Atmosphere, are more punk than most punk. The concept of DIY is one of the things that made American punk rock unique, and that's what I see in the underground hip-hop movement. It's almost like a credo."

In the nostalgia sweepstakes, meanwhile, punk rock recently got chin-checked as the popular retro flavor of the moment by the rise in neo-'80s bands influenced by synth pop and postpunk à la Gang of Four. Bands like Louis XIV are testing pop music's tolerance for dissonance anew, appropriating the Fall's Mark E. Smith's nihilistic, confrontational snarl and sneering xenophobia for their alt-rock radio hit "Finding Out If Love Is Blind." Others like Franz Ferdinand, Interpol, and the Killers have ascended to become the quirkily approachable face of cool, and they're selling loads of records, too.

In no time—surprise, surprise—this movement has spawned pretenders to the throne like the Bravery, who retrofit their Duran Duran rhythms with self-referential *sangfroid de vivre*. Meanwhile, perpetually addled Pete Doherty, formerly of British group the Libertines, is proving a far more compelling, tabloid-worthy heir to the Sid Vicious self-destruction Olympics than anyone on the punk scene. The fact that he writes great songs (and had Clash cofounder Mick Jones produce the Libertines and Doherty's next band, Babyshambles) adds to his outlaw allure. "The time until the rehash has gotten way shorter," groans Distillers guitarist Tony Bevilacqua. "It's bizarre to me that there are already Interpol clones. It's like . . . What? Didn't they come out just a week ago?"

In the wake of the Interpol clones, punk's mighty were falling by the wayside. In 2003, Rancid released one of their more undistinguished albums, *Indestructible*. What made that even worse for punk purists was that it was Rancid's first album for a major label—they'd left Epitaph, the indie that nurtured them for a decade, for megalithic conglomerate Warner Bros., and without improving their commercial prospects to boot. Punk message groups and chat rooms erupted all over the Internet debating Rancid's "sell out" status.

The most ominous sign of the punk apocalypse, however, was the enormous prevalence of punk schmaltz on the radio, MTV, and everywhere else. On their shamelessly nostalgic, moronic, inescapable 2004 hit "1985," Texan funnypunk pop-papsters Bowling For Soup came off as punk's Huey Lewis and the News—offensively inoffensive. The British also tried to pawn off their artless, artificially manufactured punk/boyband hybrid Busted on America; thankfully, this not-so-smart bomb didn't go off. Busted's awkward Green Day-meets-'N Sync blend didn't catch on with U.S. fans, despite the marketing blast of an accompanying MTV reality show.

Meanwhile, neo-punk started resembling hair metal more than ever. Simple Plan's hit punk power ballad "Welcome to My Life" proved as cheesily sentimental and bland as any Journey lighter-waver. Canadian pop-punkers Sum 41 even joined archetypal hair-metallers Mötley Crüe on the Crüe's ballyhooed 2004 reunion tour. "When they asked us if we wanted to hit the road with them, we were like, 'Fuck yeah!'," Sum 41 drummer Steve Jocz told mtv.com. "They're one of the bands that make you want to get in a band. Their whole life is partying and having fun. Whenever any dude says, 'I want to get in a band to get chicks,' if you ask him what band he has in mind as a model, he'll say Crüe every time."

In a surprise twist, however, 2004 would prove to be the year that neo-punk was artistically redeemed. It would take an idiot, however—Green Day's *American Idiot*, to be exact. Prior to this breakthrough album, released a full ten years after the band's smash major-label debut *Dookie*, Green Day had been in the artistic slumps. While *Dookie* sold eight million copies in America alone, each Green Day album that followed, while solid, sold less and less.

By the millennium, Green Day was like classic rock for Generation Y: part of its history, no longer its vital voice. Tours with younger whippersnappers like Blink-182 attempted to reacquaint Green Day with younger audiences, but it wasn't until *American Idiot* that Green Day managed to retake the pop punk throne as their own. No band had been as reliably predictable as Green Day up to that point; *American Idiot* changed all that.

When punk began, it was a critic's genre. Neo-punk, however, had dropped off the critical radar. Many pop-punk releases are rarely reviewed in the mainstream press like *Rolling Stone* and *SPIN*—even albums that contain a hit; when they are reviewed, it is often with maximum cool-kid condescension. However, *American Idiot* proved to be a special kind of album rarely found in recent times: a critically acclaimed work that also managed to capture the public consciousness. Arguably, it is the first masterpiece of the neo-punk genre, on a par with classics from the dawn of the punk era.

On *American Idiot*, Green Day looked to—*gasp!*—a decidedly unpunk influence for inspiration: the rock operas of the '60s and '70s. *American Idiot* followed an everyman character, Jesus of Suburbia, through a sprawling song cycle that spanned the indignant rave-up societal critique of the title track through the anthemic melancholy of "Boulevard of Broken Dreams" to the ambitious five-part suite "Jesus of Suburbia."

"I think *American Idiot* is the *Quadrophenia* of our time," Brett Gurewitz states, referring to the Who's 1973 double-album epic narrative of Mod alienation that was later made into a film of the same name. "I'm friends with Billie: I'm not sure if he's a fan of *Quadrophenia*, but I bet he is. I'm not saying that he copied it in any way; I just think he captured what was good about it. First of all, it's a *rock opera*: it's got long songs, it tells stories and has an atmosphere and a mood that is tied to a culture. *Quadrophenia* had that, too: in the early '80s, U.S. punks co-opted *Quadrophenia* and grafted it onto our culture just like we did with *A Clockwork Orange*. We didn't have our own legacy, our own *stuff*, and now we do." More than a revamped *Quadrophenia*, however, with *American Idiot* Green Day gave neo-punk its own *London Calling*.

The Sex Pistols' *Never Mind the Bollocks* was so powerfully radical, it pulled off a double trick: it was so unique as to never to be duplicated, yet it managed to set the formula for punk rock anyway. *London Calling* from the Clash, however, proved to be punk's true masterpiece upon its release in 1979: it showed what punk could *really* do beyond yelling over four-chord speed trials. *London Calling* fulfilled punk's promise; it wasn't a call to arms so much as it was a design for living. It showed what might happen when punks finally figured out how to use the cultural weapons they had in their hands—if they discovered where to aim the gun most strategically, as opposed to just shooting in the air and causing a riot.

"1979: The year punk died, and was reborn" is the headline of a *New Yorker* review by Sasha Frere-Jones of *London Calling*'s 2004 box-set reissue, and it's an apt summation. Frere-Jones calls *London Calling* "sixty-five minutes of rock music that never goes wrong. . . . Hyperbole itself cannot diminish this record. Each of us is invincible when it's playing. . . . Somewhere right now . . . a kid is . . . pledging to reinvent punk rock once and for all, doubting her heroes while carrying their astonishing music in her body." Over this sprawling double album, the Clash master rockabilly ("Brand New Cadillac") and haunting dub reggae ("Guns of Brixton"), and even managed to crank out a first-class catchy hit single ("Train in Vain," hidden, to preserve punk cred, as a bonus track). Similarly, on *American Idiot*, Green Day embrace a stylistic palette far more expansive than previous efforts indicated was within their grasp. Glam-era Bowie and Iggy Pop coexist here with classic punk aesthetics, Beatlesque melody, show-tune showboating, and early Who intensity, the resulting fusion sounding distinctively like Green Day and nothing else.

London Calling impressed as well because of its intelligent political impulses: songs like the pounding, urgent title track tackled the threat of nuclear proliferation, while "Spanish Bombs" explored the meaning of terrorism—two topics especially trenchant even today. *American Idiot* approached the same kind of relevance for its time: outspoken lyrics like

"Maybe I'm the faggot America/I'm not a part of a redneck agenda" bravely named names in an uberconservative, perplexingly apathetic moment in American history. Despite being on a major label, Green Day proved to be more politically relevant than many of their most radical peers in both the underground and the pop-punk mainstream. It's shocking, actually, how politically apathetic so much current punk rock remains considering the music's revolutionary birthright.

If you listen closely to your old punk records, you might discover something familiar yet new. We're currently living in the aftermath of societal decline as presciently predicted by the early punks, one of the most volcanic, unstable moments in recent world history, and yet there is still too little social dialogue in musical form. Punk-driven activist initiatives like punkvoter.com and "Rock Against Bush," mobilized around the 2004 presidential election, were impressive, however. Alongside *American Idiot*'s willingness to be a voice of dissent within the mainstream, these actions provide hope that a change is gonna come.

"Kids are starting to care again," Warped tour founder Kevin Lyman notes. "Everything was so easy for so long. I would never say 9/11 was a good thing, but if anything good came out of it, it was when people started trying to figure out what the hell was going on. Kids are willing to learn and expose themselves to more."

Are You Ready to Be Liberated?

Most intoxicatingly, with *American Idiot*, Green Day achieved a seemingly impossible task in 2004: making a record that *matters*. This book isn't just about Green Day, however. It's also about the future of the punk movement—the artists who will potentially make the next genre-defining masterpiece. One of those artists just might be Brody Dalle.

Brody Dalle made her name as the front woman for the Distillers, one of the most exciting, vivid forces to have evolved out of what's considered current punk music. As guitar player, vocalist, and primary songwriter for the Distillers, Dalle's appeal is multifaceted. For one, she can write a helluva song: her grasp of classic pop songwriting and melody, combined with a true punk's love of dissonance and discord, makes for a crucial dichotomy unique to her.

Furthermore, Dalle possesses one of those classic rock voices that's so expressive, it's startling. Dalle's vocals are bluesier, more haunted than the typical punk bark: even her most banal antiauthoritarianism shouting reflects a mysterious inner life. When Brody speaks or sings, you're curious about what her next line, phrase, word, *mannerism* is going to be. Her vocal uniqueness causes for some random, but ultimately appropriate, comparisons. "Brody's raspy yet melodic vocal style [mixes] the styles of Stevie Nicks and [Motörhead screamer] Lemmy," Larry Lugz hilariously—but not incorrectly—noted in 2002 in *Americore Magazine*. "What if Joan Jett had really, really fucking meant it?" Brian Baker suggested of Brody's voice in a review of the Distillers' self-titled 2000 album debut in the fanzine *Under the Volcano*. "Even if Brody Dalle were a hack songwriter, her raspy rock 'n roll howl would set the Distillers apart from 99 percent of the punk wannabes that infect Southern California," Joe Warminsky III wrote in a review of the Distillers' 2002 sophomore album, *Sing Sing Death House,* for Allentown, Pennsylvania's *Morning Call*.

Dalle's no hack songwriter, though. As a lyricist, Dalle proves startlingly personal, literate even; she's also poetic, even when waxing political. She claims to be unreligious, yet her words run over with images of blood, rebirth, and redemption that suggest she's made the most of a failed Catholic education. And she's still amazed that punk has made so many inroads into "normal" society. "I saw a punk rock kid at the beach wearing a fucking SubHumans T-shirt," she exclaims, puzzled. "It's so strange—I wasn't expecting it."

Yes, punk is now everywhere. Inescapable. But what most sets Brody apart, however, is that, unlike many of neo-punk's seemingly interchangeable front men, she has an unforgettable charisma, the complicated, mercurial, arresting chemistry of a Real Rock Star. "One of the first times I saw Brody perform, she had that thing where she was pulling people in," Kevin Lyman says. "It's hard on the Warped tour: there are a lot of choices, so if you're not good, kids will go get a hot dog. But she's one of those artists who, if people started walking away, she'd make them turn around. She'd pull them *back* when she started singing."

On some level, Brody and the Distillers are an ideal case study to explore where punk has come and where it is going, simply because they embody all the issues percolating in today's punk world. They have a fervent cult that watches their every move. They've been on both an indie label (Hellcat/Epitaph) *and* a major label (Sire/Warner) over the course of three albums, each of which has featured a different lineup.

The Distillers have performed, variously, in basements, on the Warped tour, and on Lollapalooza. They've been accused of being sellouts. They've made three great albums against impossible odds. The Distillers have one day been punk's next big thing, the next day scratched off the "cool kid" list as outcasts. And as a woman, Brody has had to face some unique situations that many in the male-dominated punk scene have never had to face. She's been seen as a virgin, whore, and survivor, all at the same time.

The story of Brody Dalle, in fact, tells the story of the current punk movement and all its pros and cons, lived through one individual's trials—and more, making her both emblematic and unique. Her ex-husband Tim Armstrong of Rancid, a patron saint of the neo-punk movement, was fourteen years her senior when they met; she'd never traveled outside Australia before she moved to Los Angeles to be with him. After a whirlwind courtship, she married Tim Armstrong at the tender age of eighteen.

When Brody formed the Distillers in 2000, everyone assumed Armstrong was pulling her marionette strings. Her relationship with Tim entered punk myth as well, creating a beguiling push-pull situation that played out in the press as a neo-punk Kurt and Courtney. When they divorced three years later after five years together, her struggle got worse. And the questions didn't stop.

She was blacklisted and threatened. She was insulted, called the new Courtney Love, the Yoko Ono of pop punk. She was photographed kissing Josh Homme of Queens of the Stone Age in *Rolling Stone* while her exact relationship to Tim remained nebulous, at least to the public, resulting in a media-Internet frenzy. England's *The Face* magazine put Brody on the cover, calling her "the most hated woman on Earth" (and this is from the English, who, after Maggie Thatcher, have their "most hated woman on Earth" thing down).

And yet, Dalle perservered. She remained outspoken as ever, naming names and not giving a shit. She kept her band together. Despite incredible odds, while she hasn't yet made a punk masterpiece like *American Idiot*, she's still an odds-on favorite for the possibility being within her grasp. "She could've been, and still could become, a huge crossover à la Gwen Stefani," Kevin Lyman says.

"You know, I believe in Brody," Brett Gurewitz says. "She's a huge star, a very talented singer-songwriter, who hasn't attained her potential yet. When I first heard the Distillers play, to be honest it reminded me of Rancid. I'm really a sucker for catchy songs, and what they did was catchy. It was primitive. It had passion. It had *sex* to it." Indeed, of the bands discussed here, not all fit the classic pop-punk stereotype per se. The Distillers certainly don't always fit that mold.

That is the issue pervading punk both of today and yesterday, the tightrope tension, that balance between "populist" and "popular." Again, Green Day comes to mind. The pull between "populist" and "pop" played out epochally when Green Day won the award for best rock album at 2005's Grammy Awards after just over a decade of wading in the mainstream. But was that tension any greater after winning the Grammy for their seventh album, or after selling eight million copies of *Dookie* so soon after leaving the punk underground? "Punk sometimes has this defeatist attitude where you can't expand," Green Day's Billie Joe Armstrong has said in the wake of *American Idiot*'s success. "I look at a band like U2 that started out more or less as a punk band but kept expanding and wound up being one of the biggest bands in the world. And I think it's okay to want that."

Meet the new punk.

Definitely not the same as the old punk.

Punk rock is good music played by bad musicians who are usually drunk and don't really care how bad they play because they are drunk and they know that the audience is drunk so no one cares how bad the band plays anyway. Note: the term 'drunk' can be substituted for 'on drugs' in any one of the previous examples. Oh, and bad haircuts are a big part of punk, too.

—Fat Mike, NOFX/Fat Wreck Chords

2

Be childish. Be irresponsible. Be disrespectful. Be everything this society hates.

—Malcolm McLaren, manager of the Sex Pistols*

I always thought a punk was someone who took it up the ass.

—William Burroughs†

"What is punk?"

To the younger generation, the meaning of the word "punk" most likely involves Ashton Kutcher over anything else.

"What *is* punk?"

It's possibly the worst question in the world—but one of the most queried. Just ask any band typically categorized as punk:

"What is *punk*?"

"The worst question we get asked is 'Do you consider yourselves a punk band?'" groans Dexter Holland, front man for Orange County, California's multimillion-selling neo-punk superstars the Offspring. "I don't consider us pure punk *or* pure pop. When you talk about punk as a genre, it's so fragmented—there's so much going on in it. But punk rock talks about real things that mean something to kids. It's the same reason

---

England's Dreaming, p. 44.
†*Please Kill Me*, p. 208.

why hip-hop has stuck around—because [rappers] talk about things relevant to their audience. That's why punk has remained a relevant kind of music: it's not just about 'Let's do some hookers and party.' "

"That's our most-asked-by-journalists question," says longtime punk scenester Andy "Outbreak" Granelli of the great punk debate. Formerly the drummer for the Distillers and Nerve Agents, currently with Darker My Love, Granelli's heard it all before. " 'What does punk mean to you?' I always say I don't know. I don't want to care."*

To others, "What is punk?" is almost as annoying, elusive, unanswerable, and over-discussed as "What is art?" "I guess it's human nature to want to classify something, like 'This is going to be this and I have to be able to package it in order to process it,' " explains Offspring's Holland. "It's not really like that."

The copout answer to "What is art?" is "You know it when you see it." Therefore, defining it remains all in the eye of the beholder. And there are a lot of beholders of punk—and almost as many definitions. "Punk has become more than just music—it seems to be a set of fashion, political, and musical rules that different people will argue about 'til they're blue in the face," says Dropkick Murphys' Matt Kelly. "The great thing about punk is the diversity of sounds: the Dead Boys, Leatherface, the Happy Flowers, Crass, and Condemned 84 don't really sound anything alike, but you could consider them all 'punk.' "

The essence of punk remains a paradox: so simple to execute, so hard to describe—although everyone tries. Just check almost any music-oriented chat room or message board or fanzine; googling "punk" brings up 30,500,000 results. The great cultural critic Greil Marcus defined punk as "a load of old ideas sensationalized into new feelings almost instantly turned into new clichés, but set forth with such momentum that the whole blew up its equations day by day. For every fake novelty, there was a real one."[†]

Even in its 1970s-era beginning stages, punk struggled to be defined. For some of those taking punk's pulse, this new genre was a music *style* above all, a formal aesthetic. "As far as I was concerned punk rock was something which had first raised its grimy snout around 1966 in groups like the Seeds and the Count Five and was dead and buried after the Stooges broke up and the Dictators' first LP bombed," iconic critic Lester Bangs wrote in 1977.[‡]

*Judith Lewis, Killing the Angel in the House," *LA Weekly,* June 20–26, 2003. http://www.laweekly.com/music/killing-the-angel-in-the-house/2704/ (accessed September 26, 2006).

[†]*Lipstick Traces,* p. 77.

[‡]*Psychotic Reactions and Carburetor Dung,* p. 225.

Yet for others, punk is about expressing the proper *attitude*. "The word 'punk' seemed to sum up the thread that connected everything we liked—drunk, obnoxious, smart but not pretentious, absurd, funny, ironic, and things that appealed to the darker side . . . ," Legs McNeil writes in *Please Kill Me*. "Punk wasn't about decay, punk was about the apocalypse. Punk was about annihilation."

In 2007, it's hard to say what punk is, exactly, even though it's clear that post-9/11 and post-tsunami, we're living through the aftermath those early punks predicted: a seemingly endless war in Iraq, a real age of apocalypse and annihilation. Even those who've been toiling in punk's trenches for some time acknowledge the complexity and richness of the word's meaning today.

"I don't think I want to jump into the fray of defining punk rock, given the nebulous nature of the word and concept of 'punk,'" explains Ian MacKaye, a founding member of Washington, D.C., punk legends Minor Threat and Fugazi, and cofounder of Dischord Records, perhaps the punk-associated label most famous for maintaining its integrity. "The subject becomes etherlike under the light of examination. I don't want to get into parsing the past or speculating about the future, so I respectfully bow out. The truth is, I celebrate the elusiveness of the term 'punk': if i'm bothered by anything, it's the idea that there should be a single orthodoxy with the term."

In attempting a history of current punk rock, however, one should at least define what one's writing a history of. Without question, the answer to "What is punk?" has changed many times from the era of the Sex Pistols and the Ramones to the moment of the Distillers playing Lollapalooza and Green Day winning a Grammy for a multiplatinum album. For some, punk rock has definite rules. "I think there is a limit for [the length of] punk records," NOFX's Fat Mike writes on fatwreck.com. "None of our records are over thirty-five minutes and most are under thirty. Any longer and boredom sets in. Check out some old classics like Circle Jerks' *Group Sex*. It's like seventeen minutes, and Bad Religion's *No Control* is only twenty-three." "When I first started getting into punk rock I always thought it wasn't punk if it wasn't fast," Andy Granelli admits, "but that's not necessarily true."*

As such, for many the only hard, fast rule of punk rock is that *there are no rules*. "The best part about punk rock is you can define it however you want, and there is no right answer," states Bouncing Souls' Greg Attonitoi. "How cool is that? Punk rock is whatever you want it to be. It's a blank

---

*Gerardo Wackenhut, August 2002.

page for you to write on. It's music and style that's always ready for a new twist. Three chords can be played in countless, endless, amazing ways—but two will suffice; throw some individual guts in and you have punk. It's as shallow as the kiddy pool or deeper than the deepest ocean. You love it or hate it and it doesn't care . . . *cuz* . . . *it's* . . . *punk*."

Some constants remain, however, between the various punk eras. Punk's formative years in the 1970s saw "punk become a style, but its elements—the stiff rhythm sections, overamplified guitar and harsh, almost character-less vocals—set up a terrific contrast between this rigid, strait-jacketed formula and the raging emotions that were being expressed," Jon Savage writes in *England's Dreaming: Anarchy, Sex Pistols, Punk Rock and Beyond*. "Punk's accessibility seemed to suggest that anyone could do it."

This democratic ideal is kept alive to this day, in a new generation of punk musicians and fans still resistant to the guitar solo, even if they have a secret heavy-metal shredder past. From yesterday through today, the Sex Pistols up to Blink-182 and beyond, the punk band has represented the everydude through the sound of amateur sonics. Regardless if it's created via willful ineptitude or the real thing, punk alienation is typically expressed via the struggle to express, especially via the most primitive means. As such, in *Lipstick Traces*, Greil Marcus describes the sound of Johnny Rotten's untutored vocals—the sound of a nonsinger singing—thus: ". . . a rolling earthquake of a laugh, a buried shout, then hoary words somehow stripped of all claptrap and set down in the city streets."

"I saw the Sex Pistols," says Bernard Sumner, guitarist/vocalist with New Order and an original member of Joy Division. "They were terrible. I thought they were great. I wanted to get up and be terrible too."*

That sound of undiluted lost adolescence, all tentative, quivering voices and speedy caffeinated rush, is still evoked today by bands ranging from Motion City Soundtrack through Taking Back Sunday and Yellowcard, although it has its origins in the punk's earliest roots. "I didn't start singing till I was fifteen and heard the Velvet Underground," says proto-punk icon Jonathan Richman of his initial inspirations. "They made an atmosphere, and I knew I could make one, too!"† It's a philosophy that endures through the generations. "Punk rock is starting a band with some friends who have never played an instrument before," Fat Mike clarifies, "and people come to your shows and actually like you."‡

---

*Lipstick Traces, p. 7.
†*Lipstick Traces*, p. 61.
‡http://www.fatwreck.com.

Maintaining a state of punk rockness revolves around maintaining a sense of individuality for Tony Bevilacqua of the Distillers. "Television was a great, incredible band because you couldn't figure out what they sounded like," Bevilacqua says. "That's my definition of punk rock that I've learned over the years—that's it: being your own person. *Not* looking like every other person that's at the show with you."

Of course, "looking like every other person at the show" is a blight that seriously afflicts today's neo-punk/pop punk: where nonconformity once ruled the roost, conformity is now the norm. Watch any batch of pop-punk videos, and you'll see how hard it is sometimes to tell the bands apart—especially on the more commercial end. After an hour of watching Fuse or MTV, the patterns reveal themselves: the inane shout-a-long choruses, the dramatic loud-soft dynamics, the buildup so predictable and thumpingly thunderous it could come from a Paul Oakenfold cheeseball trance hit, the uniform of full-sleeve tattoos and piercings and Dickies shorts and baseball hats and T-shirts advertising skate brands, the self-conscious "wacky" frat-boy behavior posing as irreverence . . .

"It's a shame that most people equate punk rock only with bands like Blink-182 and Good Charlotte," says Bryan Kienlen, bass player for the Bouncing Souls. "If that's punk, then I'm not, because it doesn't represent me or anything I loved about punk rock. Most people are only aware of what they're spoon-fed on TV, unfortunately. As punk blew up, I saw more and more people dying their hair, then came the plaid bondage trousers, Mohawks—just regular people enjoying a current fad who will soon be moving on to the next thing. Everything I once thought of as somehow 'sacred,' it has become public domain.

"Each person you ask will have a different experience, and slightly different definition, of punk—I'm only an authority on my own," Kienlen continues. "Probably the single most important thing punk did for me was to help me realize that I was okay. I never really fit in anywhere completely—school, church, sports, nothing—but punk's music and lyrics inspired me with new hope. Punk was my savior as an angry, confused kid; it actually saved my life more than once. Here was an environment where I was actually encouraged to express my individuality. It became my religion when I needed one—through the years, it gave me a home to grow up in and find myself; it meant everything to me, so I dedicated my life to it. I wouldn't trade my life's experiences for anything. In this way punk—or the punk that I know—remains sacred to me."

The crisis of individual expression lies at the core, ultimately, of both the original punk movement and what constitutes it today. " 'Anarchy in the U.K.' is a statement of self-rule, of ultimate independence, of do-it-yourself,"

Malcolm McClaren said of the Sex Pistols' debut single.* "Do it for your-self," Bouncing Souls' Greg Attonitoi says. "*That's* fuckin' punk to me."

"Punk is freedom to be yourself and express yourself," says Missy Suicide, founder of the hugely successful "punk erotica" Web site suicide-girls.com. Suicidegirls.com has become such a crossover media phenome-non since it debuted in 2002, it made *Rolling Stone*'s "Hot List" the very next year. "I never felt like I *couldn't* do anything, and that's really what punk rock was really about to me: I could do *whatever the fuck* I wanted to," Suicide continues. "Nobody could tell me to do any different—nobody challenged my 'scene cred.' Punk was about pushing for accep-tance. That was the spirit suicidegirls was born out of."

Now, however, we live in an era when the idea of punk rock as an oasis of personal expression is under fire. Punk rock is big business—with all the platinum plaques bands like Good Charlotte and Sum 41 have earned, joining a punk rock band is becoming an acceptable career aspiration, a nose-pierced alternative to going to law school. Go-ing through the motions can mean a major-label contract to make music that originally contradicted the whole going-through-the-motions im-pulse.

". . . It's just too goddam easy to slap on a dog collar and black leather jacket and start puking all over the room about how you're going to sniff some glue and stab some backs," Lester Bangs wrote in 1977.† Today, it's just too goddam easy to slap on a guitar, write a song about how your girlfriend sucks/rules/both, sign a major label contract, hire the guy who produced Blink-182's last album, wear "punk" clothes provided by a stylist, and start jumping around the music video set like you've just main-lined a case of Mountain Dew. Can the individual spirit be maintained in punk rock? Or has it been irredeemably sold out? "What remains irre-ducible about this music is its desire to change the world," Greil Marcus stated in *Lipstick Traces*.‡ But is that desire still there?

"Punk means telling a story over a couple of guitar chords, much in the same way folk music does," says Dave "DAZ" Prentice-Walsh, guitar player for Boston, Massachusetts' bristling five-piece The Explosion, who evoke a latter-day Clash in both their pointed, questioning lyrics and a sound suffused with the scabrous melody of vintage punk. "Punk rock is not a difficult from of expression, but it is a powerful one. If you can do this, you are a part of the musical heritage."

Lipstick Traces, p. 9.
†*Psychotic Reactions*, p. 224.
‡*Lipstick Traces*, p. 5.

Not that every faction or permutation within punk was always toler-ated, however. The first wave of Christian punk rock puzzled some of the punk's more traditionally dissident voices. Since then, however, Christian punk has become a massive movement, with religious bands like MxPx crossing over into mainstream sales charts—and winning the hearts and minds of nonreligious punk fans. In an ironic twist, the Christian punk artists were the ones who ultimately would embody what Greil Marcus called punk's "irreducible . . . desire to change the world," making converts of spiky-haired mavens one mosh pit at a time.

Issues of religion have always percolated in punk rock, but in the genre's early history religion was typically attacked. On the Sex Pistols' "Anarchy in the U.K.," Johnny Rotten claims to be "The antichrist"; tak-ing things a bit further, the Pistols' Jewish manager, Malcolm McClaren, challenged the most open of minds by putting swastikas on the band's T-shirts. In today's world, however, Jay Bakker, the enterprising, heavily tattooed scion of controversial evangelist parents Jim and Tammy Faye Bakker dubbed the "Punk Rock Preacher," has even started a punk-oriented youth outreach ministry called, a bit too aptly, "Revolution." And in a way, punk's embrace of Christianity was so initially shocking and un-expected, it seems as much a rebellious punk move as any.

"I thought punk rock was anti-everything," Missy Suicide days. "But punk has definitely become a forum for different messages. I grew up with the guys in MxPx—I went to high school with them in Seattle. I was a bit more dogmatic when I was in high school and I wasn't so open to what they had to say. They were always an enigma to me: I was like, 'How could you be so punk rock and religious?' Their parents were very religious, so they'd always grown up with God and religion; it was always a big part of their lives. They'd been programmed—they fully believed. Just because they'd found Jesus didn't mean they couldn't enjoy skate-boarding and loud music and playing guitar."

Whether the iconoclastic, idealistic desire Greil Marcus describes con-tinues to exist in punk culture is one thing; whether it can survive the commercial pressures engulfing the genre today is another. That change-the-world philosophy has been ghettoized in favor of banal, whiny punk ditties of tortured love, lost and found, that are as *faux* as a *faux*-hawk—and aren't hard to program on Top 40 radio and alt-rock radio playlists. Indeed, just because a love song is "punk" doesn't give it any particular added intelligence or edge—in fact, it may go far in the opposite direc-tion, as demonstrated by this typical couplet from Blink-182's hit "Josie": "Yeah, my girlfriend takes collect calls from the road/And it doesn't seem to matter that I'm lacking in the bulge."

Ironically, the love song was one of punk's first fatalities. "Banishing the love song, people discovered what else there is to think about," Marcus notes. "The love song had draped their lives in cheap poetry; maybe now other matters might poeticize their lives."* But cheap poetry sells, especially when it sports the right punk rock fashion signifiers. "They're saying Avril Lavigne is punk rock but she's just a young Alanis Morrisette," Andy Granelli grumbles.†

"People like Avril Lavigne can wear a few spiked bracelets and be considered punk by the general public, even though, in my mind, she's extremely far from it," notes Agent M, the dynamic female vocalist for Northern California pop-punkers Tsunami Bomb. "From what I gather, punk used to be about attitude more than anything else. People believed in doing it yourself, and being part of an underground musical community together. Punk was anti-corporate, anti-racism, and anti-rock star—with a few exceptions, as always."

Then again, from the moment the Sex Pistols signed their first major label deal, maybe punk's self-immolation in the world of big-business predictability—for that is what big business requires, *predictability*—was always the inevitable idea, anyway. And there's nothing more predictable than the majority of neo-pop punk one might catch on, say, MTV.

"Nowadays, it seems like punk is more about *image*," Agent M continues. "It's dissipated into rockers with Mohawks. Since everything happens in cycles, eventually punk will go out of style and then come back as an underground sound again. I won't be sad. Punk has changed so much over time, it's difficult to even conceptualize what it's become."

The great nineteenth-century political thinker Alexis de Tocqueville advocated that the centrality of the individual was what made America great and, above all, a unique society. Individualism holds independence and integrity as its highest goal. Now the decline of individual expression in American punk rock was threatening to render it obsolete as a cultural force. "Punk is anything that really sticks out these days—anything that makes me feel exactly the same way I felt the first time I heard Bad Brains' *Black Dots*," says Andrew Black, drummer for the Explosion. "Anything that's not *streamlined*. Which is fucking impossible, I know."

Punk is also in danger of getting outpunked by outsiders—and not in

---

* *Lipstick Traces*, p. 77
† Kelly Wilson, "Purifying punk: Dishing with The Distillers drummer about his punk rock roots and his band's constant Rancid comparisons," *State Press*, November 14, 2002, p. 9.

the aforementioned Ashton Kutcher sense. Is Bono getting in the face of world politicians and telling them what really needs to be done more punk than most of the so-called punk one might hear on commercial radio, in between Budweiser commercials? Apparently so—Geoff Rickly, front man for leading emo-punks Thursday, told *SPIN* magazine, "anything U2 does is a model of what a good band can possibly be—with Bono being involved in politics and being able to translate lofty ambitions to actual real-world political change."

So was the revolution coopted when it was finally televised? Or was it ever cooptable in the first place? "Was it that, in the beginning, punk was indeed a sort of secret society, dedicated not to the guarding of a secret but to its pursuit?" Greil Marcus once wrote. "Once people knew what to expect, once they understood just what they would get when they paid their money, or what they would do to earn it—[was the story] ready for its footnotes?"* Critical opinion of punk rock's current wave might suggest it's ready for the dustbin. "Can anyone cite a good example of new school punk rock?," writes Kevin Hopper in a 2002 column for the *Albuquerque Journal,* articulating an all-too-common opinion among music journalists. "You in the back with the MTV T-shirt. Sum 41? Sorry. Anyone else? Blink-182? No, sorry."

Apology accepted. In the end, individualism appears to remain at the core of the "What is punk?" question. But in the end, it's unclear what it means to be an individual in this confused day and age. "Punk means being yourself and not letting someone else tell you how it is, or how it's supposed to be," claims Alkaline Trio's Matt Skiba. "To me, its not a hairstyle, but a frame of mind. But you can have a cool hairstyle if you want . . ."

Then there are those artists who struggle to keep the embers of what made punk great in the first place still burning—even as they navigate their way around the implications of mainstream success. And they're not afraid to claim punk as their own, either.

On the press release announcing the Distillers' 2004 North American tour, head Distiller Brody Dalle spelled out her philosophy loud and clear for all the haters who had come out of the woodwork upon the release of her band's 2003 major label debut, *Coral Fang*: "We're still a punk band, we still play punk music, and we still hate you." Surprisingly, the critics agree with Dalle's self-assessment. "Punk rock, it turns out, is not dead," *Arizona Daily Star* critic Anthony Broadman wrote in a review of a 2003 Distillers tour stop in Tucson. "We have the Distillers to thank."

Lipstick Traces, p. 36.

"I had never heard anything like [punk] before and it moved me like no other had before . . . It was a language I could understand,"* Dalle declares. "Is punk rock really just having a Mohawk? It has nothing to do with how many studs you have on your fucking leather jacket or what color your Mohawk is."† For Brody, the only thing we have to fear is the lack of fear itself. "Art isn't dangerous anymore. I hardly ever see art that makes me go, 'Holy shit!' I want art to be dangerous again,"‡ Dalle says. "[But] you'd have to be really conceited to think you're going to advance punk rock."§ "Punk rock started as an artistic movement. I'm trying to bring that back a little bit . . . [but] I'm not gonna be a martyr for punk rock and I ain't gonna save it either."**

There is desire among Punks to be a community, but there needs to be some shape imparted on the foundations of the punk ideology, and where it comes from. The current Punk stereotype is scarred by mass-marketing and an unfortunate emphasis on style over substance. But these ills don't destroy the Punk sentiment, they merely confound the education of the new generations of people who know they are punk, but don't know what it means. It is a long road to understand what it means.

—Greg Graffin, singer of Bad Religon,
from his essay "A Punk Manifesto"

I don't know what the future of punk is, but it sure-as-hell could use a good kick in the ass.

—Matt Kelly, Dropkick Murphys

---

*"The Distillers," *Reserved*, no. 5.
†*Revolver*, December 2003, p. 82.
‡Judith Lewis, "Killing the Angel in the House," *LA Weekly*, June 20–26, 2003. http://www.laweekly.com/music/killing-the-angel-in-the-house/2704/ (accessed September 26, 2006).
§Darrin Fox, "Buzz: The Distillers," *Guitar Player*, Issue 386.
**Gray Matter*, October 2003.

3

OUT COME THE WOLVES: 1994—THE YEAR PUNK REALLY BROKE

Record company's gonna give me lots of money . . .

—Reel Big Fish, "Sell Out" (1996)

Punka-Cola Adds Life

In the spring of 2005, a Coca-Cola ad began running on national tele-vison. Shot in ersatz cinema verité style, the Coke spot followed a pair of young, brash kids crashing an *American Idol*-type talent contest. The commercial concludes, "Punk rock's not dead."

In punk's early days, such a flagrant big business cooptation of punk counterculture would've been taken as heresy—or at the very least, ridicu-lously unthinkable. Impossible. But twenty-eight years later, midway into the millennium's first decade, punk rock was indeed "commercial" enough to be the focal point of a major national commercial. Punk was now man-ufactured, bottled, and sold for mass consumption—not unlike that ad's true opiate of the people, Coca-Cola.

So how did this cultural phenomenon come about?

Bad Religion: Punk's Second Wave Regenerated

In 1987, mainstream interest in all things punk verged on "nil," ac-cording to Brett Gurewitz. In fact, three years earlier, Gurewitz's own punk band, Bad Religion, flamed out. Bad Religion took a chance on their second album, 1983's *Into the Unknown*, by branching away from their rabble-rousing punk sound. *Into the Unknown* experimented with prog-rock keyboards, trippy flourishes, and slower tempos. As a result, it received a hostile reaction from the punk underground (the album remains out of print, apparently disavowed by Bad Religion as an aberration, yet has taken on mythical status among punk aficionados).

In additon to *Unknown*'s tepid reception, Gurewitz had developed a nasty heroin habit, ultimately causing him to quit the band he'd been playing with since high school. As well, Gurewitz folded up the label, Epitaph, he'd built to release Bad Religion's music. After one more EP release sans Gurewitz—he'd been replaced by another California punk luminary, ex-Circle Jerk guitarist Greg Hetson—Bad Religion called it quits, too.

It indeed proved a turning point in his life: seemingly stuck in a rut by his early twenties, Gurewitz cleaned up his drug issues and struggled to find some kind of employment. After taking some vocational courses and a raft of odd jobs, Gurewitz became a studio engineer and owner of a recording studio. "Anything other than a square job was gonna be okay with me," Gurewitz recalls now. "I really enjoyed, still enjoy, being a recording engineer, but I had a terrible time trying to make any money. And my hours were horrible. I just knew I wanted to be in music. Then, in 1987, Bad Religion said, 'Hey man, why don't we get the group back together?' "

Going Underground: Succumbing to the Forbidden Beat

In Bad Religion's absence, popular music was going for baroque. Nascent grunge and the alternative rock of Jane's Addiction had nabbed the interest of rock tastemakers. On the pop charts, slickly produced R&B like Janet Jackson and canned hip-hop à la MC Hammer started making inroads into world domination. Near-forgotten-today hair-metal atrocities like White Lion received multiplatinum sales and major MTV exposure. Punk, meanwhile, had truly gone underground, concentrating into small, regional scenes linked by the grassroots DIY touring and distribution circuit that bands like Black Flag had trailblazed earlier in the decade. By the late 1980s, punk was no longer the shocking media phenomenon it was in its '70s inception. Instead, the genre was driven by a cult of enthusiasts that, despite their off-the-radar status, was growing. And growing. Slowly, yes. But growing apace. "The mainstream's attitude, if it even thought about punk rock at all—which for the most part it didn't—was that punk was this crazy fad that happened back in the '70s, and that anyone who still called himself a punk in the late '80s was probably kind of retarded," explains Lookout!'s Lawrence Livermore. "The major labels were completely uninterested in what we were doing way beneath the radar—which was an advantage, in my opinion. It gave us a chance to grow and develop without the distortion and feedback that major media exposure inevitably creates."

"Punk was this monster that grew behind everyone's backs," Gurewitz says. "It was the thing that wouldn't die. It was viable, even though the major labels didn't have the patience to incubate it." They didn't need to. More than anything, punk rock proved viral, infecting almost every corner of the United States in its wake. And nowhere was punk growing faster than California.

After Bad Religion reunted in 1987 and released a comeback album, 1988's *Suffer*, Gurewitz noticed punk's submerged yet ongoing resurgence. *Suffer* was the band's best effort yet, combining a sharper, mature musical rigor with an even more intense, brutal attack. Diatribes in song form like "You Are (The Government)" crucially solidified Bad Religion's anti-authoritarian persona in under two minutes flat, while "Forbidden Beat" gave a name to hardcore punk's distinctive *oompah! oompah!* drum thump. Surprisingly, the album sold like the proverbial hotcakes. "*Suffer* was what brought it back," Gurewitz says. "It was very successful. In its first year, *Suffer* sold 20,000 units. Which was, you know, *huge* back then. There wasn't a lot of money to go around from those kind of sales, but it showed it could be done."

In the wake of the exhaust from Bad Religion's tour van, like-minded souls found themselves "succumbing to the temptations of the forbidden beat," as Bad Religion's Greg Graffin intones so passionately on "Forbidden Beat." *Simpatico* bands began popping up and down the California coast—many of whom would end up on Gurewitz's Epitaph label. These new punk bands created their own local scenes, honing a catchy, rough-hewn sound in backyards, all-ages clubs, churches, and VFW halls.

California wasn't the only place where where punk was following Bad Religion's role-model example and quietly renewing its base. In Montreal, Canada, Bad Religion had started infecting the teenage minds of future pop-punk superstars Simple Plan, who would become a multi-million-selling band off albums like their 2002 breakthrough debut, *No Pads, No Helmets . . . Just Balls*. "We were around thirteen or fourteen years old when we first started playing music in bands. We didn't have any specific direction—our influences were Pearl Jam, Guns N' Roses, and Rage Against the Machine, and every kid our age loved those bands," explains Chuck Comeau, Simple Plan's drummer and unofficial "minister of information."

Comeau was born in 1979, just one year before Bad Religion formed, yet he still felt their impact on first listen. "It's funny—I was listening to an alternative show called 'Rave' on this local Montreal modern-rock station,

and they played this song called 'American Jesus' by Bad Religion,"
Comeau recalls. "I had never heard of this band, but I freaked out and
bought the record next day. Funnily enough, Eddie Vedder sings on 'American Jesus' and I didn't even know that, you know?"

The Punk Rises in the East . . .

America's East Coast, meanwhile, was also reasserting itself as a regional center for neo-punk, an unsurprising legacy as New York City was
punk-as-we-know-its undeniable ancestral home. Already home to legendary bands like Lodi, New Jersey's Misfits (largely credited for the
gang-vocal 'whoa whoa' choruses so prevalent in neo-pop punk) and vital, longstanding scenes in New York and Washington, D.C., the East
started unleashing in the mid-to-late '80s a slew of bands that would
prove vital to the next generation of punkers.

New York's Madball, formed in 1989 (and affiliated with longtime
scenesters Agnostic Front), made state-of-the-art New York hardcore en-
livened by brutal musicality. Sick of It All, probably New York's most
beloved hardcore band, formed in 1984 and continues to this day. S.O.I.A.
shows became notorious as out-of-control audience-participation sweat-
fests. The band further became associated with violence when in 1992,
college student Wayne Lo went on a murderous rampage in rural Massachusetts wearing a Sick of It All T-shirt.

The short-lived Gorilla Biscuits remain probably Gotham's most influential band of the era, however. The straight-edger combo's classic second
album, 1989's *Start Today*, combines shouted singalong hooks, tense
musical interplay, and outspoken attitude; its influence on contemporary
mainstream punk was demonstrated years later when Chad Gilbert, guitarist for late-'90s-era pop punkers New Found Glory, busted out a cherished, valuable first pressing of *Start Today* from his record collection on
MTV's "Cribs."

Meanwhile, over in New Brunswick, New Jersey, the Bouncing Souls
were beginning their reign as one of neo-punk's longest-running legacies.
Combining shoutalong choruses and a joyous energy with a hard-working
independent ethic, the Souls began as a quartet of punk-obsessed high
school kids in 1987. Ultimately, Bouncing Souls would embody the pop
punk aesthetic that would top the charts starting in the mid-'90s more
than any band in the East Coast region; their popularity would skyrocket
when they eventually signed to Gurewitz's Epitaph label in 1997, coming
nearly a decade after their first practice. "One band I can think of that
still holds original punk values is the Bouncing Souls," says Agent M of

Tsunami Bomb. "The Souls are all about playing shows for the kids and for themselves, and are very community-oriented. They are all heart, which is how all musicians should be."

But the most important movement for next-generation punk rock to come out of the East Coast would hail from a couple states over, in Washington, D.C. "I actually grew up in Maryland and D.C.," says Andrew Black of the Explosion. "There was just so much stuff that came out of D.C., I felt that I needed to look no further than my hometown. I would go see local bands like Las Mordidas, Severin, Cupid Car Club, Slant 6, Hoover, Kerosene 454, Jawbox, Fugazi, Junkyard Band, Lungfish; I completely lost my shit the first time I heard Bad Brains. I was so fucking blown away by this completely under-the-radar music."

In 1987, Fugazi was born Phoenix-like out of the ashes of two legendary D.C. groups: proto-"emocore" quartet Rites of Spring and seminal hardcore act Minor Threat. Fugazi had all of the things that could make a band succeed: an incredible live show that demanded audience participation in its dynamism, along with a distinctive musical interplay that propelled punk sonics to innovative heights.

More than anything, early Fugazi material featured catchy hooks that all the band's angularity couldn't smother. The song "Waiting Room" off Fugazi's eponymous 1988 EP is an instant smash, much like, say, Nirvana's "Smells Like Teen Spirit"—its "I am a patient boy/I wait, I wait, I wait" refrain is impossibly infectious, hard not to chant along with. However, riven by Ian MacKaye's and the band's unwavering integrity— Fugazi never charged more than ten dollars for their concerts, and ignored all big-money major label offers—the band would refuse to participate in neo-punk's commercially successful resurgence in the early-to-mid-'90s. There were many who would, however.

Everything Goes Orange: The O.C.'s New Punk Offspring

California in the late '80s and early '90s, in particular the beachside suburban area known as Orange County, would, in fact, prove to be the hothouse for the bands that would become the forefathers of the neo-punk/pop punk's commercial resurgence—and beyond: rap-rock pioneer Zack de la Rocha of Rage Against the Machine fame got his start fronting Orange County hardcore band Inside Out back in 1988. 'Eighty-eight proved to be a crucial year for California punk, as it was the year that Pennywise formed.

Still going strong, Pennywise remain one of the foremost bands of the neo-punk movement, but how far they would come wasn't so clear when the band first got together. Pennywise was born in the city that had become Orange County's legendary punk rock crucible, Hermosa Beach. Hermosa Beach was where iconic bands like Black Flag, the Descendents, and the Circle Jerks all first burst out locally before earning national notoriety.

Pennywise consisted of four baseball-hat-wearing surf-punk bros, guitarist Fletcher Dragge, singer Jim Lindberg, drummer Byron McMackin, and bass player Jason Thirsk. In 1989, the band put out its recorded debut, an EP titled *A Word from the Wise,* on local label Theologian Records, quickly sending buzz through the Southern California punk circles. Building to a roar, Pennywise's buzz got the attention of Brett Gurewitz, who signed the group to Epitaph one year later.

Upholding their Hermosa Beach legacy, Pennywise created "a sound that functioned as edgy, post-punk frat rock—it was speedy and occasionally stupidly catchy, with heavy, propulsive rhythms and positive, optimisitic lyrics that stood in pointed contrast to their grunge-addled peers," Stephen Thomas Erlewine writes on allmusic.com. Indeed, Pennywise's self-titled 1991 album debut was a call to arms for those who wanted to stay "pure" in the face of alt-rock orthodoxy: the band's official bio calls it a "middle finger directed at the grunge movement of the time."

Regardless of their antimainstream stance, Pennywise soon found themselves moving toward mass acceptance. Following its release, Pennywise's 1993 *Unknown Road* album sold in excess of 200,000 copies; in Southern California, the band would eventually grow to sell out 14,000-seat stadiums. "We were kind of starting to feel like we were doing something that really counted," Pennywise guitarist Fletcher Dragge notes in the documentary *The Epitaph Story.*

Also growing was the band's reputation for bad behavior, as extreme as the surfing and skating they loved. For one, Pennywise was hardly a straight-edge outfit—if anything, they grew to embody the opposite. Bassist Thirsk commited suicide in 1996 at the end of a long bout with alcoholism, and was replaced that year by Randy Bradbury. Dragge, meanwhile, was becoming known as the O.C.'s Sid Vicious: he was prone to vomit on audiences and occasionally on celebrities, like when he puked on radio/TV personality Riki Rachtman while Pennywise was performing at a KROQ-sponsored concert. (Radio shows seemed to bring out the worst in Dragge. Backstage at a KROQ "Weenie Roast" in 2000, Dragge attempted to strangle me, the author of this book, for no apparent reason—I had never met him or spoken to him before I felt his fingers gripping my throat.)

It was The Offspring, though, a band that used to open for Pennywise, that would become neo-pop punk's biggest sellers next to Green Day. The Offspring actually began three years earlier than Pennywise, a couple towns over in an undistinguished O.C. suburb called Garden Grove; their future success seemed unlikely considering the band's humble beginnings. The band that would become one of the biggest neo-punk groups in the world—in fact, one of the biggest groups in the world, period, regardless of genre—was formed in 1984 by two high school classmates, vocalist Dexter Holland and bass player Greg Kriesel, after the duo attended a particularly intense Social Distortion show in Irvine, California. Soon after, the pair recruited drummer Ron Welty and guitarist Kevin "Noodles" Wasserman, the custodian at Holland's and Kriesel's school.

The Offspring embodied—and continue to embody—the suburban style of classic O.C. punk. It's easy to spot Offspring's influences: in their trademark humor, there's the zippy funnypunk of O.C. punk originators the Vandals, who started in 1981 in Huntington Beach and whose 1982 debut EP *Peace Thru Vandalism* made them the first band other than Bad Religion to be signed to the Offspring's future home, Epitaph Records. In the Offspring's trademark rave-ups, meanwhile, one finds the surf-inflected twang, catchy gang choruses, and speedy rifferama of O.C. bands like the Crowd, the Adolescents, Agent Orange, and T.S.O.L (who would later sign to the Offspring's label, Nitro, in the decade following their '80s prime).

In addition to sonic aesthetics, however, what the Offspring shared most with those bands was a point of view shaped by their suburban surroundings—all palm trees, golf courses, chain stores, real estate developments, well-paved roads, and beautiful coastline (the term "golf punk" is an O.C. phenomenon). "I was really inspired by punk, but especially by the Orange County punk bands. That's what got us started in music," Offspring's Dexter Holland says. "I grew up on a suburban street. I love living where we live—I'm not going to move to France and wear a beret." "The appeal of suburbia is the safety; the problem is that the suburbs are boring, mundane, and monotonous," explains Fall Out Boy's Pete Wentz, whose own band is a product of the 'burbs. "It's the perfect place to launch a white leftist feel-good movement that is primarily based on crowd surfing and fashion."

It took some time, however, for the Offspring to make it beyond the suburban-punk borders. In 1986, the band pressed up 1,000 vinyl 7-inch copies of its first single, "I'll Be Waiting," by themselves, without the help of an established record company, to little fanfare—or fans. Three years later, Offspring's self-titled full-length album debut appeared on the indie label Nemesis/Cargo, produced by legendary California punk producer Thom Wilson, renowned for his knob-twiddling for bands like the Vandals, the Dead Kennedys, and T.S.O.L. *The Offspring* would go on to sell a mere 3,000 copies; it wasn't until the band signed to Epitaph Records in

1991 that the Offspring's success became any kind of possibility—and a remote one at that: in 1991, punk bands just didn't sell records on a mass scale. It would take a "smash" three years later to reverse that long-held music biz maxim, effectively changing punk from an underground cult to a mall-ready phenomenon.

Punk Rock Steady: The Sublime Ska-Reggae Revival

Unlike Pennywise and the Offspring, however, not all California punk bands ascribed solely to the rule of loud and fast rules! The jittery, offbeat rhythms of ska music, for one—always popular in the California music underground via bands like Fishbone and the Untouchables—soon grew in popularity alongside burgeoning neo-punk.

Ska, also known as "bluebeat" or "rock steady," began in 1960s Jamaica as a reggae subgenre. Groups like the Skatalites played it as a faster, more dance-floor-oriented version of popular West Indian music, driven by staccato horns and guitar. The sound subsequently spread internationally: ska took hold in the '60s with the Mod movement in England, and a ska revival occurred simultaneously around the beginning of the U.K. punk movement and the near-simultaneous rebirth of the Mod and skinhead movements there in the late '70s. The edgy, syncopated sounds from this era of U.K. new-style ska via bands like the Specials, the Beat (known as the English Beat in North America), and Madness crossed over to all factions. As well, thanks to movies like the ska documentary *Dance Craze* and supportive radio stations like Los Angeles's KROQ, ska soon crossed the Atlantic.

As such, ska began appearing alongside and within the punk resurgence of the mid-to-late 1980s, sometimes referred to as the "third-wave ska revival." "Skanking," the jerky, arm-waving dance associated with ska, had already found its way into the hardest of hardcore mosh pits; also, bands like Voodoo Glow Skulls and Sublime began incorporating "riddims" of Jamaican provenance with a distinct SoCal punk approach to create a new-school punky reggae party. Regionally, the SoCal ska swap meet produced the Voodoo Glow Skulls—formed not in Orange County but in the neighboring inland area, the Inland Empire, in 1988—who best represented ska's innately inclusive, multicultural approach. The Voodoo Glow Skulls combined the genre's high-energy beat with California's colorful *Chicano* flavor, complementing the bluebeat with equally syncopated Latin percussion and hornplay, as well as Mexican "Day of the Dead"–style imagery.

Naturally, Voodoo Glow Skulls signed with Epitaph in 1995, following the explosion in popularity of Green Day and Offspring the year before. As such, ska sounds proved wildly influential, spreading across the country through the '90s—bands like Boston, Massachusetts' Mighty Mighty Bosstones, New York's Slackers (featuring my old Carleton College classmate, T. J. Scanlon, on guitar), Gainesville, Florida's Less Than Jake, and Detroit, Michigan's Suicide Machines soon began appearing alongside typical Cali ska-punkers like Reel Big Fish and Goldfinger. Before they became pop superstars of today, No Doubt actually started as an O.C. ska band back in 1987 in their hometown of Anaheim, California; Rancid (and especially its predecessor Operation Ivy) have also brought bluebeat riddims into their sound.

The most important and influential of the SoCal reggae-influenced punkers, however, remains the Long Beach, California, trio Sublime. Formed in 1988, Sublime mixed the lilting rhythms of ska and reggae with indelibly catchy pop-punk hooks, a sunny yet debauched beach-party sensibility, and rap-influenced wordplay courtesy of charismatic frontman/guitarist Brad Nowell.

A Cali cult fave for some time with the skate 'n surf set they represented to the fullest, Sublime started attracting national attention for its song "Date Rape," a catchy but wildly politically incorrect ditty with possibly unironic overtones of homophobia and sexism. Despite—or maybe because of—the song's controversial content, "Date Rape" became a hit on major California alternative rock radio stations some years after appearing first on Sublime's indie 1992 debut album, *40 Oz. to Freedom*.

It wasn't until the band's eponymous third album was released in 1996, however, that the band fully broke through on a national scale. *Sublime* featured the band's biggest hit, the surf-campfire singalong "What I Got." Insanely hook-filled and instantly recognizable, with "What I Got" Sublime came as close to creating a genre-crossing pop standard as a punk-oriented band could; its trustafarian beach-bum *irie* can still be heard in the similarly inclined balladry of surf troubadour Jack Johnson.

Tragically, Brad Nowell died of a heroin overdose in May 1996 in San Francisco, a mere eight weeks before *Sublime* would be released to the public. Nowell's legacy continued, however—first by Sublime's rhythm section, drummer Bud Gaugh and bass player Eric Wilson, in a new collective, the Long Beach Dub AllStars, and then in a series of posthumous Sublime albums dredged up from unreleased material, making Nowell a sort of pop-ska-punk twist on Tupac. With such tragic protagonists and intense twists and turns that resembled the group's rhythmic pulse, the

Sublime story could make for a fine book unto itself—a new-school punk *Trainspotting*.

California Punk: Two States—North and South

The underground punk/ska revival of the late '80s also exploded in California's northern cities. Helping with the statewise cross-pollination was an L.A. scenester named Mike Burkett, who would eventually become a punk household name under the alias Fat Mike.

Circa 1986, Fat Mike had moved from Los Angeles to San Francisco's Bay Area to attend college. "I came out of the L.A. early '80s punk scene, so the defining word for punk was 'violence,'" Fat Mike recalls. "It was for sure the most violent and deadliest scenes ever. I'd witnessed two murders, one rape, one shooting, several stabbings, and countless severe beatings. After that I moved to San Francisco around '84 and things were much cooler."

Fat Mike's band NOFX had started some three years earlier in Los Angeles, but its growth would escalate following Mike's Northern California move. "I would say our peers were RKL, SNFU, Blast, Justice League, Dr. Know, Ill Repute, Don't Know, Scared Straight, and the Grim," Fat Mike explains. "All of those bands were better than us at the time, but we kept playing while they kept breaking up." NOFX in some way became the soul of this next wave of neo-punk, with Fat Mike becoming, along with Rancid, the conscience of the "scene" in the way Ian MacKaye had in Minor Threat's early '80s prime—if with slightly different personal politics.

The title of NOFX's 1992 album, *White Trash, Two Heebs and a Bean*, alone signaled the band's raunchy political incorrectness. *White Trash* even featured an irreverently bluesy, boozy cover version of Minor Threat's clean-livin' hardcore anthem "Straight Edge" that let everyone know that this new generation wasn't just punk and disorderly, they were *drunk* and disorderly, too. Per that example, testing the limits of freedom of speech in both the punk community and the world at large, NOFX left no sacred cow unslaughtered in a career that persists to this day.

Alongside bands like Pennywise and Offspring, NOFX followed the late-'80s resurgence of Bad Religion and signed with Epitaph Records. NOFX specialized in short, sharp shocks mixing a metallic KO punch with skanky ska, sloppily endearing vocal hooks, and provocative yet hilarious subject matter: lesbianism ("Liza and Louise"), venereal disease, vegetarianism, animal rights, race relations ("Kill All the White Man"), drugs ("Drug Free America"), plastic surgery ("New Boobs"), homelessness

("Hobophobic"), mean people, and even Fleetwood Mac covers ("Go Your Own Way" gets massacred deliciously on NOFX's 1989 Epitaph debut, *S&M Airlines*) all get sliced up by NOFX's cynically tongue-in-cheek bullshit detector.

Indeed, Fat Mike's pun-happy fat lip spares no idols, ruthlessly and willfully enraging the punk police throughout his band's history, even entitling one song "It's My Job to Keep Punk Rock Elite." Yet Fat Mike and NOFX have proven hugely influential to the next generation of neo-punks. For one, NOFX has remained a staunchly independent operation, free of major label interference or commercial concerns, releasing records on Epitaph and NOFX's own label, Fat Wreck Chords. "We avoided major labels by starting our own label," Fat Mike explains. "If you put out your own records, you don't need to sell that many to make a decent living. The temptation to sign to a major was there in the mid-90's when punk 'broke,' but after a few months of band discussions, we all agreed that going to a major was a terrible idea for NOFX. The subject has never come up since."

Fat Wreck Chords has proven so vital that it rivals Epitaph as the leading indie label documenting current punk rock. "When people criticize Fat, it's usually for producing a cookie-cutter sort of punk rock, where all the bands and the production values start to sound the same," states Lookout!'s Lawrence Livermore. "At the same time, it's been of a consistently high quality, and there's a large number of people who love that stuff."

Fat Mike & Co. have also held up punk's political end amid much apathy, releasing the successful *Rock Against Bush* compilations on Fat Wreck and working with punkvoter.com to mobilize against the establishment ruling powers. As well, even before they were popular, NOFX toured relentlessly, spreading the neo-punk gospel to impressionable youth throughout the States, into Europe, and beyond—even French-speaking Canada.

"Our first ever punk rock show was NOFX, who were touring with Ten Foot Pole and Face to Face," recalls Simple Plan's Chuck Comeau. "We were really impressed by how amazing and powerful the show was—and the energy. NOFX proved that you could get onstage and you didn't have to have a huge production; you didn't have to be the best musician like Steve Vai. You just had to play hard, jump around, go crazy, and above all be passionate about the music. That was really influential for us when we started out. Musically, we were influenced by all the Fat Wreck bands—we wanted to come up with our own version of them. Around the same time we'd been watching snowboard videos, and they had this new band called Offspring on the soundtrack. All those bands sort of came out all at the same time."

"I discovered punk rock in the mid-'90s when Fat Wreck Chords was really booming and No Use for a Name and NOFX were putting out, what I consider, some of their best records," Ryan Key, front man for pop punk superstars Yellowcard, said in a *Billboard* interview. "That was a big influence on me when I started sort of trying to become a songwriter."

Gilman Street Blues: Journey to the End of the East Bay

Ironically, NOFX landing in San Francisco's Bay Area put neo-punk's most politically incorrect whippersnappers into the center of punk's anticommercialist, anticorporate, most politicized bastion.

The greater San Francisco area has long existed as a poster city for counterculture movements—each one typically gets its distinct Bay Area spin, unless it started there in the first place. In the 1950s, the subversive Beat culture of music, literature, and poetry erupted out of San Francisco institutions, its leading lights like Allen Ginsberg and Lawrence Ferlinghetti making a scene around the venerated bookstore City Lights. In the '60s, the Bay was the center of the hippie/yippie "Summer of Love" uprising, centered around the Haight-Ashbury district. And in the '70s, Northern California's urban center became known as a home for pop music's most out-there movements, with sonic theater of the absurdists like the Residents, Tuxedomoon, and Snakefinger setting the area's experimental tone. Naturally, punk was ripe for a Bay Area radical makeover.

"I think what set the Bay apart most of all was its irreverence and youthful spirit: we often mocked the macho, hardcore attitudes of the older punk bands and made a direct appeal to the younger kids, almost as if we were saying, 'This isn't your older brother's punk rock,'" explains Lawrence Livermore. "And there are probably more punk shows per capita in the Bay Area than almost anywhere in the world."

Even before the dawn of neo-punk, San Francisco was already legendary in the punk diaspora for housing the West Coast version of CBGB's, a Filipino restaurant turned punk venue, the Mabuhay Gardens, and for the Sex Pistols' final performance ever in 1978 at Winterland. The Sex Pistol's S.F. swan song featured locals the Avengers as openers. The Avengers were a powerful unit fronted by the dangerously androgynous, shock-haired Penelope Houston, who commenced the region's era of punk controversy with the Avengers anthem "White Nigger." Jello Biafra would continue the iconoclastic tradition started by the Avengers: allegedly after witnessing the Avengers and the Sex Pistols at Winterland that fateful night, Biafra formed one of America's most popular second-wave punk groups, the Dead Kennedys.

The Dead Kennedys' influence proved huge both nationally and internationally: with their 1979 single, "Holiday in Cambodia," they verged on having an unlikely hit single, and their back catalogue still sells annually in the hundreds of thousands. But the legacy the Kennedys left on the Bay Area, particularly the East Bay area centered around Berkeley, was the outspoken radical political stance especially espoused by the band's leader and front man, Biafra. Collective-oriented institutions like the fanzine *Maximum Rocknroll* and the East Bay all-ages concert venue 924 Gilman thrived in this environment (started first as a radio show, *Maximum Rocknroll* entered the print domain with an insert for *Not So Quiet on the Western Front*, a punk compilation released on Biafra's Alternative Tentacles label).

"To me at the time (and I think to many of the other people involved), Gilman was far and away the most important thing happening in punk rock—just the fact that it *worked* set it apart from almost everything else that had gone before," explains Lawrence Livermore. "I'd seen dozens of attempts at nonprofit, volunteer-run institutions over the years, dating back to hippie times; almost without exception, they fell victim to infighting, self-indulgence, laziness, or corruption in a relatively short time. Gilman is over eighteen years old and still going strong. What was especially exciting about Gilman was the way it empowered people, especially young people, to do things and try things they never imagined they could do before. You had fourteen-year-olds seeing their friends start bands and a few weeks later be up onstage having the time of their lives. The next thing you know, those kids are asking themselves, 'What's stopping me from doing that too?'"

Institutions such as these provided a real alternative—and challenge—to mainstream culture: Gilman and *Maximum Rocknroll* proved that one didn't have to be coopted by mass culture to survive. "In terms of musical and cultural values, Gilman Street and the East Bay represent a very DIY, idealistic, and political strain of punk rock, one which was easily and immediately distinguishable from the more hedonistic and commercial strains of punk rock that had previously dominated the agenda," explains Lawrence Livermore. "Gilman, especially in the early days, challenged and broke down many of the established preconceptions of what punk was supposed to be about. No longer did you have to be the toughest or the meanest or the ugliest or most violent to qualify as a 'real' punk. It was an upwelling and flowering of culture that only happens every decade or two, and I consider myself extremely fortunate to have been a part of it."

Ironically, the East Bay's punk Petri dish of anticommercialism would prove to be the spawning ground for the bands that would turn punk into a true mainstream phenomenon. "The closest parallel to the East Bay scene was Washington, D.C., but D.C. bands had a reputation—not entirely undeserved—for being overly earnest and self-absorbed, whereas many of the East Bay bands took themselves a bit less seriously, and consequently, were more likely to resonate with a wider audience," Livermore explains. "As popular as Fugazi were, they were never going to launch a generation of Fugazi soundalikes who were even more popular; however, the punk scene today continues to be dominated (or afflicted, some might say) with the bastard offspring of Green Day and Operation Ivy."

Operation Ivy's significance to the transformation of neo-punk can't be denied. Many bands passed through Gilman St. in the late '80s, but they were the band that would unwittingly jump-start punk's rocket ride into the big time. Operation Ivy was formed in Berkeley, California, during the summer of 1987 by guitarist Lint (who would become better known under his government name, Tim Armstrong), bassist Matt Freeman, drummer Dave Mello, and vocalist Jesse Michaels, a quartet of like-mindedly open-minded young punks in their late teens and early twenties. Most of Operation Ivy's members had done time in unsung local bands, but with their new outfit their reputation would grow, eventually sung into national, and then international, legend.

Operation Ivy had found kindred spirits in the syncopated, uptempo dance-floor thump of ska and the racing rhythms of punk. While that wasn't a new pairing per se, in Op Ivy's hands it proved a volatile musical chemistry. Part of that appeal was the glue that Op Ivy used to bring these two genres together: passion and energy. To this day, Operation Ivy's reputation as an incredible live band remains vivid, that rep starting from their very first show at Gilman. In fact, Op Ivy signed to local imprint Lookout! Records after Lookout! founder Lawrence Livermore saw that first Gilman show. According to Livermore, "Operation Ivy, who I'd worked with almost since the beginning, were Lookout's second biggest band after Green Day. And how did I discover them? By going to shows at Gilman. They played there all the time in 1987 and 1988. As much as I came to like Rancid later on, I was a much bigger fan of Operation Ivy in the early years. They just had an almost incandescent ability to connect with and ignite a crowd. Seeing them onstage at Gilman in their prime will probably always be among my most memorable musical experiences."

In fact, before Op Ivy, Lookout! Records barely existed. A former columnist for *Maximum Rocknroll*, Livermore started Lookout! first as a fanzine, then jump-started its label imprint in order to release Operation Ivy's first single, "Hectic," in 1988. Lookout!—which took its name from Livermore's own band, the Lookouts, which featured future Green Day skinsman Tré Cool as its twelve-year-old drummer—would go on to put out early efforts from bands like Green Day, the Donnas, the Mr. T Experience, and the Alkaline Trio, among many others. Regardless, Operation Ivy was undeniably the spiky-haired spark that started it all.

"Lookout! never had the stated job of representing the Gilman scene in its entirety, but to the rest of the underground music world at that time nationally, Lookout! was the Gilman Street label," explains Chris Appelgren, who began at Lookout! as a fifteen-year-old intern, rising to become the label's president and eventual owner. "It made for an interesting relationship with our local scene, where many expectations of the label were likely not met."

To the world, however, Op Ivy represented Gilman incarnate—everything good about the East Bay punk incubator. In addition to its explosive musical attack, Operation Ivy also appealed due to its ethical stance; the band was never afraid to display its intelligence and views shaped and simmered in the East Bay's polemical crock pot, and audiences responded with respect. On songs like "Knowledge," "Jaded," and "The Crowd," front man and lyricist Michaels self-consciously pushes the punk scene to better itself and become more self-aware with the primal eloquence of Ian MacKaye's lyrics in Minor Threat. But the passion for music is never far: with "Sound System," Operation Ivy creates an ineffaceable ode to the joy of music, the ecstatic rush that makes everything all right, while the instrumental "Bankshot" showed the band's musical adeptness at harnessing ska's tricky rhythms.

Operation Ivy lasted two short years, following a number of local shows and a national tour. The band was killed, alas, by success: as Op Ivy's reputation rose, so did, paradoxically, major label interest in signing them. Operation Ivy had always operated from an East Bay–style grassroots perspective, from releasing records on a local indie label and playing anyplace, anyhow, anywhere to designing their own artwork (the band's infamous "skanking man" logo remains a strong T-shirt seller).

This pressure drove the band apart in 1989; Operation Ivy's debut album, the aptly titled *Energy*, would be released posthumously a short time later in 1990. Rancid, the band that would evolve from Op Ivy's ashes (and ultimately eclipse them in popularity), would pay hindsight tribute to their previous band's rise and fall on the stirring anthem "Journey to the End of the East Bay" off Rancid's 1995 breakthrough album, . . . *And Out Come the Wolves*: "Too much attention unavoidably destroyed us. . . ."

Despite Op Ivy's untimely demise, no premonition could've predicted how they had managed to lay the groundwork for a new generation of East Bay punk vitality. One of Operation Ivy's biggest fans was a kid named Billie Joe Armstrong, who had started a band in 1986 called Sweet

Children with a pal, Mike Pritchard (who would later change his stage name to Dirnt), when the pair were barely old enough to be high school freshmen. Armstrong and Dirnt lived in a small waterfront town, Rodeo, California, population 11,000, a working-to-middle class hamlet with a median income hovering around $50,000. Technically part of the Bay Area's eight counties, Rodeo's sixteen square miles lie in fact nearly 30 miles southwest of San Francisco's urban center, but the clarion call of Gilman Street's "forbidden beat" still made itself known to Rodeo's disaffected youth.

Having added drummer Al Sobrante (born John Kiffmeyer) in 1987, Sweet Children played their first show in 1988 at a barbeque restaurant called Rod's Hickory Pit, making the Gilman Street scene soon after. But it was at a high school house party that Sweet Children would make their most significant impact. The gig headlined Lawrence Livermore's more established band, the Lookouts (whose youthful drummer, Tré Cool, would later join Green Day).

Livermore's connection to Sweet Children came from his acquaintance with Kiffmeyer, who had previously played in Lookout! band Isocracy. But when Livermore saw Sweet Children's scrappy, generator-powered performance, however, the future was quickly laid out for him. According to Livermore, at that nascent Sweet Children concert, the men who would be Green Day "played their hearts out anyway, as if they were the Beatles at Shea Stadium, and I immediately decided I wanted to make a record with them, even though it was only their third or fourth show ever." Livermore quickly signed Sweet Children to Lookout! Records.

Displaying a tendency that would continue when its members later started Green Day, Sweet Children trafficked in the pain of the outcast's lost innocence, as demonstrated on the band's eponymous anthem, singing about a tortured young protagonist who is running from the light of day.

That song appeared on an eponymous 1990 EP on Minneapolis' Skene imprint, a small indie label known for releasing singles by Bay Area bands Crimpshine and proto-emo heroes Jawbreaker as well as local Minnesotan alt-rock power trio Walt Mink and jazzbo Chicago post-punkers Trenchmouth. "The Sweet Children" EP also presciently features a young, loud, and snotty cover of the Who's "My Generation"; that release would prove Sweet Children's last, belated hurrah, however, for soon enough the Green Day generation would make itself known.

The *Sweet Children* EP actually came out after the band had already transformed into Green Day, taking their name from what greenday.net claims "is Bay-area slang for a day with lots of green bud where you just sit around taking bong hits, hanging around. Billie Joe picked the phrase up from friends while chilling in his 'habitat' (in the basement of a Berkeley University building), and wrote the song 'Green Day' about his first pot experience." The lyrics to "Green Day" emphasize the stoner interpretation: "My lungs comfort me with joy . . . My eyes itch of burning red."

"Green Day" appeared on the official release of Green Day's debut album, 1991's *1,039/Smoothed Out Slappy Hour*, actually a collection of the band's early EPs on Lookout! *1,039 . . .* proved undeniably catchy, distilling intact, with some rough edges, the bright, speedy pop-punk sound and vision that would make Green Day famous. As well, Green Day's album debut manifested what would become the band's ideal trademark— capturing of all the awkwardness of tortured, protracted adolescence in songs like "16."

Already, a major part of Green Day's allure was becoming clear: while Green Day trafficked in three-chord minimalism, unlike many of their punk peers, they maintained a keen sense for imbuing those three chords with classic pop song structure and melody. And did we mention they're cute? Still, despite the infectious promise of *1,039 . . .* , Green Day's future success was hardly assured: if they had remained forever in the indie, East Bay punk-rock ghetto, no one would've been surprised. "When Green Day's first album appeared, anyone predicting that fame, MTV, top-selling albums, and more would be on the horizon in the near future would have been happily patted on the head and then sent to the insane asylum," writes Ned Raggett in a review posted on allmusic.com.

The same year that Green Day released their debut album, ex-Operation Ivy members Tim Armstrong and Matt Freeman formed what would become neo-punk's third biggest wheel after Green Day and Offspring: Rancid. Following Op Ivy's breakup, Armstrong and Freeman had dallied in other bands popping out of the Gilman scene. For a short time, the pair acted as the dominant creative forces in the more expressly ska-oriented combo Dance Hall Crashers; they also briefly joined the band Downfall with Op Ivy drummer Dave Mello. Yet it was with Rancid, who also featured yet another Gilman scenester, Brett Reed, on drums and in 1993 added ex-Slip/U.K. Subs guitarist Lars Frederiksen, that the pair would create what for many was the perfect template of a '90s neo-punk band.

Rancid's Armstrong and Freeman shared a lot in common with their peers: like Green Day's Billie Joe Armstrong and Mike Dirnt, they, too, were Gilman scene insiders who hailed from a small East Bay town, Albany, on the wrong side of the Bay Area tracks. Both bands played punk with a retro-revivalist's spirit from the get-go: many a critic has compared the singing of both of neo-punk's most famous—if unrelated—Armstrongs to that of the spittle-garbled roar of the Clash's Joe Strummer (Green Day typically gets some Buzzcocks comparisons, too).

Also like Green Day, Rancid released their debut recordings on Lookout! In 1992, Rancid put out a self-titled 7-inch EP featuring five brief yet blistering street-punk anthems (one, "The Sentence," clocked in at just over a minute and a half). Rancid proved to be a refreshing new voice, and in 1993 they joined Brett Gurewitz's growing Epitaph stable of future punk stars.

"It wasn't that Rancid left Lookout!," Appelgren says. "We had no contracts. We made them no offer. We loved Rancid, and would've been happy to release their albums. Epitaph, however, was far more developed as a business and made a very compelling offer to the band." Lookout! founder Lawrence Livermore proves less sanguine on the matter. "Rancid really only did their first single on Lookout!, and although I was pretty upset when they decided to go to Epitaph for their album, I can't say that I blame them," Livermore states. "The simple fact was that I wasn't that enthusiastic about the band in the early days and Brett from Epitaph was. I was a huge fan of Tim and Matt's earlier bands, especially Operation Ivy and Downfall, but something about early Rancid struck me as a little too harsh and macho—for instance, their wanting to put a gun on the cover of their first album. I didn't think that was cool."

It's no surprise what appealed to Gurewitz to sign Rancid, though. On the sixteen tightly wound songs off the band's self-titled 1993 album debut on Epitaph, Rancid demonstrated all the intensity of Op Ivy's punk-oriented material, but with an even rawer attack—and even catchier, shoutier hooks. This was no-brainer music with a brain—and bravery, too: on "The Bottle," Armstrong sings frankly about the life-destroying alcoholism that he needed to conquer in order to make Rancid a reality. Once in recovery, however, Armstrong still spit out his gutter poetry with a distinctively garbled drunken master slur that evoked, say, the Pogues' Shane MacGowan, or, of course, Joe Strummer after a couple pints.

Most significantly, the band, with their uncompromising sonic aesthetic and full-on punk gear—tattoos, Mohican 'dos, spikes, boots, leather, bristles, studs, and acne—demonstrated that they really lived the punk life to the fullest. On record, onstage, and at home, they were the same: real—and *real* punk. When Rancid was onstage, it was hard to tell them from their audience, epitomized especially by Lars Frederiksen's unwavering devotion to punk's gutter roots. "That's his job," Brett Gurewitz says of Frederiksen's everypunk persona. "I love Lars. He'd say it's more than his job, it's his life. It's . . . *who he is*."

At the same time as they kept the flame of "true punk" burning, Rancid poised themselves to take Operation Ivy's stylistic fluency even further.

"As far as Rancid goes, I think we're all from the same fucking thing—ska, reggae, punk rock," Rancid guitarist/vocalist Lars Frederiksen explains of his band's trademark sound. "That's all a part of our growing up, so there you have it."

1994: The Year Punk Really Broke, Part One

In 1992, a scruffy, roughly handmade documentary entitled *1991: The Year Punk Broke* was released. Centered around Sonic Youth and featuring tour footage of fashionable indie-alternarock bands of the time like Babes in Toyland and Dinosaur Jr., . . . *The Year Punk Broke* was most notable as it captured Nirvana smack in the midst of their unexpected rise to grunge superstardom. Nirvana's surprising, seemingly overnight hugeness (in fact, years in the making) was the root of the title: no one from rock's real underground had made it before Nirvana, and with so little compromise. Yet by 1991, even experimental-rock gods like Sonic Youth were signed to major labels and appearing on MTV.

The "punk" in the title was there because Nirvana and Sonic Youth were outsider music, but no one really thought they were really "punk"; if anything, the title was ironic, tweaking more than anything the sellout of underground rock's ideals. Both bands had descended from punk rock, certainly—these were the children of '80s punk who had moved on. Yes, Sonic Youth came out of New York's post-CBGB era, and had recorded for Black Flag's SST label, and Kurt Cobain didn't hide his love for San Francisco noise punks Flipper and Portland, Oregon's Wipers. But while there was barre-chord fury in Nirvana, Kurt Cobain's vision couldn't be limited strictly to the punk genre. While their rise though the '80s into the '90s was nearly simultaneous, Nirvana stood apart from bands like Bad Religion, Pennywise, Offspring, NOFX, Green Day, and Rancid, who pledged allegiance to a more purist punk aesthetic.

That said, it often took a purist to distinguish between grunge and neo-punk. After Nirvana whisked away the hair-metal generation with the megasuccess of "Smells Like Teen Spirit" in 1991, the '90s grunge revolution was upon us. Suddenly record companies, MTV, and radio station programmers couldn't find enough grunge bands to fill up the airtime. All at once America had a new and improved appetite for loud, aggressive guitars; disaffected, angry vocals; and cute, if distraught, frontmen, regardless of genre.

Enter Green Day. Green Day was not the first punk band to have big radio singles and MTV videos. That honor would go to Social Distortion—iconic, longstanding Orange County bad-boy punkers who had released the second-wave California punk masterpiece *Mommy's Little Monster* in 1983. (Social Distortion is so O.G. O.C., the band's original bassist and guitarist, Frank and Rikk Agnew, would go on to form the area's pop punk thrashers bar none, the Adolescents. Social Distortion persevered, however, sans the brothers Agnew.) As the band matured, Social Distortion's sound got more accessible, incorporating Stones-style rock and roll and classic country influences into their classic O.C. punk style. Newfound musical maturity found Social D. eventually scoring a hit with the track "Bad Habit" during 1992's wave of alternative rock mania.

1992 also saw the release of Green Day's second Lookout! album, *Kerplunk!* (and the band's first with former Lookouts drummer Tré Cool). *Kerplunk!* had solidified the elements that made up the band's appeal. Opener "2000 Light Years Away" blasted out what would become Green Day's foolproof formula: all unrequited, nostalgic yearning, but with a beat you can mosh to.

The Green Day sound had it all: a retro, Buzzcocks-style, angsty pop-punk fizz, 1960s Beatlesque chiming pop melody, and *chunka-chunka* guitars that were one part Hüsker Dü and two parts heavy metal. There was both humor (check out *Kerplunk!*'s country S&M hoedown "Dominated Love Slave") and hope in the Green Day sound.

Ultimately, Green Day didn't intimidate, eluding the violent hardcore clichés of punk that still made up America's media conception of the genre. Instead, Green Day's friendly, bruised, yet humorous pop punk proved a welcoming call to all like-minded outcasts (putting themselves into the literary outsider tradition, Green Day even includes on *Kerplunk!* a song entitled "Who Wrote Holden Caulfield?"). You didn't have to be the toughest pseudo-Henry Rollins guy in the pit to get Green Day. Indeed, it was possible to like the Smiths and still get Green Day. *Girls* liked Green Day. Especially girls.

Alt-rock fans found it was indeed possible to like Nirvana and Green Day at the same time as well. With his whine filtered through a fake English accent, frontman Billie Joe proved irresistible—troubled and sputtering melancholy like Kurt Cobain, yes, but more likely to bust a grape in a food fight than blow his head off with a shotgun. As such, *Kerplunk!* held the key to both Green Day's future and past—where they were going and where they had been. The album included the original *Sweet Children* EP as bonus tracks, as well as "Welcome to Paradise"—the only song from *Kerplunk!* that would make it to the band's major label debut, Green Day's massive 1994 breakthrough album *Dookie*.

Warner Bros. A&R executive Rob Cavallo had been scouting Green Day for some time. In the wake of the grunge explosion, major labels had looked to underground labels like Sub Pop, who had nurtured Nirvana, as potential treasure chests holding the next big thing. Furthermore, bands weaned on an underground grassroots approach had already developed their sound—with them, labels didn't have to spend millions on the kind of pop-star industrial production they way they might on, perhaps, a marketably pretty girl who couldn't sing *or* write songs, but just might be the next Mariah Carey. Most importantly, some indie bands had built a substantial following to exploit: both of Green Day's indie albums had sold upward of 50,000 copies—not blockbuster numbers for a major label, but strong enough to build a blockbuster on.

As Rob Cavallo advised, Reprise/Warner Bros.—home to alternative rock megastars like R.E.M. and the Red Hot Chili Peppers—signed Green Day. Cavallo went on to produce *Dookie* (and most of Green Day's albums, for that matter). Any lo-fi, indie, DIY fuzz was scraped away—the songs remained the same, but Green Day now had the freeze-dried, massive sound of Nirvana's *Nevermind* that was all over the radio.

In no time following *Dookie*'s release on February 1, 1994, Green Day was on the radio, too. More significantly, punk rock was on the radio. Not grunge—*punk rock*. Catchy punk rock, yes, but still recognizable as punk. In one fell swoop, punk had become pop narcotic, the new opiate of the young people. Amidst chugga-chugga rifferama, *Dookie*'s first salvo, "Longview," describes an ennui that proved universal to '90s kids: "I'm so damn bored I'm going blind."

Another of *Dookie*'s hits, "Basketcase," continues in this vein: "Do you have the time to listen to me whine?" Meanwhile, "When I Come Around," *Dookie*'s biggest smash, served as the uncynical, romantic cousin to Nirvana's "Come As You Are," featuring Billie Joe memorably moaning "I'm a loser and a user, so I don't need no accuser." These were losers' anthems—and suddenly everyone wanted to be a loser. "When I Come Around," *Dookie*'s fourth single, ended up spending seven full weeks as modern rock radio's most popular song, at a time when modern rock radio was still ruling the airwaves.

Mainstream critics were not uniformly kind to *Dookie*, however. Many clubbed Green Day's sonics as too self-consciously retro in their punk aesthetics—Armstrong's sneering ersatz English accent was drubbed as second-rate Clash mimicry. But to young America—and soon enough, the world—*Dookie* was an instant generational classic on the scale of *Nevermind*; it may prove even more influential, ultimately. "Green Day made a huge impact on alternative-rock music," explains Agent M of Tsunami Bomb. "They started my personal concept of punk—before I heard them I listened to stuff like Stone Temple Pilots and Nirvana. Then Green Day came and paved the way for *our* generation of punk rockers—in fact, the current wave is still riding off Green Day, down to Good

Charlotte." "My initial punk role models were Ben Weasel [of the band Screeching Weasel] and Billie Joe," confesses Fall Out Boy's Pete Wentz.

The unfolding of *Dookie*'s success felt much like *Nevermind*'s—a shot from out of nowhere, exploding in the sky for all to see. As *Dookie*'s singles ricocheted around radio and MTV, the album sold over one million copies. And then another million. And then another. And then another shot came from out of nowhere: Kurt Cobain killed himself exactly two months and one week to the day of *Dookie*'s release, leaving pop music all too void of rock stars who didn't buy into the generic fame machinery hook, line, and sinker.

Unwittingly, Green Day were one of the very few around to fill that void. Representing the youngest, loudest, and snottiest generation, Green Day was a surprise hit at the hoariest (and whoriest) of rock festivals, 1994's mud-spattered return of baby-boomer-defining Woodstock. Their reach extended far into America, deeper than any punk-oriented band had before. "The first punk band I heard was Green Day because I lived in middle-of-nowhere central California," says Tsunami Bomb's Agent M. "The only music we had coming in was mainstream radio and MTV. After I heard Green Day there, I loved the music so much I did research and discovered other bands like Operation Ivy and Rancid, whose records I'd special-order."

All in all, *Dookie* would end up moving *ten million* units worldwide— some eight million of those in the United States. Punk rock would never be the same. Cries of "sellout" began rumbling in punk rock cultural centers: to them, Green Day was the new corporate evil, on a par with, say, McDonald's. Still, most were assured that it wouldn't happen again—one punk band on the radio was all America could handle, the purists figured.

Then the punk-rock lightning struck twice.

1994: The Year Punk Really Broke, Part Two

When the Offspring made the big move and signed with Epitaph Records for their second album, the results didn't kick in right away. According to the band's official timeline, the record release party in Fullerton, California, for the Offspring's sophomore full-length, 1992's *Ignition*, lured a crowd of just twenty-five people. But the band's next album, *Smash*, released only thirteen months after *Ignition*, would change all that.

Punk pundits saw the success of Green Day as a fluke. Another punk band on the radio? Impossible. The major labels had been taken by surprise by *Dookie*'s megawatt success—they were still scouring the country for the next Green Day when they got caught off guard yet again. The next Green Day would not come from the major labels, however, but from punk's indie label minor leagues—which proved to be more than just a minor threat. Offspring would prove to be the "next" Green Day, thanks to their uncannily titled *Smash* album.

Epitaph's biggest seller before the Offspring's *Smash* was Bad Religion's 1992 release *Generator*, which has moved roughly 150,000 copies over the years. Hopes for *Smash*, released on April 15, 1994, most likely hovered well below those levels, especially for Offspring vocalist Dexter Holland. Holland was an unlikely rock star: actually born Bryan Keith Holland, he took the stage name Dexter to represent his authentic geek stink—before he attained stardom, Holland was a graduate student in genetics and molecular cell biology on the Ph.D track. (Holland represents a strange minor trend among neo-punk luminaries: advanced degrees in science. Descendents front man Milo Aukerman also holds a master's degree in genetics, while Bad Religion vocalist Greg Graffin has a master's in geology and a Ph.D. from Cornell in biology.) Holland was actually struggling to balance his science career with the band, but *Smash*'s success made his decision easy.

Like *Dookie*'s rise, *Smash*'s lived up to its name, coming in from left field. Before it became a hit, even punk's most righteous Bible, *Maximum Rocknroll*, called it "the punk record of the year!!!" *Maximum Rocknroll* wouldn't be so enthused, though, as *Smash* entered the mainstream.

The buzz on Offspring began when trend-setting Los Angeles alt-rock radio station KROQ started playing "Come Out and Play (Keep 'Em Separated)" off *Smash*. "Come Out and Play" wedded grunge's loud-soft dynamics with shouty call-and response O.C. punk and hard rock heft; a freaky-deaky Middle Eastern–inflected surf-rock guitar line made the song additionally memorable. The whole package, down to Holland's deadpan yelp, was inexplicably hard to resist; this was grunge *sans* the emotional content, metal without the guilt. Meanwhile, the lyrics' social commentary in "Come Out . . ." reflected current events via the Offspring's suburban origins—the song ironically describes a not-in-my-backyard fear of urban gang warfare typical in O.C.-style hamlets.

Soon the song was inescapable. MTV even put "Come Out and Play" 's bargain-basement video—filled with cheap stock footage, cheeseball psychedelic video effects, and numerous shots of Holland throwing his ridiculous braids through the air—into heavy rotation. *Smash* wasn't as obviously pop-friendly as *Dookie*—tracks like "Bad Habit" reflected a combination of breakneck, metal-influenced second-generation U.K. punk à la GBH and the expected O.C. influences, with some variation; the guitar heroics of "Gotta Get Away" reflected a secret suburbanite love for Van Halen, while "What Happened to You?" was a catchy, caffeinated ska-pop-punk workout.

Regardless, the *Smash* hits kept coming: "Gotta Get Away" and "Self-Esteem" proved equally omnipresent. *Smash* would rise to number four on *Billboard*'s top albums chart. Its sales would go on to eclipse even *Dookie*'s stratospheric numbers; reaching over eleven million copies sold in the United States and internationally, *Smash* became the bestselling record on an independent record ever released. Punk was now officially a mass phenomenon thanks to Green Day and Offspring: both bands became united as punk's first mainstream ambassadors in the eyes of a new generation of punk bands coming up behind them.

"It's funny—at the same time, all those bands started popping out. Some were more mainstream than others, like Green Day and Offspring, but a lot of them were very underground; it was all definitely a huge part of our growing up," says Simple Plan's Chuck Comeau. "Green Day was absolutely important: we saw the 'Longview' video first on our local station—it wasn't even MTV, it was called 'Music First Montreal'—and it all made sense. *Dookie* was such a huge influence, we then went back and bought *Kerplunk*. We bought *Ignition* by the Offspring first, and then *Smash* came out."

No one was more shocked by the Offspring's success, however, than the Offspring themselves. "It's always a shock," Dexter Holland clarifies. "I don't think anyone can put out a record, have it do great, and not be a little surprised. I don't know—maybe U2 can. You just never know what people are going to like; it's amazing to us, it really is."

Even more amazing was how quickly punk was coopted by the corporate pop music conglomerates, the coup de grace of punk's acceptance by the music industry delivered when Green Day won 1994's Grammy Award for Best Alternative Music Performance. Even before that honor was bestowed, the call had gone out to A&R executives everywhere: find the next Green Day—or else! The hysteria even hit the neo-punk indie labels that had birthed the movement. "Other bands, whether they were already affiliated with Lookout! or only wanted to be, got it in their heads that we should be able to manufacture the same kind of success for them," Lawrence Livermore says. "I had to expend a great deal of time and energy explaining to them that Green Day had created most of their own success, and that merely being on Lookout or spending large sums of money on promo and PR couldn't guarantee that kind of success for other bands."

If anything, the post-1994 moment felt like the earlier '90s, a repeat of when music-biz types swarmed, say, Nirvana's Seattle hometown to find the "next" Kurt Cobain or rifled through Smashing Pumpkins' Chicago neighborhood in the hope of finding another Billy Corgan. "When *Smash* did well they said, 'Oh, it's the new punk thing.' There are scenes, like

L.A. punk in the 1980s and the Seattle grunge thing, that are legitimate scenes, but what they called the punk explosion in 1994 wasn't like that at all," Dexter Holland recalls. "It just so happened that we had a record that did well, and Green Day had a record that did well."

"Of course it affected the local scene," Lookout's Chris Appelgren notes of life on Gilman Street after punk finally broke in 1994. "Attitude-wise, the Bay Area and East Bay scene's response and reaction to the new mainstream success of punk music was no different than anywhere else in the country." According to Lawrence Livermore, the backlash proved immediate: "Many Gilman bands and kids deliberately tried to move in the opposite direction, becoming more anti-commercial and reverting back to the more nihilistic values and styles of early-'80s punk." Despite the raw, uncompromising nature of those following in Green Day's wake, Appelgren claims, "There was still a feeling that maybe Berkeley could somehow be the next Seattle—an idea that now seems so ridiculous."

Music-industry professionals, however, were going to make Berkeley the next Seattle by any means necessary, whether it was or not. Eventually, corporate rock's representative vultures found themselves swooping around another band made up of East Bay scene heroes: Rancid. A&R types from numerous labels collectively decided that Rancid would be Pearl Jam to Green Day's Nirvana, a phenomenon that Rancid parodied in the title of their 1995 breakthrough album, ... *And Out Come the Wolves*. The wolves represented the major label music industry, the wolves' prey Rancid. And the wolves weren't entirely wrong, either.

Out Come The Wolves, Indeed . . .

Times are gonna change, change or step aside.

—Rancid, "Avenues & Alleyways"

Rancid released their next album, *Let's Go*, on June 14, 1994, just as America was feeling the full grip of neo-punk mania. Rancid's first album had done well for a pre-*Dookie* punk album—it sold around 200,000 copies—but now the band was poised to hit the big time. *Let's Go* would do the trick, but without compromise.

Recorded before punk had hit its big-time apex, *Let's Go* was pure, uncut Rancid: the album showcases the band's punk classicism like never before. Basically, the basic critical complaint about Rancid was that they remade the Clash's first album over and over, with a smudge of gutter-punk mascara—and this was the album that started all that. The exuberant "Radio" even name-checks Clash songs like "This Is Radio Clash" and "The Magnificient Seven."

The rabid fans who bought *Let's Go* didn't care about the critics, though. They loved songs like "Nihilism," "Tenderloin" and "Side Kick," where Frederiksen and Armstrong traded verses about living *la vida punka*—from Armstrong's battle with the bottle to the violence, poverty, and dangerous romance of East Bay street life.

Let's Go's intrinsic appeal, though, came from songs like "Radio," the title track, and "Salvation," all of which revel in the cathartic, life-saving release of punk music. "By example, Rancid was saying 'Punk rock is a viable music art form—it's unique to our culture, and we're gonna achieve *greatness* with it,'" Gurewitz confirms. "Salvation," meanwhile, was the closest thing *Let's Go* had to a hit single: Rancid still wasn't as radio-friendly as Green Day or Offspring, but this song still cut through to inspire the kids who needed to hear it. "You can get into what Rancid are saying on 'Salvation' no matter who you are—it really speaks for all of us," says Bert McCracken, front man for "screamo" punk stars the Used, who was just twelve years old when "Salvation" was released. "Rancid live to play music, and that's the message of a lot of their songs. They've inspired so many kids to do what they dream to do."

In 1994, Rancid inspired at least 500,000 kids—that's how many copies *Let's Go* sold in North America, earning the band its first gold record certificate. Such strong sales earned the band even more rabid attention from major labels—gossip circulated in the punk underground about how many thousands Madonna's record company, Maverick, was spending on sushi dinners at Nobu for the band—and beyond. "Along with the offers came scores of rumors as well: Rancid allegedly convinced an Epic A&R man to shave his head into a dyed-blue Mohawk, and Madonna reportedly sweetened the pot with naked pictures of herself," journalist George B. Sanchez wrote in a 2003 Rancid profile in the *East Bay Express*.

Rancid chose to stay with Epitaph, but the feeding frenzy definitely affected them, demonstrated by the title of their next album, . . . *And Out Come the Wolves*. Rancid's third album would surpass even the gold ranking awarded to *Let's Go*, rising to platinum with a million sold. It remains, arguably, the band's masterpiece. "Rancid is the greatest punk band to come out of the second wave, and . . . *Out Comes the Wolves* is probably the best American punk record," Brett Gurewitz notes. "It's the *Born to Run*, the defining moment of the time: the Ramones were the defining American punk band, but Rancid made the defining album of *my* generation. They lived the life the way they portrayed themselves on the record. Every day. Rancid eat, drink, breathe, *sleep* punk rock." "They're proof you can be one of the biggest bands in the world and still be cool, down-to-earth, quality dudes," says Dropkick Murphys drummer Matt Kelly.

. . . And Out Come the Wolves succeeded largely by capturing the sound of a band embracing and celebrating its roots. The album featured some of Rancid's best ska-oriented songs: "Roots Radicals" pays tribute to reggae legends like Desmond Dekker in both sound and words, while the natty "Time Bomb" is a ranking, skanking bluebeat rave-up bar none. Nostalgia for the past is an ongoing theme: "Junkyman" features CBGB's-era punk poet and *Basketball Diaries* author Jim Carroll, while "Journey to the East Bay" teems with wistful fondness for the band's Gilman Street days, days that seem so innocent now that punk is big business.

And then there's "Ruby Soho," the song that would prove the album's biggest hit on radio and MTV. With its infectious (if nonsensical) singalong chorus "Destination unknown, Ruby, Ruby/Ruby, Ruby Soho," Rancid distilled the vagabond romance of punk life into anthem form. "Ruby Soho" shows Rancid to the world at the band's most rollicking and exuberant best. While *Dookie* and *Smash* sold better, . . . And Out Come the Wolves made Rancid heroic role models to the next wave of punk bands. "When you're hanging out with Tim Armstrong, and Matt Freeman is wearing a Simple Plan shirt onstage, it's the best feeling," Simple Plan's Chuck Comeau exclaims. "I mean, what else could you want? Rancid's where we come from."

Stranger Than Fiction: The Aftermath

Business man, come shake my hand.

—Rancid, "Disorder & Disarray"

The success of Green Day and Offspring set punk's new gold standard at multiplatinum; expectations were now high for a genre for which just a few years before mainstream success wasn't even an option. Rancid had graduated to a spot on the 1996 Lollapalooza tour, the most prestigious summer event for almighty alternative rock. Playing the main stage alongside nonpunk grunge stars like Soundgarden and heavy metal gods Metallica, Rancid's stage time was slotted in right before punk originators the Ramones. Even the bands that were too raw, too fast, too *silly* to be prime time players were getting a leg up via association from their platinum-dipped peers: NOFX saw their 1994 *Punk in Drublic* album shoot past 500,000 copies sold to attain "gold" status. The Offspring even managed to sell a million copies more of their pre-*Smash* album, 1992's *Ignition*, off the buzz.

According to Lookout's Chris Appelgren, this was proof that the times, well, they weren't a changin'—the damage was already done. "In the wake of Green Day, Rancid, the Offspring and other punk bands' successes, punk rock was understood as commercially viable," Appelgren says. "Over the course of the next three to five years, a junior major label–style punk industry developed. Punk as a musical culture began to have more in common with the hip-hop music scene—developing a symbiotic role within the mainstream music business, as opposed to being a social, cultural, and poltical response to it."

The most shocking such development to punk purists occurred when Bad Religion signed to major label Atlantic, which released the album *Stranger Than Fiction* in 1994. In the purists' eyes, this was sacrilege: Bad Religion were the originators, the outspoken political voice that refused to be silenced, the DIY crew who released their own albums and booked their own tours. Punk bands signing to major labels had proven controversial from the get-go: how could the voice of a revolution be broadcast from an evil multinational conglomerate? History, the punk peanut gallery grumbled, was doomed to repeat itself.

"Punk died the day the Clash signed with CBS," British fanzine scribe Mark Perry wrote in 1977.* Black Flag, meanwhile, had spiraled into a half-decade of legal woes that prevented them from releasing music under the band's name when a deal with an MCA subsidiary went sour. Jawbox, a noisy Washington, D.C. band who made their name recording for the righteously independent Dischord label, raised eyebrows when they signed with Atlantic in the mid-1990s. They were the first band to exit Dischord for supposedly greener corporate pastures, but the move's repercussions ultimately broke Jawbox up after two releases.

"The majors couldn't even break the Clash, remember?" Gurewitz says. "But now they were like, 'Hey, punk—this is the next big thing.' Spiky hair, kooky clothes . . . All it took was a hit song. Just a hit song. When it happened, the world was looking at grunge in Seattle; little did they know about this punk-rock thing that had sprung up organically at indie labels like Epitaph and Dischord, that had flourished under radar for the last fifteen years; all it took were a couple of hit songs to pierce the surface. Then all hell broke loose—in '95, punk rock *exploded*. And we were there. The good news is, Epitaph survived it."

---

*Sasha Frere-Jones, "1979: The year punk died, and was reborn," *The New Yorker*, Nov. 1, 2004, p. 108.

If just barely. At first, the most vicious attacks were started coming from the punk community itself. Following *Dookie*, with each successive punk band cannibalized by the majors, the punk police's cries of "Sellout!" increased exponentially as well. And not just at major labels anymore—totally independent Epitaph was now a target, too. "That's what turned *Maximum Rocknroll* into the punk police," Brett Gurewitz says with no small tinge of bitterness. "Unfortunately, it's a self-fulfilling prophecy. You know, punk rock is underground music, but if it gets too popular, then whatever band in question must be rejected. Right?"

Despite its major label status, however, *Stranger Than Fiction* sounded just like any other Bad Religion album, for the most part: the one stab at a Nirvana-be hit song, "Infected," is actually pretty great, with a midtempo pop-rock shine reminiscent of Cheap Trick. The title track, meanwhile, is a classic of furiously strummed guitar riffarama that recalls the Jam's 1977-vintage Mod-punk fury.

Still, while *Stranger Than Fiction* managed to go gold, it was at a cost: guitarist and co-founder Brett Gurewitz left the band soon after its release. For one thing, he was uncomfortable with Bad Religion's major label status; as the band's stature grew, he wondered why they even needed to be on a major when it was now clear that the indie-punk legions could hold their own in the marketplace.

While he would never have predicted the punk revival, in retrospect Gurewitz saw the new interest in punk as following the cycles of nostalgia that culture goes through in each era. "There's always cultural recycling," he explains. "When I was a kid in the 1970s, it was all about the '50s: *American Graffiti* was the big movie, right, and then *Happy Days* was the big TV show. From the '50s to the '70s, that's a fifteen-to-twenty-year cycle."

In fact, the math in the aftermath of the neo-punk explosion wasn't so easy. At the same time as it was celebrated, the success of the Offspring, and then Rancid, was threatening to destroy those who built it. Struggling against new, unimaginable pressures, Gurewitz and, in the process, Epitaph almost fell off the ledge. "It knocked me off-kilter as a person. It knocked me off-balance, because I wasn't expecting it," Gurewitz says. "Everybody prepares themselves in life for failure, but you never really prepare yourself for success. I had to kind of check myself, because all my life I had been writing these very, *very* anti-establishment songs, and then all of sudden I found myself this wealthy, successful guy in society writing a big giant tax check to the federal government. It made me question what it's all about and all that; it was kind of a tough time for me."

So tough, in fact, that Gurewitz fell back off the wagon into the destructive addiction that had so destabilized him in the previous decade.

"I lost seven years of sobriety and ended up addicted to heroin again," he says. "I lost my way a little bit. After a few years I got back on track, but I just really had to do some soul-searching." At the same time, an overdose of success was threatening to shut down Epitaph's life support. "Lots of indie labels don't survive when they have hits," Gurewitz explains. "We were forced to grow so much, so *fast*, in every possible way, to accommodate 'the hit.' We had to add people; I had to mortgage my house, just to have enough money to press enough records to sell. Just to keep going, I had to borrow money from the bank."

Epitaph wasn't alone amid the punk indies nearly crushed by this unexpected windfall. "Lookout!, which had been growing steadily for six years already, suddenly grew very rapidly, and that kind of expansion can often be risky or traumatic for institutions and/or the individuals involved," says Lawrence Livermore. "I found for me it created a great deal of pressure that I didn't necessarily want or need. Up until that time, Lookout! had been fun as much as it was work; suddenly it was in danger of becoming all work and very little play."

To Gurewitz, the Offspring's success was a do-or-die moment for Epitaph that evoked bad memories: Bad Religion's stylistically diverse second album, *Into the Unknown*, had been a failure so large, it ended the nascent Epitaph's ongoing commercial activity at the time. And here he was again, only this time the situation was perversely reversed. In the documentary *The Epitaph Story*, Gurewitz jokes thus of *Into the Unknown*: "To give you the official numbers, we shipped something like 10,000, and I think we had 11,000 returns—I don't know how that happens. We had a huge flop." That a similar scenario could happen again plagued the mogul in the making. "I had huge orders, yes, but you know, in the record business, sales are two-way, not one-way," Gurewitz says. "What the store doesn't sell, they send back to me. I had put everything on the line, and I could have gone up like *that*."

Epitaph were also in danger of losing their bestselling band: The Offspring were still contracted to Gurewitz's indie, but after *Smash*'s unbelievable numbers, major recording companies were willing to open the vault to get the band's next record. The Offspring started receiving big-money offers just as tension started to grow between the group and Epitaph.

Rumors floated around regarding the Offspring's annoyance that Gurewitz was giving Rancid so much attention when they were the top-selling band. Included in the grudge were offenses like Gurewitz flying to every Rancid show he could and getting a Rancid tattoo. Today, Gurewitz doesn't deny either charge—he proudly rolls up his black T-shirt to show the "Let's Go" lettering ink-carved onto his arm—but it doesn't keep him up nights, either. "I think that's all water under the bridge, to be honest with you," Gurewitz admits. "I said some nasty things about them that I regret, and they said some nasty things about me at the time. I thought after we broke the *Smash* record, I would have liked for them to stay at Epitaph."

When Offspring inked a massive deal with Sony's Columbia imprint, however, the infighting escalated. "Yeah, I was mad at them, they were mad at me, and we got in a fight," Gurewitz says. "We aired our dirty laundry in public, but in retrospect it was a lot of to-do about nothing. I don't think we could have handled it more professionally—we were both pretty green."

In fact, Gurewitz admits that "at the end of the day, the relationship hasn't come to hurt either of us. They've gone on to be big rock stars, I've gone on to have a great, wonderful living owning an indie label. And I got paid a *fortune* when they went to Sony, because they owed me one more record."

Pay the Man: Pretty Fly for a Punk Band

In the years that immediately followed, the shine started peeling off punk's new bloom. Earlier, pop music consumers had grown tired of endless ersatz variations on the grunge template—Candlebox, anyone?—and now it appeared that neo-punk might be on the decline. The attempt to find new neo-punk stars in *Dookie*'s wake seemed to be stalled for progress: highly hyped New York punk band D Generation—poised in the media as the next big thing—failed to capture a mass audience with any of its three major-label efforts released between 1994 and1998.

Even established neo-punk stars were having trouble holding onto their audience—let alone matching previous sales figures. The Offspring's first major label album for Columbia, 1997's *Ixnay on the Hombre*, proved a relative disappointment compared to *Smash*'s multimillion-selling success. While the album (which paradoxically features ex-Dead Kennedys vocalist/punk activist Jello Biafra) reached number nine on the charts, it only went "platinum" (one million units sold) in the United States, selling just a couple more million worldwide—numbers not commensurate with the expectations inherent in the Offspring's big Sony deal.

1998 saw another misstep in pop punk's comedown: Rancid released *Life Won't Wait*, a sprawling, slightly messy album that sonically reflected its many different recording locations (Los Angeles, Jamaica, New Orleans), with a different genre feel for each one—blues, reggae, and so on. As such, if . . . *And Out Come the Wolves* was Rancid's *London Calling*, then *Life Won't Wait* was the band's *Sandinista*. The album proved some-what overblown and dilettantish, with an oversized guest list: the diverse cameos included reggae greats like Buju Banton and Dr. Israel, members of Brit ska legends the Specials, Mighty Mighty Bosstones' Dicky Barrett, and New York hardcore legend Roger Miret of Agnostic Front. With just 250,000 sold versus . . . *And Out Come the Wolves*' platinum plaque, *Life Won't Wait* represented a 75 percent drop from the previous album released three years earlier. What was supposed to be a triumph proved more of a blip.

Even the mighty Green Day, the band that blew the scene wide open for all to see, suffered precipitous sales drops in the post-*Dookie* boom times. *Insomniac*, 1995's slightly harder, edgier follow-up to *Dookie*, entered the charts at number two but would go on to sell just a quarter of what its predecessor did (although *Insomniac* is redeemed by its inclusion of fan favorite "Geek Stink Breath"). The band's biggest success of that year would actually come from a soundtrack contribution called "J.A.R.," but it was no "Longview," alas. 1998 saw Green Day release *Nimrod*, the band's most experimental album yet—as close to the anything-goes spirit of *Into the Unknown* or *Life Won't Wait* as Green Day gets. Unfortunately, with all its nutty instrumentation and variance, *Nimrod* wasn't as fun to listen to as it sounds like it was to make.

That said, *Nimrod* does feature one of the band's most indelible, enduring hits, "Good Riddance (Time of Your Life)," another pop-punk campfire singalong ballad whose theme of nostalgic remembrance still gets it played at proms and graduations today. Regardless of a hit single, *Nimrod* continued the band's downward slide, selling even less than *Insomniac*; by the band's fourth album, 2000's *Warning*, Green Day sounded tired.

Warning's minor hits with "Misery" and "Minority" in no way prepared for the Grammy-winning greatness of *American Idiot* four years later. Despite a street cred–returning headline spot on the 2000 Warped outing and a tour with Blink-182 meant to introduce them to new fans, Green Day struggled to reach *Dookie*'s heights until *American Idiot*'s success.

Some fans, meanwhile, were becoming disenchanted with the neo-punk movement in the conflict between its revivalist tendencies and commercial success. While the new punk aped the aesthetics of the old school rather closely, in the eyes of some it had drifted too far from punk's original raison d'être. "The original punks were fighting against something. It was the same with the Reagan years—they produced some of the most incredible punk rock ever," says Brody Dalle of the Distillers. "But, you know, when punk rock had its resurgence in the '90s, *Clinton* was in the fucking White House. It was the golden years—like, 'What the fuck do you have to complain about'? Punk became more about music and style than any political or social motivation. There's no catalyst—there's nothing driving it."

Social commentary, however, was the basis of the album that turned neo-punk's fortunes around on the pop charts: *Americana*, the 1998 album by the Offspring. The thematic concerns of *American Idiot* would be presaged six years earlier by *Americana*, a loose concept album about how American society had been corrupted as it veered toward the millennium, selling itself out to the plastic, the suburban, and most of all, the unhealthy and disposable. "When we first started writing for this record, there was this theme emerging about the sense of disillusionment with modern-day American ideas," Offspring front man Holland explains. "A generation ago, what was being exported was the idea of fighting communism. What's being exported today is McDonald's."

To get at the theme, Holland and the band approached every track as if it were a short story told from the point of view of a different perspective. "Each song represents a different vignette from American life: when you think of 'Americana,' you think Norman Rockwell, white-picket fences, and *Leave It to Beaver*," Holland says. "Now it's *Married...with Children*—it looks like *Happy Days* on the outside but feels like *Twin Peaks* on the inside."

The Offspring succeeded in tapping into middle America's fears and frustrations—so well, in fact, that songs like *Americana*'s huge single "Pretty Fly (For a White Guy)" found their titles becoming pop culture buzzphrases. Prophetically released just a few months before Eminem would make his album debut, "Pretty Fly" discussed the phenomenon of white kids from the suburbs adopting the mores of inner-city hip-hop gangstas, taking what they see in music videos as real life.

Throughout *Americana*, Offspring satirize everything from victim-defense feminism ("She's Got Issues") and criminals who blame their upbringing for their crimes (the title track, "Walla Walla") to slackers dragging down the economy who need to pull themselves up by their bootstraps ("The Kids Aren't Alright," "Why Don't You Get a Job?"). Throughout, like on "Pretty Fly," Holland assumes the character being satirized, and in the quest to take down political correctness, he's usually pretty hard on his subjects. Amidst all the politically incorrect spoofing, it's hard to tell where the Offspring's sympathies lie, exactly.

Sometimes, in fact, it appears that the point of view on *Americana* isn't really a critique of suburbia as much as it is the embodiment and expression of neoconservative suburban beliefs about the "have-nots"; the fact that the Offspring are products of a homogeneous, upper-class suburbia seemingly adds credence to this perception. While this contrarian vibe gives *Americana* a certain vitality, such an interpretation makes Holland bristle. "I'm a Democrat, and there are elements [in *Americana*] that could be perceived as left-leaning. At the same time, when we're talking about personal responsibility and anti-P.C., those could be perceived as Republican kind of ideas," Holland says. "We just wrote the album to be a commentary on American culture today. Like 'Pretty Fly'—kids in suburban Orange County, where I live, adopt the gangsta identity by going to the mall, where they buy FuBu, Tommy Hilfiger, and Ice Cube's latest record."

Whether *Americana* struck a nerve entirely on the pop audience's appetite for social commentary is debatable, however. Cleverly, the Offspring packaged their message in a novelty package: surely more people bought *Americana* for "Pretty Fly" 's Def Leppard sample and insidiously catchy "Give it to me baby!" refrain than for any cultural critique.

Selling over ten million copies, *Americana* returned Offspring back to the level of success it had enjoyed with *Smash*. In a new-world, dot-com era kind of way, *Americana* may have gone beyond the earlier album's triumph: after a bootleg MP3 of "Pretty Fly (For a White Guy)" found its way onto the Internet in advance of the full album's release, it was illegally downloaded over *twenty-two million times* over two and a half months, setting a record and landing the song at the top of *Rolling Stone*'s chart of "Top Pirated Internet Songs."

That there was even a chart for "Top Pirated Internet Songs" signaled that this was the beginning of a whole new era. And if the Offspring were the ones who renewed neo-punk's commercial viability in this new era, it was Rancid that would step in to save its soul.

In 2000, Rancid released their second self-titled album, some seven years after their eponymous debut. Self-titled albums often signify a particular statement of purpose over a lack of imagination: giving an album the band's name in lieu of any other title suggests that the album represents the band's true, uncut essence. With 2000's *Rancid*, the archetypal neo-punk band of neo-punk bands did just that and more: as well as capturing their own essence, now they seem to have bottled the essence of punk, *period*.

Both Rancid's overcooked punk classicism and tendencies toward self-indulgence were checked here: this is pure expression in the loudest yet most minimal means, utterly from the gut. When I reviewed *Rancid* for *Rolling Stone* upon its release, I immediately sensed its importance, awarding the album four stars (which got cut down to three and a half in the editing process). The feelings I expressed in my original review stand today: "Throughout their career, Rancid have been accused of attempting to mimic the Clash's first album. [But] on *Rancid*, the band and its co-producer, Epitaph label head Brett Gurewitz, have gone back to the garage. The album has twenty-two songs, clocking in at just over thirty-nine minutes; *Rancid*'s sonic reduction leaves only rip chords, thundering double-time drums, and shout-along choruses screamed with desperate abandon by Rancid vocalists Tim Armstrong and Lars Frederiksen. With *Rancid*, the band's mix of American thrash minimalism and Brit punk's sound and fury have transcended revivalist mimicry once and for all. . . . In the words of the late Johnny Thunders, you can't put your arms around a memory, but you never want to let go of music this powerful."

The artistic and genre purity of *Rancid* was, sadly, not a trendsetter. *Rancid* was, in many ways, the antithesis of a trend that had already sprouted out of garages throughout America straight onto MTV: the mall-punk phenomenon.

It's Mall Gone Wrong: The Children of Blink-182

In the wake of the success of Green Day, Offspring, and Rancid, a seemingly endless parade of bands began springing up to compete in the challenge for neo-punk's brass ring. Down by Law. Unwritten Law. Lagwagon. Hot Water Music. H2O (started by a former Sick of It All roadie in 1994). Bracket. Dropkick Murphys. No Use for a Name. The Nerve Agents. The Smoking Popes. Face to Face. Avail. Anti-Flag. Pulley. MxPx. The Explosion. Some of these groups actually started before the wave ignited by Green Day, some of them after; some had stayed righteously indie, some went direct to major labels. All, in this new environment, had the potential to be stars—either in their own minds, or in that of excitable record company lackeys.

From yet another small Northern California town (Ukiah, in this case) came AFI, whose initials stand for "A Fire Inside." AFI worked their way up from Gilman St. to the major labels, largely on the Goth-inflected, tortured poet charisma of singer Davey Havok and the wrenching hooks of songs like AFI's biggest hit, 2003's guiltily pleasurable "Girl's Not Grey." "AFI is my favorite band—they're very intense and emotional," says Bert McCracken of the Used. "Davey Havok pours his heart out, but it's *tasteful*."

Another band that represented a potential underground breakout was Boston, Massachusetts' Dropkick Murphys, whom Tim Armstrong signed to his Epitaph-subsidiary Hellcat label in 1998. The Dropkick Murphys stood out in their full-on embrace of their Irish heritage, as well as a boozy, loud merging of British "Oi" skinhead music, gruff, American-styled hardcore, traditional Celtic nuance, and insanely catchy everyone-in-the-pub-sings-along chants. While never crossing over on a mass/MTV level, the Dropkick Murphys managed to sell over 700,000 records over six releases on Hellcat/Epitaph and are still going strong. In the process, they've managed to grow while maintaining their integrity with the core punk audience. The Dropkicks' profile actually increased in 2006, thanks to Martin Scorsese's using their track "I'm Shipping Up to Boston" as the centerpiece of his hit film *The Departed*.

Not all bands were so concerned with maintaining their integrity, however, as the rise of what became derisively known as "mall punk" made clear. Some might argue that the beginning of mall punk began with bands like Offspring and Green Day signing to major labels and playing big package tours like Lollapalooza; that's when punk T-shirts and haircuts started appearing at the mall on a regular basis. When stores like Hot Topic starting multiplying exponentially in malls across the land, any middleman between mainstream and underground was eliminated in the process. "There are a million stereotypes [of Neo-Punk]," explains Pete Wentz of Fall Out Boy, "most of them involving the words 'my space' or 'hot topic.'"

But there was a new kind of band coming out, bands whose presence on the pop-cultural radar resulted primarily from the wave of record executives scouring the country in the wake of *Dookie* and *Smash* on the hunt for the "next Green Day." This type of band typically epitomized everything, in sharp focus, that made Green Day commercially viable. "It wasn't punk rock to me anymore—it was jock rock," says the Distillers' Tony Bevilacqua. "It really was."

They were called "mall punks" because they, well, resembled kids who hung out at the mall. A sort of mall-punk uniform developed somewhere in the chasm between the actual mall and what was worn in videos on MTV; often there was no distinction. The style of the mall punk typically drew from a few variations of the uniform: like the military, each variation held its own cultural signifier identifying what version of punk the band/fan was down with. "Everything I once thought of as somehow sacred has all become public domain," groans Bryan Kienlen of Bouncing Souls. "Few of these people who look 'punk' are lifers: most are just regular people enjoying a current fad."

One aspect of the uniform was a sort of ordered-off-the-Internet version of Rancid's update on 1977 punk style: all spikes, leather, tattoos, and *faux* hawks. Then there was the sort of "regular guy" punker—a sometimes preppy variation on the clean-cut skater/"straight edge" look: jeans, T-shirt, maybe an ironic polo, Converse All-Stars or Vans, short hair—that signified through style a self-conscious disinterest in style. If a band was really "edgy," maybe a member or two would show signs of "individuality" by aping the style innovated by AFI's Davey Havok: half stage-diving hardcore rat, half Marilyn Manson-style Goth, the piercings, fishnets, and chipped black nail polish contrasted with torn jeans and scuffed boots.

The pressure to conform, or at least to define one's place in punk's spectrum and draw a line in the sand, was now paramount. The same kind of high school caste system that punk initially purported to criticize has in fact always been present within any punk scene; now that millions of dollars and the chance for MTV to play your video were on the line, however, this aspect stood out in high relief. "It's the whole uniform thing," says Distillers guitarist Tony Bevilacqua. "You know—the Mohawk, the spikes, the fucking Exploited T-shirt. It's *retarded*—like, what are you rebelling against? Society? That you have everything you ever wanted? It's bullshit—the uniform is what punk was originally rebelling against. I don't know how kids today have Mohawks and listen to fucking bullshit like Good Charlotte."

"Clichés in punk today are full arm sleeves of tattoos, three-row studded belts, Spock haircuts, and nail polish," explains Matt Kelly of the Dropkick Murphys. "It seems the L.A. fashion-punk aesthetic has become 'what punk is.' It's acceptable now to have funny-colored hair and stupid clothes."

The band that put mall punk on the map was known first as Blink, until a legal threat from a similarly named group forced them to change their name to Blink-182. This trio from San Diego had been marinating in the punk underground since the early 1990s, releasing albums and EPs of bratty, obnoxious pop punk on smallish punk labels like Kung-Fu and Grilled Cheese: a survey of early Blink song titles like "Does My Breath Smell?," "Dick Lips," and "Ben Wah Balls" indicates the kind of frat-friendly humor that would bring the band fame. "It's hard to admit actually liking Blink," admits Warped tour honcho Kevin Lyman.

Blink-182's big breakthrough came with their fourth release and major label debut, 1999's *Enema of the State*, which featured a porn star on the cover dressed as nurse, strapping on a glove with glee in preparation for some creative erotic proctology. It wasn't much different from earlier Blink, aside from that canned, highly produced big radio sound that seemed to be a prerequisite for being on a major label. The breakout single, "What's My Age Again?", set up the classic Blink paradigm: utterly basic pop punk littered with insidiously catchy, whiny hooks. It was the video for "What's My Age Again?" that truly made the band stars, however: in it, the band parodied the visual tropes showing up in teen-pop videos from Christina Aguilera, Britney Spears, and "boy bands" like 'N Sync and Backstreet Boys. The basis for satire was thin, though: to seasoned ears, Blink-182 sounded and looked just as manufactured as the pop idols they were poking fun at.

In no time, Blink-182 eclipsed Green Day as the biggest pop-punk band around, and proved nearly as influential. The fact that *Enema of the State* sold four million copies didn't go unnoticed by endless amounts of ambitious garage bands. Not every punk-oriented group that made it onto the charts post-*Enema* was as juvenile, but as successful punk role models, Blink-182 raised the bar just high enough to graze the lowest common denominator. "The biggest compliment of all is a kid saying we opened his eyes to a new style of music," Blink-182 bass player/songwriter Mark Hoppus told *Rolling Stone* in a 2000 cover story on the band. "We're kind of like Fisher-Price: My First Punk Band."

Suddenly, MTV's *TRL* was filled with videos from those kids in predictably adorable "wacky" pop punk bands; personal ads on Web sites like craigslist.org advertising for "cute punk guys" became the norm. First up was Sum 41, a quartet of spiky postadolescent Canadians who searched for the missing link between early Beastie Boys brattiness and Blinkian scatology on hits like "Fat Lip." After an initial rush of popularity, hard-partyin' Sum 41 kept themselves in the tabloid headlines thanks to front man Deryck Whibley's high-profile romances with Paris Hilton and Avril Lavigne, to whom he is now married.

Next up were Good Charlotte, a Maryland pop punk five-piece distinctively fronted by a pair of raffish blue-collar twins, Benji and Joel Madden. Good Charlotte skipped the indie minor leagues and went straight into the majors; while their 2000-released self-titled first album proved still-born, Good Charlotte scored smashes with the good-time power-pop of "The Anthem" and "Lifestyles of the Rich and Famous" from sophomore effort *Young and the Hopeless* two years later. The photogenic Maddens paid their corporate dues, serving as VJs on MTV, while Joel kept himself in the gossip column by dating teen star Hilary Duff. At the same time, Good Charlotte were approachable. They wore their working-class background like a badge of honor, which made them easy to identify with; they were not so different from the mall rats who bought their records and attended their stadium tours. Good Charlotte loved partying, piercings, punk rock, and video games, just like their audience: they were living the mall-punk rock and roll fantasy. "I just love things that aren't real," explains Billy Martin, Good Charlotte's spindly, Goth-styled guitarist. "If I could jump off a building, grow wings, then fly and shoot arrows at the monsters underneath me, I'd be set. But you can't do that, so I live in a video game world. I'll continue to be in a band, or I'll turn into a video game character."

Pop-punk bands began replicating exponentially, so much so it was hard to tell them apart. Furthermore, while many of the new pop-punk bands hailed from different cities, many were now deracinated from any regional scene identity or sound—wherever a band came from, too often they looked and played like they originated in O.C. "I don't know that there are any vital punk rock scenes today, at least not in the sense of coming up with creative new ideas," says Lawrence Livermore. "I'm not expecting history to repeat itself in another location, and honestly, I'd just as soon it didn't. I don't see much of anything new or different coming out; it's more like a case of the true believers keeping the faith alive and continuing to draw in new converts to an old religion. Once a style of music becomes as successful and ubiquitous as punk has, it's very difficult for musicians to go against the grain and try new things; it's now developed firmly held views about what is and isn't acceptable under the rubric of 'punk rock.' If you stray too far from that style, you're just not going to get heard."

As a result of O.C.-ification, it's hard to divine what distinguishes New Found Glory from, say, Story of the Year, or the All-American Rejects from Sugarcult, or Sugarcult from the Ataris. Hunky punk dudes from the ritzy California beach town Santa Barbara, the Ataris *did* score a minor hit with a somewhat witty pop-punk retrofitting of Eagles drummer/vocalist Don Henley's 1984 solo hit "The Boys of Summer." Chicago's Alkaline Trio, meanwhile, continue as one of the best of the late-'90s punk pop wave: more convincingly angst-ridden—and openly alcohol sodden—than most of their contemporaries (although the band's drinking has been reduced), since their earliest releases Alkaline Trio mixed effective, unabashedly trad pop songwriting with the jagged workin' man *chugga-chugga* kick of great, unsung Windy City bands of older vintage like Pegboy. The next new kids on the punk rock block to really go after Good Charlotte's spot, however, were Yellowcard, a group of attractive, well-scrubbed young'uns from Jacksonville, Florida, who enhanced their punk career options by moving to Southern California at the dawn of the millennium.

Yellowcard did vibrate out a bit ahead amid the static nature of their pop-punk peers—and not just because they rock a violin and their drummer, Longineu Parsons, remains one of the few African-Americans, let alone minorities, to play for a high-profile neo-punk act. Sure, singer Ryan Key has the aw-shucks good looks and sensitive whine that even the little girls understand, but it was the band's musical virtuosity that made Yellowcard distinct on the *TRL* countdown: the band features a full-time violinist, for one, and an impressive command of Cobainesque hooks that resonate with stop/start, loud/soft dynamics to boot.

Aside from these quirks and small triumphs, however, Yellowcard represented the even greater encroachment of suburban American values on punk's once anti-establishment bent, down to their name. Punk's outcast stance has long been considered "anti-jock," with popular, preppy athletes usually the antithesis to the punk crowd in the lunchroom. That distinction is now gone, as Yellowcard's name, taken from the soccer term for fouling, suggests; that "Yellowcard" is actually interband slang for someone who makes a fool of themselves partying too much and must be removed adds further to the jock vibe, which the band don't disavow. It sounds like they've earned some "Yellowcards" themselves with their party-harty sports bar hijinks.

"Our bass player and myself are pretty *disgustingly* into college football," Ryan Key admits. "We definitely had our worst show on a weekend during the big game between Georgia and Florida. It's the biggest game on the planet to us—it's like our World Cup. We were in Chicago playing with No Use for a Name that weekend, and we hit a bar at 3:30 P.M. to watch the game before the show. We drank all day, and believe me, I never played a show that intoxicated before in my entire life—we were absolutely *disheveled*. It was so bad our bass player threw up on stage, while we were playing; I managed to sing only about twenty percent of the lyrics. The rest of the band wanted to murder us, and I vowed to never do it again. I still apologize for that night whenever we play Chicago."

Perhaps the most controversial of all the post–Blink-182 bands to become popular is Montreal, Canada-based Simple Plan. Next to Yellowcard and Good Charlotte, Simple Plan may be simultaneously the biggest of the newer pop-punk outfits and the most hated. Each of the band's albums, 2002's *No Pads, No Helmets . . . Just Balls* (note: another jock-punk joke) and 2004's *Still Not Getting Any . . .* have sold nearly two million copies in North America, and even more worldwide.

Each Simple Plan album percolates with perky, unintimidating pop punk hits like "I'll Do Anything," with a power ballad or two like "Untitled" thrown in for good measure. Everything Simple Plan does holds a distinct, regressed-adolescent cast—"I'm Just a Kid" is a typical title—and the band's sound is booming, clean, precise, and radio-friendly (big-time rock producer Bob Rock, helmsman of legendary, huge-selling albums from the likes of Metallica and Motley Crüe, was behind the boards for *Still Not Getting Any . . .*).

Simple Plan proved so cuddly and adorable, not only were they *TRL* favorites at MTV (singer Pierre Bouvier even hosted an MTV show), they were chosen to appear in kidflick icons the Olsen Twins' 2004 film *New York Minute* and have their songs played on Disney Radio. It's not surprising, then, that the trash-talking cognoscenti driving punk message boards across the web anointed Simple Plan the biggest sellouts in neo-punk.

Simple Plan have indeed been called terrible things in the media and on the Internet. In a 2004 cover story on the band in *Threat* magazine, writer Dan Epstein notes how Simple Plan remain "the preeminent whipping boys of punk-pop haters everywhere . . . Their detractors accused the band of being everything from 'lightweight' and 'gay' to 'a punk-rock version of the Backstreet Boys.' To many, Simple Plan's songs were too catchy, too clean, and too full of generic teen angst to truly qualify as punk—as if the term hadn't already been subgenred into irrelevance years ago."

It's the "Backstreet Boys of pop punk"-type of name-calling—the accusations implying the band is the mere product of devious, crass major label Darth Vaders—that truly irk Simple Plan's members. "That's probably the biggest misconception about Simple Plan," Chuck Comeau says. "It makes me the most angry—not angry, *disappointed*—to see people say 'Oh, those guys are puppets, they're manufactured, the label put them together.' You don't have to like the music, but the reality is this band has worked so fucking hard."

The "sellout" tag landed on Simple Plan largely because of the reputation of Reset, the previous band that Simple Plan frontman Pierre Bouvier and Comeau started when they were just high school kids. Reset evoked the influence of the technical, brutally fast, metallicized roar of edgy, nonmainstream 1990s-era neo-punk bands like Ten Foot Pole and Strung Out. "We just wanted to play fast," Comeau recalls. "We were young kids—fifteen, sixteen years old—and just wanted to play aggressive, in-your-face music."

Reset became semilegendary on the scene, playing both DIY national tours with bands like MxPx and spots on the Warped tour. The band ended up selling twenty-some thousand of their indie releases with no promotion. When the aggro dissonance of Reset evolved into the cheery melodicism of Simple Plan, punk's keepers of the flame smelled a corporate rat.

According to Comeau, however, Simple Plan's pop-friendly sound was just the result of maturity—a wish to grow beyond the speedy racket of their youth and communicate. The band did just that, inspired as much by the breezy, uplifting alternative rock of the Foo Fighters as by, say, the jolly infectiousness of the Doughboys, longstanding pop-punk favorites from Simple Plan's Montreal hometown.

"Maybe we didn't want to do the same kind of superfast all the time, in-your-face, aggressive, hardcore punk rock," Comeau says. "We just wanted to do something a lot more catchy, melodic, and memorable than Reset—something that people could sing along to, rather than just be impressed at how technical and fast we are. Simple Plan was just more . . . *rock* than Re-set. Just because it's commercial doesn't mean it isn't from the heart. If there was no record label, I'd make the same record."

Regardless, being more "rock" and commercial resulted in accusa-tions of "sellout"—and some mud in the face, literally: at one particular Warped tour stop in Calgary, bottles and mud were relentlessly thrown at the band. The whole Simple Plan/"sellout" controversy even found its way into the band's songs, like "Shut Up" and "Me Against the World."

"In the 'pure' punk-rock world, you're not allowed to be successful—we've got onto Top 40 radio and *TRL,* and people resent it. It's stupid," Comeau says. "I've made the same mistake—when I was fourteen, I got bummed when Green Day went superbig; it was almost cool not to like them. But when you start performing, your dream is to be heard and have fans across the world. I want my band to be the biggest in the world—if that's a sin, then fuck it, I'm guilty."

For Comeau, "selling out" all depends on staying true to one's original ideals. "We never said we wanted to stay underground. We were never on an indie—we signed to a major from day one," he says. "Selling out is when you say, 'We don't care about the mainstream,' but then you change when the money comes in. We always said we want to be a big band—we don't want to stop at being just a punk band. We're not the critics' fa-vorite band; we're the people's band. It means more to me to hear ten thousand kids screaming at my show than being on the cover of *SPIN* or getting a five-star review in *Maximum Rocknroll.*"

Pop punk further annoyed purists because many of the bands broke with one of punk's basic tenets: thou shalt play thine own instruments and write thine own songs. Even if the results of such a maxim were amateur-ish, they at least guaranteed in some measure an authentic, honest musical expression. When ringer songwriters and substitute virtuoso musicians are called in, the grind of the pop machinery can be heard all too loudly: to genre purists, it can seem like such moves indicate that the band is all too pliable to the commercial whims of their major label—not so much a real band as a creation.

No surprise, then, that Good Charlotte courted the punk police's wrath when, for their most successful album to date, they brought in ringers to enhance the sound and songwriting. Rancid's Tim Armstrong helped write one of . . . *Hopeless'* biggest hits, "Lifestyles of the Rich and Famous"; he's also helped cheese-punkers Bowling for Soup on "Here We Go," their con-tribution to the *Scooby Doo 2* soundtrack. Vandals drummer Josh Freese, meanwhile, raised eyebrows when he subbed as studio drummer on Good Charlotte on *Hopeless.* An incredibly versatile, powerful musician, Freese has become known as the go-to session guy for punk's drummer-challenged unable to perform due to major-label pressure. He's played with punkers and nonpunkers alike, however, sitting in with bands spanning Offspring, Liars Inc., Humble Gods, OK Go, and Unwritten Law to 3 Doors Down, Devo, 311, Suicidal Tendencies, and Avril Lavigne—even wretched boy band O-Town has benefited from Freese's musicianship.

"The drummer gets fired, and they 'Captain Midnight' it. That's something you hear about from producers and studio engineers all the time," says Distillers guitarist Tony Bevilacqua. "They'll tell you stories about how the the band goes home from the studio one day, and then the next the original drummer is gone and some 'ghost drummer' like Josh Freese comes in and really does the track. It's like, that's just the way it is."

Why Can't We All Just Get Along?: Welcome to the Warped Generation

On the radio, on MTV, pop punk has proven the most dominant sound. "Pop" is short for "populist," meaning that it's designed more than anything to reach the masses. To that end, pop here also indicates musical style—an emphasis on traditional (i.e., predictable) songwriting structures and repetitive, melodic hooks that lodge into the memory like an addictive drug. Pop implies a certain polish and efficiency, a key infectiousness where noise and discord lose out to melody, as well as a deference to accessible subject matter. Of the original punk tribe back in the 1970s, the Buzzcocks were the original punk pop progenitors: the closest of their peers to embody, say, the Beatles' melodic gifts, the Buzzcocks wrote classically simple, succinct, catchy songs expressing romantic angst (a classic pop trope). In the contemporary punk diaspora, Green Day epitomized this now-classic pop punk aesthetic with gusto and made it their own, proving wildly influential in the process. In Green Day's wake, the "emo" generation (Dashboard Confessional et al.) have picked up the pop-punk torch and recast it in their own heart-on-black-T-shirt sleeve image.

But pop punk isn't just the only game in punkadelica: its popularity, however, has created a bigger pond for everyone in the punk pool to wade in—and not just the shallow end, either. Always more diverse than given credit for, even in its formative days in the '70s, the various strands encompassing punk today—covered under the umbrella term "neo-punk"—offer up a different flavor for every taste and ideology. Among neo-punk's loosely defined genre choices are the horror-show punk-rockabilly hybrid 'psychobilly' (represented by bands like Tiger Army and Nekromantix); metal punk (Avenged Sevenfold, From First to Last, Strung Out, Atreyu); neo-hardcore (Converge); ironic retro garage (New Bomb Turks); metallic yet uncategorizably odd (Coheed and Cambria); street/gutter punk (The Casualties); Christian pop punk (Relient K, Further Seems Forever); proto-punk revivalists (River City Rebels, an ex-ska band who hired former New York Doll Sylvain Sylvain to give them an authentic glam-punk makeover); noise punk ([International] Noise Conspiracy, Rye Coalition); politically aware punk (Avail, Anti-Flag, the Explosion); and even an indie-rock–influenced variety (Say Anything, the Forecast, Melee).

"The subgenres of West Coast jock rock," groans Distillers' Tony Bevilacqua. "That's so funny, man. You could be a gutter punk and listen to fucking Rudimentary Peni, or the AFI California goth punk, or you could be a rockabilly punk. Choose your uniform—which one do you want?" No genre splinter has caused as much consternation in the neo-punk world, however, as what's become known as emo. "Fat Mike says it's a fact that if you're talking about how if you lay naked on the beach with an erection and these birds fly down and start fucking you . . . Oh, wait, I think he was talking about *emus*," jokes Alkaline Trio's Matt Skiba.

The infamous emo movement began in the mid-to-late 1980s with bands like Washington, D.C.'s Rites of Spring and San Francisco's Jaw-breaker. Such proto-emo outfits trafficked in a highly potent combo of su-peraccessible melodic punk with a screaming, confessional intensity that would inspire a nation of melancholy youth to pick up guitars and start bands as therapy. Bands like Thursday, Taking Back Sunday, Get-Up Kids, Saves the Day, and Jimmy Eat World have come to epitomize this more sensitive interpolation of punk's mission, with catchy, heart-wrenching songs of failed romance providing the classic emo template.

This subgenre is best embodied by emo-punk troubadour Chris Carabba, best known by his stage alias, Dashboard Confessional. At first, Dashboard Confessional got rid of the distortion associated with punk rock, playing his songs solo, just voice and guitar; this minimalism of ex-pression both made his songs more accessible and connected him to the traditional idea of the singer-songwriter. "I had to get out the stuff that sucks about life, so I would write a journal and find these lines that would become a song. Eventually, I phased out the journal, and my songs are what was left," Carabba says.

However, when he took Dashboard Confessional on the road, Carabba discovered how the personal could be transformed into the universal. His concert appearances demonstrate how deeply the emo audience identifies with the performers and their lyrics: Dashboard performances assuredly end up in mass singalongs, with many in attendance openly weeping in cathartic joy. "When I started going out and playing shows, these small crowds were singing along like giant crowds," he says. "Maybe they're finding some release and some solace that there are other people out there like them."

Emo, meanwhile, has produced in neo-punk a new trend: some particular emo children are spearheading a return to the charismatic, mercurial, mesmeric front man in a more conventional, long-haired rock star mode. In particular, My Chemical Romance's Gerard Way and the Used's Bert McCracken (an innovator of "screamo") are returning the focus to center stage after so many years of bland pop-punk front people. Onstage, McCracken in particular channels his personal demons and Cobainesque mythology into performance nitroglycerine. And McCracken even had his run in the tabloids thanks to a doomed romance with Kelly Osbourne that played out its drama, naturally, in front of MTV's reality television cameras.

"Bert McCracken is the first of the new rock stars who came out of the emo world," says Kevin Lyman, founder of the ultrasuccessful punk-focused summer tour package, the Warped Tour. "Emo was always about everyone being faceless, but if you notice, the front guys are stepping up, like Adam Lazzara from Taking Back Sunday, and Bert. They have dynamic personalities again, and that's what made the rock bands of the eras. Bert is dying for music and rock and roll."

While emo has become a true phenomenon among punk audiences—it's even spawned an (excellent) book on the subject, *Nothing Feels Good: Punk Rock, Teenagers, and Emo*, by journalist Andy Greenwald—not all in the broader punk community are dying for it. In the wake of emo omnipresence, every punk band on MTV seemed to sing with that same sensitive whine, dressed in minimalist but oh-so-fashionable black. Some are sick and tired of it, and just don't want to take their jagged little emo pill anymore. "I think the answer to the 'emo question' is 'shit,'" says Matt Kelly, drummer for the Dropkick Murphys.

"I always thought that bands like Rites of Spring and Embrace nailed it so good; then by the time the Promise Ring came out, emo was way over," says Explosion drummer Andrew Black (ironically, the Explosion released their early sides on Promise Ring's emo-oriented label home Jade Tree). "Now you have massive amounts of whining pricks with haircuts in black T-shirts—they just make me wanna *puke*."

Emo's black T-shirt uniform has become its badge of defiance, its line in the sandbox at the punk playground. "I have never seen a bigger split in the punk scene than right now with emo," Warped tour founder Kevin Lyman says. "I see 'I hate emo' shirts—there's a real backlash, which sucks. People either love it or hate it: last year on Warped, bands were prejudiced either for or against emo. It was the first time I saw such juvenile hostility backstage among bands. I think it was alcohol-fueled. But emo's still punk."

"There are still the bullies and the nerds," Fall Out Boy's Pete Wentz explains. "You can guess what lunch table we sat at."

The World Comes Tumblin' Down: Meet the Distillers

Yes, punk rock is no stranger to controversy, and neither are the Distillers. On April 25, 2000, a bomb with a pretty face went off in the neo-punk world: the Distillers' first, self-titled album was released.

The Distillers are a band that has always stood out on the neo-punk scene. Like most things in society, the neo-punk scene is dominated by men. However, the first incarnation of the Distillers was unrepentantly fronted by three young, badass women—guitarist Rose Casper, bassist Kim Chi, and the band's magnetic vocalist, guitarist, and songwriter, Brody Armstrong (male drummer Matt Young rounded out the band initially). To see three women losing their mind on stage amid neo-punk's testosterone monotony felt revolutionary in itself.

The Distillers also had a backstory nearly as compelling as their lineup. Brody Armstrong had entered the neo-punk world as an outsider with the ultimate "in." For one, she was a native Australian—there was no Orange County in her. Most significantly, by the time the Distillers first got together, Brody had married into punk royalty, literally: at just nineteen years old, she was already the wife of Rancid front man Tim Armstrong.

Brody's romance with Tim Armstrong began when she met him in 1996 at a massive outdoor rock festival in Australia, where both Rancid and Brody's former band Sourpuss were performing, alongside the likes of Sonic Youth, the Foo Fighters, and the Beastie Boys. Brody was actually celebrating her seventeenth birthday that day; a year later she would be celebrating a marriage, and moving to the United States. The thirteen-year difference in age between the Rancid front man and Brody—he was born in 1966, she in 1979—made tongues wag in punk gossip circles.

As far as rock and roll scandals go, it wasn't up there with Jerry Lee Lewis marrying his underage cousin, or even Woody Allen getting with his stepdaughter. Still, the Brody-Tim union was scandalous enough. It was official: neo-punk finally its own Kurt and Courtney, a pair to replace the void Sid Vicious and Nancy Spungen left in their bloody wake. This improbably punk fairytale romance would give Brody a media hook other neo-punks didn't have—whether she wanted it or not.

Immediately, Brody felt the distrust in the punk community. She was living a Mohawked version of *Willie Wonka and the Chocolate Factory*: she'd got the punk-rock golden ticket, and no one was going to let her forget it, especially the jealous punk Bettys who wished they were her. "Gonna get their hooks in, gonna drag you way down/Yeah, you wanna go home soon?" she sang about the caustic experience on "L.A. Girl" off *The Distillers*. Things proved even harder when Armstrong started performing music with the Distillers. It's one thing to be a rock star's wife; it's another to be in your late teens-early twenties and just oozing ambition. Brody had been a fairly well-known underground musician in Australia, but in America, the cards were stacked against her: to some, she was seen as an opportunist riding her husband's coattails. To others, the music spoke for itself.

The Distillers stood out in the neo-punk universe. For one, it was no easy listen: the Distillers didn't play pop punk per se, but instead crafted a roiling sound that was equal parts uncompromising hardcore street punk and chunky, rollicking rock and roll. Brody's singing was as raw as any male punker's—maybe more so—with a tinge of the "drunken master" slur made famous by her husband in Rancid.

But on songs like "Gypsy Rose Lee," however, Brody displayed both a beguiling command of hooks and melody and a bruised vulnerability without sounding too pop, evoking comparisons to the complicated gifts of say, Courtney Love (such comparisons would endlessly haunt the Distillers). Meanwhile, the album's lone cover, a gritty, aching revamp of Patti Smith's "Ask the Angels," suggested there was more to the Distillers than mere revivalism. The Distillers made punk that wasn't afraid to be intelligent at the same time as it was brutally confessional. Brody was giving neo-punk an uncut hit of complicated eroticism, one that it desperately needed. This was a star in the making, regardless of genre. "To be honest, the first Distillers album reminded me of Rancid," says Brett Gurewitz, who released the album on his joint-venture label with Tim Armstrong, Hellcat. "It was primitive, but it had a sexuality to it. It had passion, and it was hooky. It had catchy songs—that's really what I'm a sucker for, catchy songs."

"I don't think anyone can sing like her," Gurewitz told *SF Weekly* in 2001. "She has an amazing voice. She sounds like a gravel truck with a missing axle, but she never misses a note. She sings right in key, but she's really got a super-intense, rough edge. It's amazing. . . . This is one of the best new bands to come out in a long time. People oughta pay attention." And they did, slowly. According to Gurewitz, the first Distillers album sold reasonably well, moving around 20,000 units initially. However, with the band's second album, 2002's *Sing Sing Death House*, the Distillers' star starting far rising more precipitously.

The sound was as uncompromising as ever, made clear by the opening track, "Sick of It All": over jittery warp-speed guitars recalling second-wave U.K. thrash punks Discharge, Brody sang lyrics evoking Columbine-style shootings: "I went to school today with an Uzi/There's this kid, he teased me, so I shot him in the face." But there were also hooks, and potential hits, amid the loud 'n fast rifferama: the video for "The Young Crazed Peeling" got some play on music television, while "City of Angels" became the number-one requested song on KROQ. "When you're number one on KROQ above System of a Down and Linkin Park . . . that's weird," Brody told *Modern Fix* fanzine.

Sing Sing . . . would go on to sell over 200,000 copies—not exactly Offspring numbers, but enough to suggest big-time potential. The band even opened up a stadium tour with Garbage and No Doubt. The Distillers' ascent had begun, and with the driven Brody Armstrong at the helm, world domination seemed certain.

Then the bottom fell out.

In 2002, Brody split from Tim Armstrong, eventually divorcing him—and in the process unwittingly divorced herself from the neo-punk community. "It was obvious: she was a man-using career opportunist, the greatest crime of the village law, creating a split through the heart of the global punk-rock network," went a passage U.K.-style bible *The Face* ran in a 2003 Brody cover story. The Brody-Tim divorce was a litmus test that made the scene's true colors came out. "I wasn't really moved by the Distillers," Bouncing Souls' Greg Attonitoi says. "Rose, the original second guitarist, was my favorite part of the band when we toured with them, but she's not in the band anymore."

It was a time of lines being drawn in the sand. Those Courtney Love/Yoko Ono comparisons started anew, but with an even nastier tone. The heat only increased when photos of Brody—who had by now replaced her married name with "Dalle," in homage to Beatrice Dalle, the French star of the tortured-woman film classic *Betty Blue*—were published in *Rolling Stone* showing her making out with another alt-rock sex symbol, Josh Homme, the enigmantic mastermind of Queens of the Stone Age. The Internet exploded with gossip and speculation.

Things got worse. When Brody left Rancid's Hellcat label for the major label comfort of Warner Bros./Sire, cries of sellout only increased, reaching epic proportions when the Distillers ditched a spot on the Warped Tour to play Lollapalooza. The feeling was that Brody and the Distillers had ditched the punk community for greener pastures—green meaning money, of course.

That idea was enhanced with the actual release of *Coral Fang*, the Distillers' third album and major label debut. While *Coral Fang* featured ragers like "Die on a Rope" that are as hard and fast as any Distillers song, its material is far more nuanced than that of a typical punk album. Recorded with new, unexpected sophistication by Brit producer Gil Norton—who'd twiddled knobs in the studio for the likes of the Pixies, Foo Fighters, Patti Smith,

and Echo and the Bunnymen, and would later record Jimmy Eat World—
Coral Fang featured slower tempos, like the Nirvana-influenced "The Gallow Is God," and even a ballad in "The Hunger." Furthermore, the opaque
lyrics seemed to split the difference between coded jabs at ex-hubby Armstrong and passionate declarations for Homme.

Coral Fang was a masterful, textured album full of assured songwriting, but it got lost in the ensuing media controversy around Brody Dalle's
life choices. "They put a ton of money into that album," Kevin Lyman
notes, "but they went too far into the publicity." "It was kind of weird—
they had so much buzz, and then it didn't materialize," says Simple Plan's
Chuck Comeau. "I don't know what they mean to the scene right now,
because they're not really in it," says Agent M. "I was hopin' the best for
them, you know?" says old pal Gurewitz, who'd lost his hottest new band
in the process.

Regardless of sales, Brody Dalle had been transformed from cult punk
into a media celebrity—in 2004, she made number ninety-five on *Maxim*'s "Hot 100" list of the most attractive women (down just four from
Desperate Housewives star Eva Longoria) and starred in an *Entertainment Weekly* poolside photo spread with alternative rock godfather Perry
Farrell. "They wanted me to wear a bikini. I refused," Dalle says. "I don't
care how many records I sell, me getting in a fucking bikini isn't going to
happen in *Entertainment Weekly*. I am not your 'entertainment.'"

Bikini killed or not, *Coral Fang* didn't match its hyped expectations.
It would go on to sell little more than the Distillers' previous album—but
on a major label's fattened budget, it needed to be a smash. Still, the album showed that Brody wanted to smash out of punk's calcified stylistic
hegemony—and could. "Brody's songwriting really changed," Tony
Bevilacqua recalls. "She was writing different kinds of tunes, ones that
weren't punk rock songs." If anyone was going to revitalize neo-punk,
Coral Fang showed that it just might be Brody Dalle.

Neo-Punk: No Longer Indestructible?

The genre, meanwhile, was showing growing pains potentially symp-
tomatic of a fatal disease. Rancid, the torchbearers of neo-punk's indie integrity, abruptly left Epitaph after twelve years for a major label deal
themselves, contradicting earlier proclamations that they'd never do such
a thing.

"The one good thing about Rancid is that we never signed to a major
label," Rancid's Lars Fredericksen told *SPIN* magazine in 2001. "We've
shown that you don't need some fucking big major label who you'll end

up taking it in the ass from, eventually, to make music." Before going to Warner—Green Day's label home—Rancid held special antipathy for the business moves of their Gilman Street/East Bay rivals. "Yeah, they're a sinking ship," Tim Armstrong said of Green Day in a 1998 *Guitar World* feature. "I wish them all the best, but they're on a major label, which means they have to sell a lot of records just to survive and that's scary. I mean, nobody wants to go out like M.C. Hammer."

When Rancid's about-face hit the net, however, the fans brought the hammer down. The Web site punknews.com received over two thousand hits within forty-eight hours of posting the news that Rancid had dropped Epitaph for Warner, as punknews' one-named founder Aubin told the *East Bay Express* in 2003. "For a lot of people, it's a big deal," Aubin is quoted in the article. "We reported the news because we knew it would be something people cared about, and the wealth of comments that that story generated within such a short amount of time showed that a lot of people really did take it seriously. Signings are usually the biggest and most controversial stories we report on."

"RANCID HAS SOLD OUT!!!! THEY ARE FUCKING SELL OUTS!!!! THEY HAVE GIVEN UP ALL THIER PUNK ETHICS, ALL THIER BELIEFS, JUST FOR MORE MONEY!!!! THEY'VE PULLED DOWN THEIR PANTS AND ASKED WARNER TO SHOVE THE CORPORATE BOOT RIGHT UP THIER ASSHOLES!!!! DONT BOTHER DEFENDING IT!!!! RANCID HAS SOLD OUT!!!! AND YES, IT DOES MATTER!!!!" read a typical post on the matter. Another wonders if "the bible mention this (sic) as one of the signs of the end times?"

Those closest to Rancid, though, were the most shocked. There's a rule about getting a tattoo of a girlfriend's or boyfriend's name: it usually portends a future breakup—think of Johnny Depp's love-induced skin-ink immortalizing of Winona Ryder. When Brett Gurewitz got a Rancid tattoo on his arm, he may have set the same wheels in motion. "I don't wanna talk about it," Brett Gurewitz says. "*They* don't even admit it happened, so . . . you know."

The resulting album, 2003's *Indestructible*, was typical Rancid material (and included some jabs back at Brody Dalle). *Indestructible* started strong, setting a record for Rancid's highest chart entry at number fifteen, with 51,000 sold (the band had never scored higher than number thirty-five). Still, Rancid's major label debut was no major success, and disappeared from pop-culture consciousness far faster than any of the band's previous releases.

Rancid even starting making the typical major label moves they'd often criticized, like packing their videos with tabloid celebrities like Kelly

Osbourne and Good Charlotte, alienating the band's core fans further. Rancid even seemed conflicted about the move in their album art—the Warner Bros. logo was nowhere to be found on *Indestructible*'s packaging, but the kids figured out the real deal. "This just in . . . there will be NO Warner Brothers imprint (logo) on the record . . . only the Hellcat logo! You know what this means? PUNKERS BEND OVER; THE MAN is trying to trick you," read one of many passionate fan responses on the Internet. "Not only have they left their home (Epitaph) that claimed they would be partners 'for life' but RANCID are too pussy to have the WB logo on their record! Geeze guys comeon, if you are going to get a divorce, take off the fucking ring. C-Ya in the board meeting!"

As the first decade of the millennium winds on, neo-punk seems like it's in a precarious funk—hardly indestructible. The ability to distinguish between an increasingly anonymous crop of new pop punk bands gets harder with each new video on *TRL*. Alternative rock radio, champion of the airwaves in the 1990s and one of pop punk's main outlets, is now severely weakened, with many station closings across the country, including some of the format's biggest, like WHFS in Washington, D.C. And what actually goes on the radio is seemingly arbitrary—an obscure indie punk band like Horace Pinker are just as catchy as any major label act, erasing distinctions even further.

Elsewhere, Anti-Flag, (International) Noise Conspiracy, and Rise Against, some of the most outspoken and raw of the indie neo-punk bands, have all signed to major labels, while Tim Armstrong's side project the Transplants (with ex-Blink-182 drummer Travis Armstrong) put out an album with Atlantic; Armstrong didn't quell the sellout hosannas, either, when he collaborated as a songwriter-for-hire with Top 40 pop starlet Pink. Seattle, Washington's Acceptance disguised their pop-punk sounds to consumers with a first single that's a Coldplay ballad soundalike. Jimmy Eat World moved further away from their punk origins on the 2004 album *Futures*. Recent albums from Good Charlotte, Yellowcard, and Sum 41 didn't meet high expectations. And Brett Gurewitz has yet to sign another band as big as Offspring, or Rancid—or even the Distillers—to Epitaph; his biggest current band, Poughkeepsie, New York, pop-punkers Matchbook Romance, has sold around 200,000 copies of its 2003 album *Stories and Alibis*.

During 2005, meanwhile, Blink-182 announced what appears to be a permanent hiatus, with the band's formerly most shy, least obnoxious member, drummer Travis Barker, getting his own cheesy reality show on MTV documenting his marriage to a Playboy playmate. By 2006, Blink co-front man Tom DeLonge had announced his new band, Angels & Airwaves (featuring ex-Distillers bassist Ryan Sinn), making Blink's demise official. By 2005, Green Day and the Offspring had become neo-punk's *eminence grises*, classic rock for a generation born too late for the classic rock of Led Zeppelin and Cream; a summer "Greatest Hits" album from the Offspring only reinforced this notion. Meanwhile, drugs returned to the scene—that is, if they ever left. "Every band in this town does drugs—everybody," says Distillers guitarist Tony Bevilacqua. "It's amazing to me how weird it is. Cocaine is like the new beer."

Opinion varies on what it was exactly took punk rock so far from its roots as it swam up the mainstream. Some blamed MTV. "MTV got ahold of it and ran wild," says Bryan Kienlen of Bouncing Souls. "It's scary how much power that channel has to singlehandedly create new fads out of whatever it chooses at will. Gosh."

Some said it was the radio. Of course, how could we forget the Internet? "The Internet was really the mighty unifier of the music world," states Bouncing Souls' Greg Attonitoi, "and of the world in general." Maybe it was just what the kids like. Was punk now a brand more than a movement? "All the mall punk bands have spawned their own imitators," Bevilacqua continues. "Now the younger kids are getting into *those* bands—it's as if they prefer the fake ones. They're just moving down the line. Then, in three years, kids will be into something new."

All it will take is a hit song.

Just a hit song.

And maybe it would take another hit album to save it. In 2005, *American Idiot* showed that punk could be saved, but could it be saved again? Would punk rock ever be as vital as it once was? Now fans want to know who is going to release the *next* genre-redefining masterpiece and carry on the punk flame.

4

Would the Distillers be punk's new saviors? Or the first to leave it behind? The Distillers have always stood out amid their brethren in the neo-punk movement. Admittedly, they've had a hard time fitting in: on one level, they're too hard for pop punk, too catchy for hardcore, too rock and roll for street punk—they're no fans of genre rules and boundaries. And in Dalle, the Distillers have a front person so compelling she rises above genre constraints. "I'm not the Distillers," Brody Dalle claims. She pauses for a moment to reflect. "Well, in some sense I am," she clarifies. "The Distillers always will be and always has been Brody," says her bandmate and longtime partner-in-crime Tony Bevilacqua, co-guitarist in the Distillers. "It's just one of those bands. It's her thing—her songs, her lyrics, her guitar, her voice, her face. It's like Nine Inch Nails: Trent Reznor is the band. If there was a Distillers show tomorrow with three new members plus Brody, the same amount of kids would show up."

The Distillers have those things that a great band needs: an arresting visual persona, songwriting that mixes punk fury and energy with literary craftiness and classic melody, and an utterly distinctive, beguilingly expressive vocal style. Alas, Dalle is probably best known from the gossip columns. Such is the complicated drama that makes up this band. It's a story that, on the one hand, provides an insight into the archetypal experience growing up inside the neo-punk industrial complex. The fact that the Distillers prove to be anything but archetypal, however, is what truly makes them compelling. Theirs is a partly voyeuristic, partly cautionary tale—based on a true story, or some interpretation thereof.

Indeed, a large aspect of Dalle's appeal is the autobiographical. Dalle's story has in fact fallen into mythology. It's not for nothing that she's endlessly compared to Courtney Love in terms of living out a rock narrative that's like a car wreck: you can't take your eyes off it, even when it's veering into danger. But Brody's not Courtney Love. Then again, she wasn't always Brody Dalle, either.

Brody was born Bree Joanne Alice Robinson of Irish and Sicilian blood (Pucilowski, an Eastern European name, came later from her stepfather, while Brody was a school nickname). Her birthday is January 1, 1979—a day that would prove even more prophetic than a typical birthday for Dalle some seventeen years later, when she would meet her first husband, Tim Armstrong. She grew up in Melbourne, Australia—Fitzroy Melbourne, as she clarifies on the autobiographical song "The Young Crazed Peeling," first on Bell Street, then on Bennett Street in a Quonset hut along the Merri Creek. This alternately humble and exotic environment would set her apart from the West Coast American punk rock peers. Melbourne indeed is a totally appropriate spawning ground for a maverick like Dalle. The city has its own history of iconoclasm, musically and otherwise, from its outlaw beginnings to a genre-shattering musical tradition ranging from AC/DC's twisted boogie to the early Aussie punks Radio Birdman. "Melbourne has a rebellious characteristic—there's an Old West aspect to its personality that's fiercely independent," explains Missy Suicide. "And there's a big punk rock and indie scene there—it's where Nick Cave is from, after all."

Dalle's turbulent childhood has proven a fertile source for the Distillers' lyrics, giving similarly distressed young outcasts an icon to identify with. In fact, she's already attempted her memoirs in song a few times—songs like "The Young Crazed Peeling" detail a wayward youth that's alternately thrilling, uplifting, and scary: "My mom kicked out my dad for battery/Found a way, found a way, she found a way out of spiritual penury/Working single mother in an urban struggle/Blames herself now, 'cause I grew up troubled." Brody was raised by a single mother; Melbourne's bohemian world, however, was never far away. "My mom is not a psychiatric nurse, as has been printed before—that drives me fucking crazy," Dalle explains. "She is just a *nurse*, right—has been a nurse for thirty years. But before all that she was an artist. First and foremost, she was a photographer, a sculptor, and painter; that's what she wanted to do with her life. She ended up being a single mom on a nurse's salary, but my mom is really a beatnik."

In appropriately beatnik fashion, Dalle's mother met Brody's birth father in photography class. "They started going out and dating, and my mom got pregnant," Dalle explains. "I wasn't planned and she wanted to keep me. And that was that. Here I am." Her natural father, an expat from Birmingham, England, left soon after that, although he continued to "spread his seed" all over the globe (Dalle estimates she has "five or six" siblings). Dalle never really got to know her real father, and in fact considers herself to have been truly raised by her stepfather (when she wasn't busy raising hell, that is). "My real father has nothing to do with my life," she explains. "Or any of my brothers' and sisters' lives, for that matter. I know for a fact that blood means nothing, because I was raised by a man whose blood I don't have in my body. He is the reason that I think that I am so strong. I went to him always—he's my *real* father. He was my salvation, this man."

Dalle always gravitated toward music as a young child. Her first album, eerily, was a compilation called *The Bad Girls*, incongruously bringing together femme-fronted 1980s new wave like the Go-Gos with Top 40 pop like Miami Sound Machine. U.K. stripper-turned-pop-dance-diva Samantha Fox was a favorite, and the *Ghostbusters II* soundtrack definitely got some spins by young Brody. But the artist who really galvanized her was a true '80s icon, an individual, independent woman prone to quirk and idiosyncrasy. "My first concert ever was Cyndi Lauper," Dalle admits today. "It was the 'She's So Unusual' tour—my dad took me to the Tennis Center to see it when I was seven years old. She was the biggest thing. Since then, I've always wanted to cover "Money Changes Everything" and 'When You Were Mine.' I liked Cyndi better than Madonna."

Dalle's musical influences took a turn for the darker, however. "We had some Beatles records, which I used to be fascinated by because my mom told me that one of them blew their heads off," Dalle explains. "I thought John Lennon killed himself." Music began to take on associations that transcended the sonic for the nascent rocker. "My parents' speakers would burn when they would play it really loud," Dalle says. "I associated the burning smell with the music. It was really strange—that smell would kind of put me into a weird trance."

The music that would truly burn into Dalle's preadolescent soul, however, arrived in her life circa the age of twelve. It would prove to be the music that transformed Dalle into who she is today. By chance, Dalle found a copy of an indie Nirvana 7-inch single, well before that band exploded into global consciousness. It was a very rare Nirvana release, made up of only five hundred pressings, the number of each individual release scratched into the vinyl. "That single is probably worth a thousand dollars today," Dalle says. "I played it over and over again for hours. I'd just keep listening to it and wouldn't stop. I still have it."

In the wounded soul, aggressive guitars, and indelible melodies of Kurt Cobain, Dalle found a kindred spirit. The conflict and confusion in

Cobain's lyrics spoke deeply to Dalle, mirroring the turbulent feelings she was feeling as a young, self-made outcast. Soon, however, the world smelled teen spirit and Cobain was an international phenomenon, no longer Dalle's secret indie crush: Nirvana soon went into constant rotation at Triple R, Australia's leading alternative rock station, a pattern repeated around the globe.

Before they'd exploded, Nirvana had even booked a tour of Australia (which would sadly prove to be their only visit to the Southern Hemisphere), and was due to play at a small but legendary Melbourne venue known as the Palace. It was about to get even more legendary, as Nirvana's popularity had exceeded the Palace's capacity well before they reached Oz's shores. "By the time they got there to play the club, there were masses of people there," Dalle recalls. "I was twelve years old and wasn't allowed to go, and I was *devastated*. I was so mad."

Soon after Dalle's Nirvana epiphany came another uncanny coincidence that would introduce her to the woman to whom she would be forever linked as an adult performer: Courtney Love. "When I was thirteen, I would go to this record shop called Polyester Records on Buffet Street and sift through the leftovers on sale in the cut-out bin," Dalle says. She was struck by the cover of an album, *Pretty on the Inside*, by a band she had never heard of named Hole. "There was a picture of Courtney with blue hair—at that time, I was like, 'Yeah!,'" Dalle says.

Pretty on the Inside is perhaps Love's most aggressively dissonant record, created well before she became the queen of melodic alternative rock: co-produced by Sonic Youth's Kim Gordon, *Pretty* . . . indeed resembles a primitive recast of early Sonic Youth, a challenge to sit through thanks to loads of unrestrained feedback, distortion, and Love's then-untutored caterwaul. Dalle was astonished by Hole's addiction to noise— "I loved how the power and energy pulled together," she recalls. Brody would become even more intrigued when she learned about Love's personal life. "I found out that she and Kurt were, you know, *together*," Dalle says, "and that made it even more fascinating for me."

Soon after her exposure to the volatile Cobain-Love axis, Dalle's uncle presented her with her first guitar. "It was such a shitty piece of fucking balsa wood—a train wreck of a guitar," Dalle chuckles. "It was unbelievable. My mom and dad still have it, and every time I see it I laugh."

Dalle's adolescence, however, was about to become no laughing matter. Like many a tortured *artiste*, Dalle has Catholic school to blame for at least part of an angry, misspent youth. But what made it worse was the fact that neither Dalle nor her family was religious, immediately making her even more of an outcast than she already felt like. "I was a little confused when I was started going to Catholic girls' school at twelve years old," Dalle says. "I wasn't raised Catholic, I wasn't even baptized—my mom's an atheist! I really had no background or understanding of what Catholicism was. The Bible and all these weird concepts were just so brand-new to me; they seemed more like stories from a children's book than this iconic, historic thing. I mean, I've always been fascinated by religion; I use a lot of those metaphors, without a doubt. I never read the fucking Bible, but I love imagery—that means more to me than anything else."

The young Brody was saved from the torture of her Catholic education by Rock 'n' Roll High School (RnRHS)—not the cult movie starring the Ramones, but a feminist-based collective in Melbourne that offered young local musicians a place to make noise. Started by local Melbourne musician Stephanie Bourke, drummer for the band Litany, Rock 'n' Roll High School was a place that offered musical instruction, career guidance, and practice space for individuals just like Brody, who had just started her first band, Sourpuss.

Dalle had become even more immersed in music beyond Nirvana. She'd become obsessed with angry, challenging, dissonant punk bands like Black Flag and Discharge, and because of Kurt Cobain's endorsement, discovered San Francisco noise-punks Flipper. With these revolutionary currents raging inside her, Dalle felt it was time to actually begin living her dream. According to Dalle, the nascent elements of Sourpuss had gotten together at an all-ages show featuring the Mimis, a sort of Melbourne twist on the Ramones' blitzkrieg bop, named after the mythical spirits of Australia's native Aboriginal culture.

"There was this girl Susan, and my best friend from primary school Sara, and another girl, Cobina," Dalle recalls. "We sat on the floor and said what we wanted to do in the group—you know, 'I play guitar,' 'I play bass,' 'I want to sing.' We formed a band in theory, and then I got a guitar and amp for Christmas." Sourpuss commenced Brody Dalle's inability to maintain a stable band lineup. "I think we had admittedly *eight* female drummers," she sighs. "Later we got a succession of male drummers."

Indeed, the novice Sourpuss needed a place to work out its musical kinks and find its sound, and Rock 'n' Roll High School seemed an ideal fit. "I came across Rock 'n' Roll High School because of my uncle who gave me the guitar," Dalle explains. "He worked at a school for troubled teens and had heard about it, so I checked it out." It was an exciting time: RnRHS administrator and founder Stephanie Bourke would bring alternative luminaries like the Breeders, Sonic Youth, and Babes in Toyland to meet and greet the school's young charges; Brody even has a snapshot of herself with California punk nutters Redd Kross when they visited RnRHS. Located in Melbourne's Collingwood area, RnRHS offered seven instrument-filled rooms to make noise in—in other words, nirvana for those young Aussies who aspired to be Nirvana. At least for a time.

Brody's relationship to RnRHS and in particular its founder, Stephanie Bourke, grew to become one of the Distillers' many controversies. In a 2003 *LA Weekly* Distillers cover story by Judith Lewis, Dalle ripped into the school's feminist slant, which she claimed was oppressive. She wanted to be play music, sure, but not be pigeonholed as just a novelty *woman* rocker, which she saw as RnRHS's true mission—to indoctrinate a new generation of "women in rock." Most crucially of all, she laid into RnRHS honchos like Bourke, calling them "psychotic feminists, like Nazi sows, out of their *fucking* minds."

Dalle's comments set off a firestorm. "I was shocked and dismayed to read my name in your publication alongside hurtful and defamatory statements about 'the people' who ran Rock 'n' Roll High School," Stephanie Bourke wrote in a scathing letter to the *LA Weekly*. "To say the girl bands were not taken seriously is ridiculous." Bourke took issue with Dalle's comments about Courtney Love in the article. "Brody was a Courtney clone, covered Hole songs, and emulated her every move," Bourke wrote. "It's a bad joke that this young woman, so 'concerned' with injustice, is so mean about the women who have played a large role in her development: Courtney, who inspired her, and the community at RnRHS, who facilitated her career."

As well, a number of RnRHS supporters wrote letters to the *LA Weekly*'s editor to protest the article, cutting down down "tall poppy" Dalle. "I have been learning classical piano from Stephanie Bourke at the school for some years now," wrote Clare Chadderton, "and I can't think of any Nazi-sow moments—though one time she did tell me to practice a bit more." Even Dalle's former Sourpuss bandmates got in on the action, taunting her with her birth name Bree in the process.

"As the founder of Brody (real name Bree) Armstrong's first band (Sourpuss) and fellow beneficiary of RnRHS's tutelage, I was extremely disappointed to read her appraisal of an institution that has done so much to help so many young women—including Bree—to achieve their ambitions," Cobina Crawford wrote. "As someone who has worked closely with Bree, I have witnessed her incredible knack for creating 'butterscotch moments' with useful people—and for creating a revisionist bio that would make Stalin blush. Good on her, too. No one wants to read a 5,000-word puff piece on some middle-class kid who fixates on Courtney Love, do they now?"

Even today, the RnRHS controversy remains unresolved. Dalle seems unrepentant about her comments in the *LA Weekly* article, even though she claims she called Bourke last year to "apologize for calling her a Nazi, you know, and a psychotic." Dalle still teems with bitterness about the subject, claiming that Bourke "colluded" against her with her Sourpuss bandmates.

"I don't like that woman. I had nothing to do with her for eight years," Dalle explains. "It's like if you go to school, you don't owe your math teacher for the rest of your fucking life. . . . She'd be screaming into your face about not plugging in the amps the right way. Now she says that I am socially and politically unmotivated, that I am so disrespectful to women in rock, that I have done nothing for women in rock. She told one of my best friends that she hopes I burn in hell. I don't know what I did to inspire such hatred in this woman."

Bourke, however, seemed most hurt because Brody doesn't acknowledge the support that she and RnRHS gave her nascent rock and roll yearnings. Dalle concedes there is some truth to this, with qualifications. "She was important to the band, but there was a price to be paid for it, absolutely," Dalle says in retrospect. "She managed my career for a little bit, you know." Dalle explains how Bourke arranged for Sourpuss's first recordings, getting her boyfriend from the band No Comply to produce the demos. As well, she admits that Bourke's influence got Sourpuss booked for "a lot of great shows."

During this time, Dalle's profile grew in Australia—a teenage girl grunge band was, according to her, a "novelty" few could resist. Record labels like Sony began courting the band, seeing Sourpuss as a female counterpart to Silverchair, Oz's internationally successful trio of adolescent Nirvana-bes. "[Silverchair] front man Daniel Johns and I were the Kurt and Courtney of Australia," Dalle explains of the association. "Did we date? Fuck, no. I was fifteen."

Perhaps Dalle remains touchy about Bourke because her former mentor was in fact responsible for the most significant contribution to Brody and the Distillers' career. As Dalle admits, "Stephanie got us on the bill at Summersault." Summersault is a massive, legendary Australian touring festival that draws audiences in the range of 100,000 people, featuring the cream of the crop of big-name alternative-rock bands. Bourke had arranged for Sourpuss to play on one of the festival's smaller stages; it would prove to be the gig of Brody's life. As Stephanie Bourke points out in her letter to *LA Weekly,* "It [was] through RnRHS that Brody's band Sourpuss made it on to [Summersault with] Rancid, where she met Tim Armstrong, who subsequently took her to the U.S. and signed her to his label."

"That was the fateful day," Dalle says now of Summersault's January 1, 1996 show—which also happened to land on her seventeenth birthday. "I'd had a few fateful days before that, but this was a new path." Rancid were on the Summersault bill alongside Beck, the Beastie Boys, Bikini Kill, Sonic Youth, Pavement, and emo forbears Jawbreaker.

"I was hanging out with Thurston and Kim from Sonic Youth, talking to Ad-rock from the Beastie Boys—I didn't know who Rancid was," Dalle says today. "I had never heard of them before in my life." Musically, she felt no kinship with the neo-punk icons. "I had already kind of rejected punk rock at that time," she says. "Punk rock was so cliquey: you know, your hair had to be a certain way, and you had to have the right patch on your backpack."

Dalle had instead gravitated to the fringes of the grunge sound, grooving to the psychedelic, fuzzed-out neo-garage trash rock of Mudhoney and Aussie stoner-rock heroes Tumbleweed. "I grew my hair out, and was wearing fucking sweaters and shit—I think I had orange and brown flares on when I met Tim," she says. "Kids then were all about long hair, zitty faces, and Mudhoney T-shirts."

Dalle, in fact, may not have seen Rancid's set that day. She can't remember, due to extenuating circumstances involving an excess of birthday bubbly. "Someone gave me a bottle of champagne, which I popped way too early—we played at noon and after that it gets a little hazy," Dalle recalls. "Yeah, it was all kind of like a big blur, man."

She does remember Tim introducing himself, however. "I'm standing there helping pack our drummer's kit, and Tim just came over and asked me if I was a drummer." Dalle remains coy about the gory details of what transpired next: "There is also stuff that is just not anyone's business" (online rumors abound that Dalle lied about her age to Armstrong; it's a rumor she doesn't dignify with a response). What she's crystal-clear about, however, is the meeting's end result.

"I knew that I had a connection with him instantly," Dalle explains. "Someone took a photo of us, and we were very natural together." Communication between young Brody and Armstrong dwindled, however, after Rancid left Australia, and Dalle found herself going through a rough patch. Shortly after leaving the group, one of Sourpuss's former drummers was murdered, causing a national scandal. And a few months after the Summersault show, Sourpuss themselves broke up. Dalle fell out initially with Bourke and her Rock 'n' Roll High School community. Increasingly rebellious, Dalle had fallen out with her parents, which caused her to move into a Melbourne's women's shelter.

"I was surrounded by fucking freaks there—it was so terrifying," Dalle says. "It really wasn't a place that I should be in, but because of the friction between me and my parents, it wasn't possible for us to live under the same roof. A lot of truth was coming out—a lot of childhood darkness was being uncovered."

In fact, Dalle wasn't sure when she'd see the light, as she had felt she had nowhere to go. She had run-ins with the a dangerous local gang of homeless, don't-give-a-fuck urchins. "[They are a bunch] of really, really abused children who had nowhere to go, led by this . . . really bad junkie," Dalle says. "They were bad, bad people. They would beat the shit out of you if you had ten bucks in your pocket."

Dalle recalls a time when she and her pal Gertie—a childhood friend who would later recur as a character in Distillers' lyrics—had a dangerously telling encounter with the gang. "We'd snuck out of my house and gone into the city at like four in the morning," Dalle says. "We were crossing the street near the train station and these girls came up and kicked the living shit out of us. They fractured my arm, then tried to befriend us so that they could get more out of us, you know."

These run-ins cured Brody Dalle of any romance about squatting (ironically, anarcho-crusty squatter punks would be early supporters of the Distillers): "It's bullshit—there is nothing romantic about squatting whatsoever. They're afraid to live their life, especially if they do it deliberately, on purpose. It's mostly rich kids who are suffering for something that's not real, with an emergency credit card from mom and dad in their pocket."

Dalle was running out of options—for her, there was no emergency credit card. She had already returned from a spell in the seedily ramshackle industrial-beach village Jalong in New South Wales, Australia. There, she lived with musician friends in a house next to the highway, never sleeping due to the constant hum of traffic noise. Upon her return to Melbourne, Dalle became drawn to the street life, hanging out with junkie punk rockers and an eccentric homeless millionaire, who stayed on the streets despite having made a fortune in business. "He was an alcoholic," Dalle explains, "and every week his daughter would pull up in a fucking Ferrari and give him cash."

In addition to a failed suicide attempt (Dalle claims she slashed her wrists incorrectly), young Brody began experimenting with drugs, which she refers to in Distillers songs like "Desperate" ("Dirty heroin, take it back a step/This is my arm, this is my heart"). She claims, however, that the extent of her drug use has been largely exaggerated and romanticized in her myth. "I was going through all these phases that really didn't last that long—like a six-month span," Dalle says. "It's just ridiculous. I'm not a junkie. I can't do it—it's gross to me: I hate needles. All I did was swallow some caps a couple of times."

Junkie or not, when Dalle received a call from Tim Armstrong out of the blue inviting her to follow Rancid on the summer '96 Lollapalooza tour in America, there wasn't much left tying her to her hometown. The age difference between them—Armstrong is many years her senior, having been born in 1966—didn't faze her. She'd already been dating older guys, like the thirty-year-old "anarchist douchebag" who owned the local punk-rock bookstore.

"Oh, I have a daddy complex, is that what you want me to say?" Dalle responds. "Do I like older dudes? I don't like younger dudes, because they're not at my level, and I don't really want to teach a younger dude how to act, how to behave, and how to treat a woman. Having a thirty-year-old boyfriend in my teens turned me on to great music and a whole culture of literature and discussions about religion. Actually, acid was the anarchist douchebag's religion."

As for her bond with the older Armstrong, Dalle believes that their instant mutual attraction stemmed from their similarities and shared backgrounds, resulting in an instant familiarity, intimacy, and trust between the two. "He saw an equal in me," Brody says. "We assimilated on a few levels, particularly about our childhoods." Their bond would find its way into Dalle's songwriting, like in the autobiographical "The Young Crazed Peeling," which documents this turbulent era with spiky vigor: "I love a man from California/He's the prettiest thing, we got the same disorder."

Not surprisingly, Brody took Armstrong up on his Lollapalooza offer: she traveled with him for two weeks on the megatour, which also featured the diverse likes of the Ramones, Metallica, Devo, Soundgarden, and Pacific Northwest psych-grunge avatars the Screaming Trees. Paradoxically, on this jaunt Dalle would meet Josh Homme, the man she now calls the love of her life (and the father of her child). Homme is currently the guitarist of innovative heavy-rock eccentrics Queens of the Stone Age. At the time of Lollapalooza '96, however, he was doing double duty as the Ramones' driver and Screaming Trees' second guitarist; Homme had a lot of free time, as his former band, the astoundingly heavy stoner-rock combo Kyuss, had recently imploded.

"It's wild that I met Joshua for the first time when he was playing in the Screaming Trees on Lollapalooza," Dalle says. "It was another fateful day. He was sitting backstage on a bench reading a book. I have no idea what he was reading; I wasn't looking at his book. But I was looking at his *book*. We talked for two hours—I was a *huge* Kyuss fan. I never saw him again after that day for years."

Even stranger was the sometimes violent rivalry between Rancid and Screaming Trees. "They fucking hated each other, dude, because of their musical differences—it was nemesis combat between them," Dalle recalls. "Screaming Trees would taunt Rancid, like 'You guys are poser English punks with a fake English accent.' There were beefs everywhere. There was an incident with this kiddie pool that all the groupies would lounge in with their clothes off. Van from Screaming Trees pulled out a knife and started stabbing the shit out of the pool in front of all the Rancid guys."

After Lollapalooza, Armstrong and Dalle parted, with her going back to Australia and him going out again on tour. Dalle didn't hear from Armstrong for a quarter of a year; young Brody was so despondent she halfheartedly attempted suicide. But when Tim finally did call, it was with a proposition: move to America, to California, to be with him. This was *l'amour fou* for the liberty spikes set—punk romance in its highest form. This was fantasy fulfillment, however, that anyone could appreciate, with a touch of the surreal: teenage girl with big dreams living in a faraway place on the edge of nowhere is plucked away by rock star to live in the Promised Land.

"It was just insane," Dalle says. "I'd probably spent two or three weeks with the guy over a period of a year and a half before I moved to America. I wouldn't do that now—no way. If my daughter did it, I would find it pretty terrifying."

I'm sitting with Brody Dalle in the home she shares with Josh Homme today as she traces this narrative's spinout down memory lane. Located on a wooded side street in a Valley suburb of Los Angeles, Dalle and Homme's house is a beautiful Spanish three-bedroom house tastefully decorated in Southwestern desert style—you just might stumble upon the kind of bovine skull Georgia O'Keefe might paint amid the guitars and vinyl albums strewn about. The house is in fact indicative of the couple's synergy. "Josh and I bought this place and did it up together," Dalle says as we sit in the dining room going through photo albums to jog her memories. "We both love the Southwestern style." Occasionally, as she talks, Brody pulls individual photos out if they are particularly apropos to the subject at hand. "Here's a picture of me wearing a Kyuss T-shirt when I was sixteen," she says, laughing. "The funny thing is, Josh told me it's a bootleg shirt! If I'd only known then. . . ."

The photo books are a record of Brody's life outside the persona, the life that the tabloids—and *NME*, and *Rolling Stone*, and *The Face*, and *LA Weekly*—don't see. One picture shows Brody at six months old, with a shock of red hair that surprisingly resembles Homme's today. "I have some big eyes there," she murmurs. There's a picture of Dalle's mom from the late '70s-early '80s, looking like a beautiful bohemian blend of Sophia Loren and Jean Seberg, an idealized yet authentic femme from the Godard-Fellini nexus. Next comes a photo of Brody and her stepdad posing with a kangaroo: "I didn't realize how handsome my father was until way after the fact."

The most shocking photo image comes from a class picture from Brody's first year of Catholic school: it features a smiling, barely teenage

Bree Pucilowski wearing a crest-emblazoned sportcoat. "I still have my baby fat and all!" Dalle marvels. Seeing this picture of Brody in such a conservative establishment garb is like discovering a long-lost photo of George W. Bush as a long-haired, tie-dyed Deadhead holding a joint. Then we enter Dalle's "punk years," commencing with a shot of her at sixteen sporting a skinhead girl "Chelsea" haircut, fringe bangs and all.

The most haunting photo in the collection, however, is the shot of Brody taken the day she's leaving indefinitely to live with Tim in America. She's with her family—mom, dad, sister—posing for a last shot at the airport. Brody looks startlingly youthful, like any other rebellious teenager out with her folks; she's wearing a halter top that says "BITCH," and she's flipping the camera the bird. It's a universal image of a punk-defined childhood being left behind, the climactic shot of the nuclear family detonated, as it was and would never be again.

"I remember the date: April 8, 1997," Dalle says. "I'd just turned eighteen. I just wanted to go, so I left. It was crazy. I think the reason I was able to do it was because I didn't think about it; otherwise, I probably would've talked myself out of it. I really did not think about it. I just went. I was in love—or at least I thought I was in love at that time. And I had no idea what to expect, or what I was getting myself into—or even that I was on a path to where I am now. I did not even think about the future once; it was just about the moment. I had no idea what I was doing."

In fact, Dalle claims she doesn't remember getting on the plane. "I don't even remember the flight over," she says. "I have no recollection of it at all. My parents were devastated. They didn't really want me to go—I found out afterward how terrifying a thought they thought it was. But if they'd told me that at the time, my response would've been that I would probably give them the finger."

The photograph is her proof. "I never planned it, I never thought about it. No, I never . . ." Dalle pauses a moment in concentration before resuming. "When I was a kid, I never said, 'I'm going to America when I'm older,'" she continues. "But I knew there was like a bigger world out there that I wanted to discover. I was living on a very faraway island called Australia down under, but I knew there was always something bigger in store for me. But I didn't know what it was. And I guess I had the opportunity when Tim asked me to move to America with him.

"I think California is badass," Dalle says of her adopted home. "I'm a total Valley girl, dude. California has got a more utopian feel than any other place." But there was some element of culture shock for Dalle, who'd never traveled far outside her native part of the world. "In Australia, we don't keep our eggs in the fridge," she explains about one unfamiliar, inexplicable American practice. "It is such an alien concept to me."

Indeed, the physical necessity of keeping herself fed Stateside resulted in high anxiety at the supermarket. "I couldn't stand how many options I was given when I went to the grocery," she says. "I literally cried when I went to the store because I had to pick fucking cereals and I was faced with, like, thirty options. I'm standing there just devastated in the aisle, torn between Captain Crunch or Lucky Charms. Which one, you know?" America's supersized culinary excess caused Brody to gain some thirty-five pounds. "I weighed one-twenty when I moved," Brody says, "After that, at one point I weighed in at one-fifty-five. I'm five-eight, so I can carry it. But I was *big*."

Adding to the surreal vibe was her new circle of friends, adopted almost entirely from Armstrong's cadre of neo-punk big shots and entourage. One of Armstrong's closest friends was also the owner of the label Rancid recorded for, and Armstrong's actual business partner in Hellcat Records, Epitaph chief Brett Gurewitz. "Tim and Brett had a really tight connection with each other," Brody recalls. "We would eat at Brett's house all the time, you know, just hanging out. We were there through the hard times and the good times."

Although Brody claims the "first time I went to Gilman Street was when I played it," it was not long after Brody had moved to America that Armstrong started indoctrinating his new girlfriend into his beloved East Bay punk scene (Andy "Outbreak" Granelli, drummer for the two most significant Distillers albums to date, also hailed from the East Bay axis, having played in the innovative, Gilman-spawned punk outfit the Nerve Agents).

Life with Armstrong was indeed an immersion course in the neo-punk scene's current events and currents. Traveling from their home in Los Angeles's cozily bohemian Los Feliz area through the Bay and beyond, the couple would check out both old-school punk rock faves like the (Glenn Danzig-less) Misfits as well as digging the new breed. Armstrong was Dalle's reluctant V.I.P. introduction to neo-punk's growing contingent that she would soon hitch her post to with the Distillers. It was a contingent that was nipping at the heels of neo-punk originators like Armstrong's Rancid even as it simultaneously revered them as forefathers.

"It was exciting around the East Bay—AFI and that whole scene," Dalle says. "It was good stuff. At that point, Rancid were like the old-timers. The early '80s punk was coming out in *my* generation."

Meanwhile, the difference in generations and nationality between Armstrong and Dalle was expressing itself primarily through Armstrong's embrace of twelve-step recovery culture. Armstrong had a troubled history of addiction that had threatened his previous musical projects, let alone his life. There was no way he was going back there again; his high was strictly punk rock, pure and uncut. Armstrong's sobriety was another culture shock for young Brody, especially coming from lager-sodden Oz—where the word "alcoholic" is Australian for, well . . . *Australian*.

"I moved to America to be with Tim when I was eighteen," Dalle explains. "You know, at that point I'd been trying to get into bars since I was thirteen years old—which was quite a struggle. And then finally when I was able to drink, I came to America to be with Tim and I can't drink anymore, you know?"

According to Brody, in Armstrong's universe one had to be a sober, clean punk if you wanted to hang fire. "They lived their lives a certain twelve-step way," she recalls. "No one could drink. It was so strict it was sick—a *sick, sick* way to control people. The addiction is never really conquered, it just gets misplaced. It manifests itself in control—controlling other people."

One gets the distinct sense after a while that the "other people" Brody's referring to actually refers to her. "I never had a problem," she says, "but Tim met me when I had been doing some drugs; he decided on the spot that I had a problem after all. Obviously, my mind is very malleable—I was, like, barely eighteen years old! I started believing that's where I belonged, but I never got a chance to find out if I had a problem or not. I thought his heart was in the right place, which I found out pretty soon it wasn't."

Dalle didn't ever feel entirely accepted within this new environment, in particular its female population, who regards Brody as an unnecessary import—an interloper. She channeled this new-world alienation into a renewed burst of creativity and focus brought on by this combination of humiliation and enforced sobriety. "I started writing songs," Dalle says. "I wrote 'L.A. Girl'—that was the first song I ever wrote when I moved here. I had to write it on Tim's guitar upside-down because he's left-handed; I learned how to play upside-down, and can still write all my songs that way."

She claims "L.A. Girl" is written specifically about a female friend of Tim's who threatened to turn Brody's world upside-down almost as soon as she got off the plane. "She asked me the first day I moved here when I was going home!" Dalle laughs. "Yeah, she was in love with Tim, but then I came and that was it. They didn't hide how they felt about me: they hated my guts. I grew a thick skin."

Then again, more than a thick skin was necessary for Dalle to survive in this new world. She was entirely supporting herself, with little financial help from Armstrong—which is exactly how she wanted it, she claims. "I had gotten a grant from the government. I received some money for something that happened to me when I was young," she notes cryptically.

"What happened to me when I was a kid, it doesn't matter. If I hadn't have gotten that money, there's no way I would have been able to move. Because I wasn't going to be supported by him. Nothing to do with him— I didn't want to take his money. Up until midway through our marriage, he never supported me financially. I was raised by a single mother—I was staunch about being independent."

Independence was all about the couple's quaint punk-centered home life. "Tim was a punk rocker—we lived in this one-bedroom apartment on Griffith Park Boulevard with, you know, no furniture. But punk rock clothes were everywhere," Dalle says. "There was never anything in the fridge. I had just come from this home life with my family, so I was like 'What the fuck?' So at age eighteen, he let me play domestic housewife: I bought the groceries and cleaned."

The problem was, at that time Dalle felt she was missing the housewife gene: "I didn't know how to do it. I was so dysfunctional and I just had *no fucking idea*. So eventually we bought a house." And with the house came marriage. Dalle became what she never expected to become ever in her life: someone's wife. Decamping to a remote Nevada location, she and Armstrong married in the summer of 1997, in what was reportedly a witch-led Wiccan ceremony. "Fuck no, I was never going to get married," she says. "To me, the whole sanctity of marriage is bullshit; I was into faster relationships anyway. It took my mom thirteen years before she got around to marrying my father."

The thing was, there was the little nagging problem of Dalle's Australian citizenship: it was either get hitched or get back to Melbourne. "My fucking visa was running out, so I had to get married," she says. "I mean, it was something that we both wanted, but it was kind of a pressure cooker."

Dalle and Armstrong got married in summer 1997. However snaked the journey it took to get there, this union maintained some traditional gender roles—Dalle even legally changed her last name to Brody Armstrong. Still, one got the sense it was underlined at the very least by real passion. When asked by the fanzine *While You Were Sleeping* if she licked "ball sack" during fellatio, the unflappable Mrs. Brody Armstrong replied, "Yeah, of course, my husband's." But all wasn't going exactly according to plan: Dalle found herself literally becoming a mall punk against her will.

"I had nothing to do, so I got a job working in the mall," she confesses. "I worked at Betsy Johnson at the Beverly Center, and it was a nightmare. I'd never worked retail in my life. I lasted four months: the mall is a fucking Antichrist." It was high time for Brody Dalle to start a band—or go insane.

Thankfully, she opted for the former route. In 1999, Dalle started up the first version of the Distillers, taking the name from a distillery sign in Melbourne. Her first bandmate was a friend she knew who worked at Epitaph, Kim "Chi" Fuelleman, a native of the O.C. punk scene who got her Korean-influenced punk name for her interest in Eastern medical and spiritual practice. The band's first second guitarist, Rose Casper, was an energetic young punk from Detroit who, while still in her teenage years, earned O.G. scenester status for her devotion to the underground. The band's lone male member, drummer Matt (sometimes "Mat") Young, was the group's veteran bridging the punk generations, having played in legendary O.C. punk-pop bands like CH3.

For Tony Bevilacqua, Distillers version one was all about the women rocking out up front, in defiance of silent neo-punk chauvinism. "Kim was just the best chick," Tony Bevilacqua says. "She has a nice voice: she, Brody, and Rose all sang really well together. It was weird having the front line being all girls, but it also was cool to see that. That is my favorite lineup of the Distillers."

The Distillers played their first show on Thanksgiving 1999 at an extinct L.A. punk hovel called the Garage on Santa Monica Boulevard on the fringe of Los Angeles' boho Silverlake district, located maybe at most two miles southwest of Epitaph's neighborhood (the Garage has since been replaced by a neo-soul/acid jazz D.J. bar). In no time, the band recording a scrappy, roughhouse 7-inch-single, which made a fan out of reluctant neo-punk scenester and future Distillers guitarist Tony Bevilacqua. "I was a fan at the time," he says. "I got their first seven-inch and I liked it a lot. This was really cool shit: I immediately was attracted to her voice and the whole energy of the band."

Bevilacqua recalls an unfortunate first meeting with Brody at an early Distillers show at the Roxy, largely due to his defying the no-drugs policy in the presence of Tim and his crew. "I don't know if it was because I was smoking pot or whatever, but she was just bummed that I was in her dressing room or whatever," he recalls. "She gave me a stinkeye, and was kind of cold to me. The second time I met her, I was rolling on Ecstasy at the annual Punk Rock Bowling thing in Vegas. She was with her husband at the time; they were talking to me and I was so fucked up. I was so high, all I remember is that she had a Mohawk."

Bevilacqua figured his first impressions had soured the Distillers on him. Then, however, he was approached by Brody while procrastinating one day in Epitaph's mailroom. "I was just slacking off listening to music, and she walked right up to me and was like 'So, you just got hired here, right?' I was like, 'Yeah . . . ,'" Bevilacqua recalls. "And then she goes, 'Do you want to go on tour with my band?'"

From that moment on, Bevilacqua would be the Distillers' official roadie, and later guitar tech, before he graduated to the second guitar slot for the recording of 2003's *Coral Fang*. Bevilacqua was there selling T-shirts, driving the van, changing guitar strings—or some combination thereof—for every Distillers tour, the amount of which seemed to be growing exponentially.

The band's first tour was a lower slot on one of Epitaph's Punk-A-rama package shows. In its early days, the band also toured with AFI and scoured Europe for a month opening for New York hardcore legends Agnostic Front in early 2000. The Distillers finally played their first headlining tour on a bill with punkabilly faves Tiger Army and Nekromantix. According to Bevilacqua, in the early Distillers days on the road "it was cool if we sold sixty bucks worth of T-shirts at that point. But they just toured a shitload, building a fan base from playing live."

The Distillers' raucous live show also made a fan favorite out of guitarist Casper, who came into her own by assaulting crowds with an outrageously exuberant guitar-tossing energy. "Rose was my favorite part of the band," says Greg Attonitoi of Bouncing Souls.

"Rose had like really awesome stage presence with the way she played," Bevilacqua says. "Distillers fans *love* Rose. They don't like me at all—and still don't—because I'm not her when I walk onstage. They still talk about her on message boards because she was a big part of the band. In a way, the kids identified with Rose because they felt like she was one of *them*."

According to Brett Gurewitz, the fan base earned from hard miles on the tour bus came out "reasonably well" for the Distillers' first album, released on Tim Armstrong's Hellcat label via Epitaph in 2000. "It sold around twenty thousand, thirty thousand copies," Gurewitz claims. "Now it's up to a couple hundred thousand."

The tough sell at first was most likely due to the uncompromising music held inside. *The Distillers*' rough black-and-white graphics suggested that the album might be more a street-punk affair à la the Casualties than a cheery, overproduced pop-punk Green Day retread. This was fight music, borrowing thrashing influences and radical societal critique from New York hardcore stars like Sick of It All, raw political American punks Code of Honor and Avail, and metallic U.K. activist street punk icons Discharge. "The first record is pretty much hardcore—you know, the 'forbidden beat,'" Dalle says today. "The first record is probably my favorite Distillers record," Tony Bevilacqua says. "It's just superfast, rad punk shit with three girls singing, and it just sounded awesome."

All the influences, however, were united by the then–Brody Armstrong's survivor spirit and expressive caterwaul. Songs like "Oh Serena" pledged a message of hope to their young, troubled female protagonists; a passionately frayed cover of '70s New York punk priestess Patti Smith's "Ask the Angels" rages toward transcendence, not against the machine.

"Gypsy Rose Lee," meanwhile, is a cathartic, autobiographical coming-of-age tale, one of Brody's most personal anthems. "That song comes from the heart—you can hear it. It's different from a Louis XIV song where they're just talking about picking up chicks," Bevilacqua states. "That's why people identify with Brody—when someone sings from the heart and talks about personal issues, people identify with that more than anything else."

"The Blackest Years," meanwhile, reveals for the first time what would become an ongoing Brody lyrical conceit: a character named Gertie Rose. Based on a friend of Dalle's from childhood, Gertie serves to symbolize in the Distillers' music the violent injustices so many young women face, but in a nondidactic way. After a couple of listens, *The Distillers* reveals its yearning human side, suggesting something bigger than just punk rock.

"The album kind of uplifts you instead of bringing you down," says Bee of Suicide Girls. "It made me feel okay about being pissed off about all the shit I was pissed off about. It helped me idealize myself and become that ideal. The Distillers make punk that reflects how I really feel."

Bevilacqua wasn't surprised that neo-punk's not-as-visible female audience was energized by what they heard. "They were playing the kind of music that dudes play, and just as good as them," he says. "That's one of the things that I miss, having the three girls singing. Me and Ryan do not do justice at all to how great those girls sing together. It was something different."

When *The Distillers* hit punk consciousness, however, was when the "Courtney clone" accusations started percolating. Brody has had to endure Courtney Love comparisons due to a series of uncanny parallels—from the similarity of their honeyed rasps to their shared preference to mate with iconic rock stars. "Someone got the Courtney Love script out and Brody picked it up," says Kevin Lyman, who claims he "backed Brody before anyone else did—more because I was introduced to her by Tim and heard her demos. I said, 'Let's help her out.'"

Tim's influence would also come to haunt Brody. Ever since the Distillers' first album, rumors have floated that Brody's had a ghostwriter in Tim Armstrong—just as Kurt Cobain is rumored to be Courtney Love's phantom ringer in the songwriting department. "She's not Courtney Love—that's so dumb," says Tony Bevilacqua. "Everyone said Josh wrote *Coral Fang* or whatever. I hate that shit. I'm mean, I've watched her sit down, write lyrics, and work out parts for *days*."

The Distillers' sophomore release, *Sing Sing Death House*, meanwhile, proved the band's breakthrough. According to Tony Bevilacqua, that's thanks in large part to a shift in personnel. Drummer Matt Young and bassist Kim Chi left before the album was recorded to join Los Angeles punk legend Exene Cervenka of X infamy in the old-school/new-school punk hybrid supergroup Original Sinners. New drummer Andy Granelli of the Nerve Agents was drafted in first as a tour replacement for Young, but stayed on for *Sing Sing.* . . . Kim Chi's replacement, meanwhile, was Ryan Sinn, a San Diego speed-metal virtuoso with a fondness for eye makeup and playing live without shoes.

"The rhythm section really stepped out on the second record. Andy is a way better drummer than Matt, and that was a huge thing," Tony Bevilacqua says. "Ryan, meanwhile, has a faster, crazier bass-playing style than Kim. Ryan is like a guitar player that plays the bass like a guitar."

The fusion of Brody's guitar and Andy's drumming became the real rhythm section, the sonic linchpin, for the Distillers' sound: they developed a musical chemistry akin to, say, James Hetfield and Lars Ulrich in Metallica. Ryan, meanwhile, would provide a rippling, speedily melodic pulse under Brody's chunky rhythm-guitar method. *Sing Sing* captures the band at a sonic peak, despite problems in the album's recording: when one key member of the production team abruptly exited the project, the recording schedule became abbreviated. The resulting urgency to get everything down on tape comes out in the songs' relentlessness.

"Someone dropped out at the last minute and I had to step in," says Brett Gurewitz, who produced *Sing Sing* at his Westbeach Recorders studio in Hollywood. "We did it so fast; I think we mixed the record in seven days. But it's a cool-sounding record. I'm still proud of it. It was a lot of fun making that album."

Sing Sing also represented a major leap in Brody's songwriting. The furious guitars heralding the album opener "Sick of It All" reflected the band's street-punk roots, with lyrics exploring everything from the roots of Columbine-style violence to anorexia. Meanwhile, heart-wrenching anthems like "The Young Crazed Peeling" showed that sophistication and rage were not mutually exclusive in Brody's world. Gertie Rouge is resurrected as well for the cautionary "Young Girl." "I Understand" is a field report from the tortured adolescence of "a misshape, mistake misfit . . . with a junkie heart": "When I was a teen girl," Brody sings with knowing versimilitude, "I walked real awkward/Like a dog with three legs."

At the same time, Brody proved she had the potential to write a hit. The video for "Young Crazed Peeling" got played on MTV, but the album's biggest success was Brody's confessional "City of Angels," which proved a smash on a big alternative radio station, KROQ. There are also interesting, complex explorations of language, like "I Am a Revenant": a "revenant" is a ghostlike apparaition who returns from death to avenge an injustice. Who knew? "There's way hooky stuff on *Sing Sing* but also weird, angular punk songs," Bevilacqua says. "As well, Brody is very well read—with her vocabulary, the lyrics are always insanely good."

While the videos and hits helped, what really drove the album to a near quarter-million in sales was the band's relentless touring. "*Sing Sing* became a success because they went out and toured the country for a year straight," Bevilacqua says. "They built that thing."

Rose Casper's tenure in the band, however, would not extend beyond *Sing Sing*, turning the Distillers into a trio of Brody Dalle, Andy Granelli, and Ryan Sinn. "Rose was really young when she joined the band," Bevilacqua says. "She was seventeen or eighteen when she joined the band, and she's kind of a wild kid—a hurricane. It just never worked; she never wanted to follow the rules. Her, Andy, and Brody used to get in tons of fights."

Meanwhile, life on the road for the Distillers was becoming increasingly ascetic: ruled by Tim Armstrong's twelve-step discipline, the band's touring machine was stripped of any hedonistic rock and roll excess—no groupies backstage, no drugs, no drinking. *Nada*. In other words, nothing juicy to capture for a future episode of VH1's *Behind the Music*.

"When the tours used to be organized by HellCat and Brody was married to Tim, no one in the band drank or did anything," Bevilacqua says. "Everyone in that whole punk rock world, they're all sober, Alcoholics Anonymous people. It's really bizarre. I smoked pot and drank beer, but I never did it on the road. On all the Distillers tours combined, I only ever drank one beer in total prior to *Coral Fang*."

The Distillers' touring machine was about to ramp up: the band had been asked to join an arena tour opening for Garbage and No Doubt (supposedly No Doubt bassist Tony Kanal personally scouted the Distillers' club shows). On tours with the likes of the Dropkick Murphys, Bouncing Souls, and the various Punk-A-Rama and Warped package tours, the Distillers had played to thousands. But on the No Doubt/Garbage tour, however, the Distillers would play to crowds bigger than they'd ever seen, *tens* of thousands of people every single night at massive venues like California's Arrowhead Pond. "We had a crew on that tour, actually," Bevilacqua continues. "It was our first tour with a bus, not a van—with a sound guy, a merch guy, the tour manager, and me. It was a big deal."

According to Bevilacqua, the Distillers were playing to quadruple the amount of people they'd ever played to before. "It was weird watching the crowd go, 'Who the fuck is this?'" he says. "Every night there were like fifty kids there to see the Distillers, all in the front row. But some fans were complaining. They were saying the Distillers shouldn't be playing with No Doubt, but with other punk bands instead."

The No Doubt jaunt had in fact set the bar even higher: the Distillers' presence on such a high-profile bill alerted major labels to the band's potential mainstream appeal. "When Distillers did the No Doubt tour, that's when record labels like Warner Bros. [who ultimately signed the band] got interested," Bevilacqua admits. "I think they were like, 'Cool, we have another band like the Used.'"

The fans, meanwhile, were growing along with the band—"mostly girls and young kids," according to Bevilacqua. "They want to see Brody and shake her hand," he says. "People always say to me 'Dude, you must get so laid on the road!' And I'm like, 'No, I don't.' In fact, I've never gotten laid on the road. Never, not once—they're all too young."

Despite the feminist-critical rhetoric Dalle throws around in the Stephanie Bourke/Rock 'n' Roll High School debacle, she's not afraid to list the women in her life she considers positive role models. "Growing up I had this older woman who influenced me so much," Dalle recalls. "She was a journalist named Jacintha Laplathier. I'd baby-sit her kids, and she'd revise poetry that I would give to her. She made a big difference in my life." But Dalle herself feels pressure as a role model due to her legion of young fans.

"They're pretty rabid sometimes, " she says of the "Distiller kids." "It's a weird concept to me. If I ever do come in contact with them, I start asking about their own life. They want to talk about cutting themselves and stuff, and about the drugs. They are so fascinated by something that is not me. It's my persona, yeah, but it's not real. So I keep a barrier there, as I can't really get real with these kids. It's not like I'm just reading fucking confessions. It is filtered through art."

The Distillers' next album, 2003's *Coral Fang*, would in fact filter through art one of the most convulsive turning points in Brody Dalle's life: the moment she got divorced from Tim Armstrong, along with her subsequent attachment to Josh Homme. For punk rockers, Dalle's divorce was the equivalent of the supposed Brad Pitt/Jennifer Aniston/Angelina Jolie home-wrecking love triangle—with an almost as sordid media aftermath.

At the same time as Brody's divorce was under way, the Distillers were going through major changes within the band, all while trying to record what would become the band's major-label debut. Brody asked her long-time confidant Bevilacqua to quit working as guitar tech and join the band as guitarist. "I was surprised, to put it mildly," he says, grinning. "I've always been the village idiot in the Distillers."

For Dalle, it was important to surround herself during this period with people she could totally trust. "Tony and I are best friends. He's a loyal dog, you know—my right-hand man," Dalle says. "Our friendship is one of the longest relationships I've ever had. There are maybe three people who have always been there in the fire with me. And he is one of them." And, of course, Brody had to divest herself of Tim's surname. She chose "Dalle" from the name of the actress Beatrice Dalle, who's best known for her role in *Betty Blue*, one of Brody's favorite movies. *Betty Blue* follows Beatrice Dalle's titular protagonist as she spirals into violence and mental illness, bloodily destroying her relationships with men. It's a provocative stage name for this period in Brody's life, certainly.

Name changed and second guitarist added, the Distillers' circle was complete. With the new major deal, however, the band was under pressure to deliver on their promise. Subsequently, the recording experience became suitably "major label." For one, Bevilacqua notes the label's terse insistence that the band have a "name" producer. "They were like, 'You *are* going to have a producer!'" he laughs.

The band settled on Gil Norton, who had was legendary for producing unique bands like the Pixies, Echo and the Bunnymen, Counting Crows, Patti Smith, and the Foo Fighters. According to Brody, the suits at Warner Bros. "didn't know who Gil was" (Norton would go on to produce Jimmy Eat World's smash 2004 album *Futures*).

However, while *Coral Fang* turned out amazingly, the experience was not all the band had hoped for. "I'll never use a click track again in my life," Brody exclaims about *Coral Fang*'s rigid recording process. "Andy is the most solid drummer—he doesn't *need* a click track," adds Bevilacqua. "Knowing what I now know about recording, I would never do a record like that again. The push and pull was all 'pro-tooled' out; there wasn't a chance for it to breathe, really."

During the recording process, the Distillers could breathe a bit easier. This time, the band wasn't going to record quickly in a ramshackle "punk" studio like Westbeach Recorders (where the band had done *Sing Sing*). Instead, on Josh Homme's recommendation the band settled into "the Site," a mountain cottage residential studio in bucolic San Rafael, California. This was serious major label recording: the Site featured a fireplace, pool, and, best of all, private chef.

"Every day the cook would make us grade-A meals—I haven't eaten that well since. I'm drooling thinking about it now," Bevilacqua admits. "It was just rad, the chillest place I've ever been: just north of San Francisco, set in wilderness on the side of this beautiful hill in the middle of nowhere. It was right up the road from Skywalker Ranch. And there was a lot of drinking. We'd go through Ketel One bottles like *that*! Recording at the Site put us way over budget.

"It's definitely an experience I'll probably never relive. It was fun," he continues wistfully. "It's the whole clichéd thing—you know, we felt like a *band*; we existed solely for the making of the record."

Despite the idyllic setting it was created in, with *Coral Fang*, this traumatic period in the Distillers musical history would be converted into musical catharsis. "I remember one time she played these songs over the phone to me from Australia that eventually ended up on *Coral Fang*," Bevilacqua recalls. "I was like, 'Wow, that's really cool!' They were different, really personal—there's a lot about what was going with her at the time, when her life was turning upside-down, and changing."

Coral Fang standouts like "Drain the Blood," "Dismantle Me," "Die on a Rope," and "The Gallow Is God" teem with images of viscera, transformation, mutilation, and rebirth—themes that echo the cover's image of a crucified, blood-spurting woman. Other songs, like "The Hunger," were achingly romantic, almost fragile—and it didn't take much detective work to figure out that these besotted words were about Dalle's burgeoning romance with Josh Homme. "I wrote it about the most special person to me," Dalle says. "It was at a time when we were on opposite ends of the world."

Musically, too, *Coral Fang* would suggest a rebirth for the band, leaving behind many of the neo-punk conventions their fans wanted to hear. This change in plan proved problematic for the Distillers' new record label. When Dalle and Armstrong were splitting up, it became clear that Dalle recording for her ex-husband's label, HellCat, whom the Distillers were signed to, would not be the best move. At the same time, hype for the band was at an all-time high—they'd bolstered their audience through higher- and higher-profile tours, and their songs got played on the radio, as well as MTV. When Warner Bros. signed the Distillers in 2002, they must have figured they had the next neo-punk gold mine on their hands.

They didn't.

"All those songs Brody wrote for *Coral Fang* while she was away in Australia, they weren't punk rock songs," Bevilacqua explains. "When they signed the Distillers, they were like, 'Cool, we just found this new Warped Tour punk band.' The record label was very worried about it."

As for the rest of the neo-punk community, bands that previously considered the Distillers to be peers, well . . . Bevilacqua claims many former friends turned their backs on Brody: "It was like, 'Oh, you divorced Tim— fuck you, you're a bitch.' And a lot of the fans did that, too. It was a huge deal, a very public breakup—it was in magazines."

"The Distillers were in that whole punk rock world. Tim and Brody broke up and that all went away," Bevilacqua continues. "It affected everyone in the band, but especially Andy. Andy lost a lot of actual friends when that thing with Tim went down. Andy had been a big part of that whole Gilman Street crew, but people wouldn't talk to him now because he was in *Brody's band*. It was very high school, really.

"For me, what happened was awesome—this whole new world came up," Bevilacqua adds. "I was like, 'This is great. These people are into cool shit.' I was surrounded by so much smarter, so much more intelligent musicians than I was in the punk scene. Now we're playing with Peaches and Eagles of Death Metal. I got to play with PJ Harvey—cool! We got to open for the *Pixies*. When Brody's world changed, the Distillers went with it."

Then again, the Distillers' new world also had its down side. "I've done interviews where all they want to talk about is Josh and Brody," Bevilacqua says with a groan. "I'm like, 'Don't you want to talk about the . . . *music?*'"

Soon, all anyone wanted to talk about was the June 12, 2003, issue of *Rolling Stone*. The cover is not shocking in itself: it presents a special "Monsters of Summer" tour issue, featuring the twelve artists most likely to jump-start the concert circuit. The front cover featured "the establishment": Ozzy, Fred Durst of Limp Bizkit, Metallica's James Hetfield, Marilyn Manson. The second page was the cool kids' table—Dave Navarro, Dave Grohl, and Josh Homme with his arm around new kid Brody Dalle (Perry Farrell, AFI's Davey Havok, Metallica's Lars Ulrich, and Linkin Park's Chester Bennington get relegated to the overleaf). The photos inside, however, were worth more than a thousand words.

While a Q&A with Homme mentions a rumor that Brody is the Queens' front man's "new flame," the adjoining photo confirms it: the image depicts Homme and Brody enthusiastically, unabashedly sucking face. At this point, Brody is still using Armstrong's name—it says "Brody Armstrong" in big type right next to the notorious photo. "The band didn't even know it had happened," Tony Bevilacqua says of Brody's *Rolling Stone* scandal. "We were working in the studio: when we opened it, we were like, 'Whoa, that's gnarly.' I remember thinking, 'God, this has been a blur.'"

Reaction from fans and the industry, however, proved immediate. "Do you think [the Distillers' management] understood the power of Tim Armstrong within this scene? Do you think, if I was a manager, I would let Brody, under my advice, stand there and let someone take a photo of her with her hand on the crotch of the guy from Queens of the Stone Age in *Rolling Stone* during that summer?" queries Warped Tour's Kevin Lyman. "Don't you think they should've put her kind of low-key for a little while?

"I don't think she was ready," Lyman continues. "I don't think Brody had that solid, die-hard fan base yet that would allow her to give up all these punk kids and go into the pop world. But they took her there anyway—featuring her in high-profile magazines, on TV; Brody started showing up at all these parties. I would've put her back in the underground a little bit—and kept whatever she was doing with the Queens of the Stone Age guy out of the press. I think it really fucked her up, and I think she's going to have a hard time. Brody's image is hardcore; I think she scares that pop crowd now."

In fact, the Distillers were scheduled to play the Warped Tour when Brody's divorce made sharing a bill with Rancid an impossibility. Instead, the Distillers swapped Warped for Lollapalooza, conveniently featuring . . . Queens of the Stone Age. "Lollapalooza was my first tour as an actual member of the band," Bevilacqua notes.

Kevin Lyman believes that the Distillers' dropping of Warped wasn't a good signal to the audience the band had spent years cultivating. "They pull the Distillers off the Warped tour, because Brody said she couldn't tour with Tim at that point, which is probably understandable," Kevin Lyman says. "Her blowing off the Warped Tour was her choice; if she had wanted to do the tour, she would've been welcome."

In truth, Brody and the Distillers had, in fact, been served notice as to where they were and weren't welcome. If the *Rolling Stone* photos were seen as huge violations by the neo-punk community, then Brody Dalle's cover story in the longstanding (now folded) U.K. style mag *The Face* was a close second. In it, Dalle lets it all hang out, clarifying once and for all her position on the whole divorce controversy.

"I never left Tim for Josh . . . I never left Tim for anyone. I left Tim for me," she confesses in the article. She claims that she and Tim "didn't make love anymore," and that she was "constantly being watched" by Tim's "people." There was mention of a near-overdose of antidepressants. Brody also reveals that Armstrong is a "founder member" of a Los Angeles punk gang called U.S. Thugs made up of "scary people," and that she took out a restraining order out against him because "the threat of violence is always there."

"I didn't like being married to the mob," Brody tells *The Face*. "I didn't marry Tim. I married all of them."

In the same article, Andy Granelli complains that "everyone thinks she's a slut and a junkie and she divorced Tim to step up the social ladder." Most shockingly, Brody reveals to *The Face* that "there have been death threats against Josh"; she claims that Tim has additionally been spreading false rumors that she's become a junkie. A media war begins: songs on Rancid's 2003 album *Indestructible* apparently address the breakup, while to mtv.com Tim Armstrong compares his failed marriage to Brody to "a nice big scab," and says of Homme, "Hate isn't a strong enough word for how I feel about him."

In a response on mtv.com headlined "Homme Blasts Rancid Singer over Dalle Treatment," Homme confirms the death threats he's been receiving. "I got all kinds of threats. They were saying, 'We're gonna kill you,'" Homme said in the story. "And I was saying, 'I'm six-foot-five and I have red hair and I'm not hiding. Go ahead.' I didn't steal anybody's anything . . . Now it's established that fake English-accent singing fucking copycat motherfucker is full of shit."

Despite the drama, Bevilacqua claims that all was stabilizing on the Distillers' home front. "Josh and Brody were totally in love, so it was cool," he says. "I'd never seen her so happy. I've always been a Queens fan, but he's a great guy, too. Josh treats Brody how she should be treated. You always want your friends to fall in crazy love with the best person in the world, and sometimes it happens."

And while *Coral Fang* did reasonably well in the United States considering the outcry and hype—it sold somewhere in the neighborhood of a quarter-million—it especially impacted listeners across the pond. "We got way bigger in Europe, especially England," Bevilacqua says. "It was weird. Brody is like a celebrity over there, a big-ass deal—I mean, they put her on the cover of *The Face*!"

Meanwhile, Brody doesn't have to worry about getting a twelve-step lecture à la Tim Armstrong from her new man Homme: Queens of the Stone Age have been known to dress in all-white for performances, the idea being that each band member represents a line of cocaine (or a rail of speed—California's Coachella Valley, where Queens hail from, is a key region for the production of illegal amphetamines).

As such, as a result of Armstrong being removed from the equation, a new hedonistic spirit has overtaken elements within the Distillers. "Up until a few years ago, I had never done hardcore drugs," Bevilacqua says. "But there was a dark moment around when *Coral Fang* came out. I had partied for three days straight, and then we had to do *The Jimmy Kimmel Show* the day the album was released. I was like a ghost; I thought I was dying."

Today, some two or three years after *Coral Fang* was released, the Tim Armstrong situation seems to have finally settled in the Distillers camp. "I haven't see that guy since this whole thing went down," Bevilacqua states. "He was a jerk."

Meanwhile, the Distillers are on hiatus, but that doesn't mean it isn't business as unusual. The last show they played as a group was with the group's heroes, the Pixies. Since then, the group has been on what Bevilacqua calls an "intense break." After Bevilacqua recently completed a stint playing bass with honky-soul freak show Har Mar Superstar, for exam-ple, he learned the break would be permanent. The Distillers as we knew them would never return.

The calm before the storm was broken when drummer Andy Granelli left the Distillers to turn Darker My Love, his side project collaboration with Tim Presley (who did the gory cover art for *Coral Fang*), into a full-time band. In October 2005, Granelli posted a statement on thedis-tillers.com announcing he was leaving the band. "I have officially quit the Distillers," Granelli wrote. "I started Darker My Love . . . as an outlet for us to play exactly what we wanted to, without compromise. So I feel now it is my time to go back to that. I will miss everyone very much, this has been very hard for me, and I am going to miss Brody, Tony, and Ryan very much. None of this comes from any ill will. The four of us are still close friends. I will miss the Distillers, but I need to move on." Sometime after, Ryan Sinn left the Distillers with an online sendoff that wasn't as friendly. "Well, I'm no longer part of the life I knew so recently," Sinn an-nounced on myspace.com. "The Distillers are no more and it feels like a weight has been lifted. However, I'll never get rid of the disgust inside from it all." Sinn would later turn up in 2006 in the Blink-182 spin-off project Angels & Airwaves.

"Andy's leaving is bad because it's the end of an era," Bevilacqua says. "I mean, me and Ryan could've been anybody, but Andy's drumming and Brody's voice *were* The Distillers—it's a big deal that he isn't going to be in the band. It's sad I don't get to play with him anymore. But change is good: you throw in new members, you throw in new chemistry, you throw in new ideas. It's always awesome to do that."

Brody Dalle is not so sure. She's distressed about the fact that every Distillers album has had a different lineup. She's not even sure if she's go-ing to credit the next music she releases to the Distillers. While she's real-istic about her leadership role in the band, the idea was always to have a *band*, not a solo project. "Doing it solo is not how I view it in my head," she says. "I'd rather it not be like that. I tried to make it a group—a group event with a group conscience. There are just too many egos involved. Nothing is democratic. People have different opinions, but someone is al-ways going to make the decisions, and that person was me. Someone will always be disappointed, that's what I found.

"Every record that I've ever made has a new lineup," Dalle continues, "and I'm back in that place again; I have to put a new band together." Only Dalle and Bevilacqua remain from the Distillers axis. "It's fascinating to me that it's just the way it is—everything runs in cycles, and now I kind of em-brace it," she says. "It definitely keeps things fresh—it's not totally inten-tional, but our next album will probably be really creative and dynamic and sound different from all the others. It's about building up new relationships again, which is not a bad thing. It's about commitment, how we treat each other. It's about family, I guess. It is so cliché, but most of us in the band come from broken homes. We are pretty much all loners."

Dalle won't be alone for much longer. Commitment is on Brody's mind a lot these days: she's just a few months away from marrying Josh Homme; just months later, she will be giving birth to her and Homme's child—a daughter, Camille. Before then, however, Brody absentmindedly toys with the engagement ring Homme gave her before she catches herself. "It's from 1924," she says of the ring, "and has two hearts. It's really rare—it's so beautiful, this thing. I love the detail work on it."

Unlike the media circus that was Armstrong and Dalle's divorce, there has been nary a mention of Dalle's and Homme's nuptials in the tabloids. The couple are open about their engagement—Homme affectionately refers to Dalle as his "finance" in public settings—but the level of hype has settled down, which appears to be a good thing. Their relationship seems like it's for real, not for the cameras.

Meanwhile, Brody has been working on some new material, which, true to form, suggests another evolution-revolution, as is her wont. "Brody played me some of her new songs," Bevilacqua says. "They're slower and more spacy, less pop; the next album is probably going to be a darker, moodier thing. And she's, like, really singing."

Bevilacqua has noticed of late that Brody's singing style has changed as well. "On the first Distillers' record, she's screaming her lungs out," he says. "Now she's more singing than screaming. She's like developing her voice more, like one does with an instrument."

In person, Brody Dalle has a wily charisma. She's charming but mercurial; she might change the meeting time of an appointment numerous times—or just not show up at all—but somehow it doesn't get on your nerves. She's totally straightforward and direct, except when she's not. She can be quick to trust and quick to distrust, sometimes within a sentence. Chances are, she's studying you. Chances are, she's in control. One tends to follow Brody's lead; she is, after all, a leader of men in a world dominated by them.

All those seeming contradictions make up who Brody is—it's what makes her stand out. She is, after all, a rock star. Not a neo-punk anti-hero. Nope, no matter how reluctant she is to embrace it, Brody Dalle is now a rock star, with all the romantic pros and cons that sobriquet embraces. She's got heartbreak down. Self-destruction. Redemption. Silliness. Excess. Moments of righteousness. Moments of narcotic abuse. Messiah complex. Moments of genius. Moments of rebirth. Of course, always be on the lookout for the inevitable rebirth.

Even after just a few years dancing around the mainstream pop culture consciousness, the ballad of Brody Dalle carries some of the weight of myth that she cadged from her idols Kurt Cobain and, yes, Courtney Love. Brody's punk-debutante entrance into mythmaking is a welcome development. For one, it feels at once unbelieveable and real. If neo-punk is ever going to have a riot of its own, it's going to need some true myth-makers again working the bullshit detectors, be they back in the garage or in an expensive recording studio complete with personal chef. It's going to take a real rock star to toss that first brick at what have become re-strictive style boundaries—even if that rock star has to ultimately leave his or her punk rock in flames.

Ring the alarm, or your sound is dying

> —Tenor Saw, from the 1985 dancehall-reggae
> classic "Ring the Alarm"

Ring the alarm, or you're sold to dying

> —Fugazi paraphrasing Tenor Saw's "Ring the Alarm"
> in their 1995 song "Fell, Destroyed"

5

"Reactionary" is probably one of the most misused, but coolest-sounding, words in the English language. According to the dictionary embedded in my computer's hard drive, "reactionary" means "opposed to social or political changes that the speaker considers liberal or progressive (*disapproving*)." Still, many think "reactionary" means someone who's self-aware, cutting-edge, "with-it," and ready to "react" to trends. Some just like the word's percussive syllables.

Recently the fashion designer Kenneth Cole ran an advertising campaign called "The Reactionaries" featuring a bunch of young, hot, multicultural urban professionals gallivanting while wearing his clothes. Which definition of "reactionary" do you think Cole was shooting for? At the same time, some make being a reactionary work for them. In politics, Ronald Reagan was the ultimate reactionary. Reagan promised a return to a dreamland version of the 1950s, the complexities of contemporary society be damned. In Reagan's vision thing, life was simple, the economy was always booming, and the forces of good and evil were clearly demarcated. But Reagan's world ran on deficits, and the bottom was doomed to fall out.

It did so in the 1990s, with the first Gulf War and a wallet-deflating recession—so much so that Reagan's successor, George Bush Sr., got voted out of a second term. In punk rock, though, suddenly it seemed cool to be reactionary again; anything was better than the crappy early '90s. As a result, neo-punkers began going after Reagan's throne as the ultimate incongruous nostalgists, hearkening back to simpler times—or rather, a brightly colored vision of punk innocence. Neo-punk became more anachronistic than anarchistic. Retro became the new orthodoxy; even the genre's self-proclaimed radicals come off as reactionary. And something somewhere got lost in the translation: just what happens, exactly, when one era's anticlassicism becomes another era's neoclassicism?

Meet the new punk.

Maybe too much the same as the old punk.

"We're probably the best Green Day-type band there is out there," Green Day bass player Mike Dirnt cracked to the Associated Press in the wake of *American Idiot*'s triumph. This is a hilariously self-aware statement coming from the gods of pop punk. Green Day realize the damage they've done in spawning an innumerable amount of *Dookie* clones. But even the clones need to stay consistent. Following up the multiplatinum success of their 2002 album *The Young and the Hopeless*, Good Charlotte released the single "Predictable" in 2004 as a harbinger of their next release, *The Chronicles of Life and Death*. But *Chronicles* was anything but predictable—there was a ballad here, a New Wave rapping song there, a symphony orchestra thrown in for good measure—and sales suffered. The fans rejected this maturity; they wanted their pop punk to stay the same.

"If you really analyze old punk, a lot of those bands sounded the same, too," Warped Tours' Kevin Lyman points out. "Today, there might be two hundred bands out there that sound like Good Charlotte, but for some reason Good Charlotte transcended. The bands that stand out, those were the bands that rose to the top. Why did the Used and Taking Back Sunday rise above? Why do six to eight bands rise out of the sixty bands playing Warped Tour every year?"

Neo-punk's secondhand-goods approach may seemingly be just another inevitable pop-cultural retread. Before they came into their own sound, Coldplay sounded like a collage of all the nice catchy bits from Radiohead before Thom Yorke and Co. got weird and discovered Aphex Twin. And how many ersatz Pearl Jam ripoffs à la Creed are there that just bite the more baroque moments off, say, *Ten*, and add even more bombast and slickness until the end result sounds like an overfed, inbred cousin of the real thing? Ultimately, a large faction of the masses don't want to hear something new as much as they crave endless variations on their favorite band's look and sound. It's as if a band's most popular moments have been frozen in time and subsequently dethawed by others whenever the fan base needs a fix. Sometimes it can happen even in the context of one band: look at how U2 returned to their anthemic '80s-era sound, the one heralded by their peak of popularity, after almost a decade of sonic experimentation. At the same time, it's also true that U2's return to their classic sound produced their strongest artistic dividends in recent years.

With the new punk, however, its derivative nature holds additionally problematic dimensions. Until *American Idiot*, Green Day was never a favorite of mainstream rock critics. For one they weren't "serious" and enigmatic like R.E.M., with lyrical mysteries to decode and layers of persona to peel off; instead, Green Day offered a juvenile, direct, spiky, yet sugarcoated take on teen pop. Green Day's biggest sonic sin to critics was how they aped their punk influences in an all-too-retro way. Typical complaints about the band ranged from "They sound too much like the Buzzcocks" to "Billie Joe is doing a bad Joe Strummer impersonation" to "What's up with the London accent when you're from Northern California?" Neo-punk's derivative nature even haunts the genre's leading lights.

"Of course it's derivative—I agree with the critics," says Dropkick Murphys' Matt Kelly. "I haven't heard many current punk bands doing anything all that different. Everything comes from somewhere. It just comes down to to how obscure or obvious a band's influences are, and the combination thereof. Punk is about keeping things fresh, putting a new twist on things, and not becoming stagnant and bloated like our predecessors."

"I totally agree that current punk is unoriginal and derivative," says Tsunami Bomb's Agent M. "There are a few select bands who succeed in making new and different music, but on the whole it's all been done before, and done better. I think punk musicians—Tsunami Bomb included—should all work harder to be more creative. We should at least try to be good at what we do and have something special about us."

The critical disdain toward neo-punk was cemented with the advent of the mall punks—the kids who discovered Green Day via *Dookie*, which came to represent the sound of their youth. *Dookie* was a kind of gateway drug for many young punks; it became a beginning and end in itself for a new generation of bands. "Green Day really started my personal concept of punk," says Agent M of Tsunami Bomb. "After hearing them and identifying them as punk, I thought of punk as fast, upbeat, poppy music with rough edges. It took me a while to realize that there are so many subgenres of punk. I still don't really listen to anything that's superheavy, most likely because of my beginnings in punk with Green Day."

Dookie became a kind of punk Cliff's Notes. "Before *Nevermind* and *Dookie*, you had to really delve into music history in order to find stuff that appealed to you," explains suicidegirls.com founder Missy Suicide. "After they came out, it was a lot easier."

"This band I work with is one of the biggest pop-punk bands in the business, but their idea of old school is *Dookie*," complains a music-industry professional who refused to be quoted by name. "They sound like the Buzzcocks, but they've never heard them—they sound like the Buzzcocks because the bands they like rip off the Buzzcocks. One time I was hanging out with one of my bands at the Warped tour, and they said 'Hey, come with us to the old school stage.' I thought, cool—maybe the Damned or T.S.O.L. are playing. I show up, and *NOFX* is onstage. I was like NOFX? Since when are NOFX 'old school'? But they are—to twenty-year-olds who don't know their history."

"People get mad that I don't bring out the Adicts or U.K. Subs on Warped, but to my audience, those bands haven't stayed relevant to the kids," Kevin Lyman says. "When I brought bands like T.S.O.L., Circle Jerks, and the Damned on Warped, they had a hard time, because they couldn't capture the kids in that setting."

The end result of this shortsighted reading of punk history on the part of neo-punk fans was a kind of retread culture cut off from its roots—a trend not just in neo-punk, but in '90s art regardless of medium. In *Spike, Mike, Slackers & Dykes*, John Pierson's landmark tome on the explosion of American indie cinema in the '80s and '90s, Pierson quotes director Kevin Smith, the art house auteur behind films like *Clerks, Chasing Amy*, and *Jay and Silent Bob Strike Back!*, about his disinterest in knowing the history behind his style. "I don't feel like I have to go back and view European or other foreign films because I feel these guys [indie film icons like Richard Linklater, Jim Jarmusch, Hal Hartley, and Spike Lee] have already done it for me, and I'm getting it filtered through them," Smith told Pierson. "That ethic works for me."

That lazy laissez-faire "ethic" also worked for the new generation of neo-punkers. "A lot of young kids don't know what a great band is, so they are easily persuaded to like bands that are just copying great bands," Bouncing Souls' Greg Attonitoi explains. "So goes the plight of our disposable society."

However, when the raft of mall punk bands started bogarting Green Day's or Blink-182's style outright, they were unwittingly absorbing that band's influences without knowing where they came from. This "borrowing from the borrowers" process resulted in a few simple elements becoming grotesquely overemphasized in the new, commercially oriented neo-punk bands. Simple songs, yet rendered in excessively huge, clean production. A catchy, shouted chorus. The singer affecting an adolescent whine, regardless of his age. Lyrics about how the singer misses his girlfriend, the lost innocence of childhood, or fart jokes—or some combination thereof. Abrupt dynamic shifts of loud/soft to introduce the chorus; according to a record company executive who asked to remain anonymous, this stylistic development occurred because "it makes the song work better for radio station promo bumpers."

Furthermore, lyrically, much neo-punk swims in the shallow end—even when trying to make a big statement. A song like Pennywise's "American Dream" presents a laudably uncompromised anti-authoritarian point of view, but hampers it with trite musings on "the end of the American dream," rendered with all the shallow poetry of a rebellious thirteen-year-old's journal entry. Led Zeppelin weren't the greatest lyricists, sure, but this kind of simplistic "anti" platitude isn't threatening to anybody.

None of this would seem so shocking to today's music fan except for the fact that punk started as an obscurist critics' phenomenon. What knowledge the mainstream had at all of punk came from fanzines and music critics who went out on a limb to loudly champion the Clash, say, or the Sex Pistols, or Black Flag. Even Nirvana and grunge were critic-enthused before they went mega. Revolutionary movements such as punk and grunge built on the shock of the new: the ingredients might've been old, but something fresh was added in the soufflé.

Fugazi, for example, stood out and made timeless music because they rejected hardcore convention. Fugazi innovatively slowed down tempos and added elements of, say, dub reggae and angular dissonance recalling post-punk legends like Gang of Four to create their own distinct aesthetic within the punk genre. Listening to Fugazi, one could imagine how punk could expand and broaden its scope. Yet the starting points for the kind of neo-punk you can see on, say, MTV—and often in the indie world as well—seems to stem from four places, whether the bands themselves know it or not: the Clash, the Buzzcocks, U.K. ska bands like Madness, and tuneful California-style punk like the Descendents or Jawbreaker—or, more typically, some combination thereof.

Today, however, punk bands are no longer expected to bring innovation, even from their enthusiasts. In a review of the Distillers' *Coral Fang* on pitchforkmedia.com, Eric Carr wrote, "The Distillers might not be able to spot a new idea with the Hubble, and no one will single-handedly save any faltering genre anytime soon"—and that was from a *rave* review! The same review complains how

> [the] Offspring can manage to garner esteem for "keeping punk alive" merely by sucking for ten years running. "Everything is so goddamned obligatory!" cries the punk relic. "The sound the look, the act—time was, this whole thing used to be about standing apart, not blending in."

Indeed, many neo-punk bands have started sounding the same, indistinguishable from one another regardless of their regional affiliations, displaying the same set of influences across the board. "I think that's maybe due to the Internet—these are modern times," Brett Gurewitz says.

"There's been a lot of revisionism. The problem now is that, it's like the snake that's eating its own tail. With some of today's punk rock, its only influences are punk rock. It's like inbreeding—it starts getting anemic and less robust because there's less diversity in the gene pool. Any band that sounds like Bad Religion today, what are they bringing?"

"After discovering those types of bands, we stepped away from all other kinds of music and just focused on that," says Simple Plan's Chuck Comeau. "That kind of music became . . . *our world*."

"I think now it's harder than ever to do something interesting and original because of the popularity punk has in mainstream music," says Alkaline Trio's Matt Skiba. "I don't think we're into anything that hasn't influenced a lot of other bands—although we were talking about Gary Numan recently, and someone in a very popular band, who will remain nameless, had no idea who he was. I think as the band's grown, so have we alongside of it. Doing something cool and different are strengths, and bands that you can't tell apart on the radio are cliché."

For Tony Bevilacqua of the Distillers, replicating clichés formed the basis of the neo-punk aesthetic. "I got lumped into this whole West Coast, Hellcat-Epitpah punk rock world, and I just found the whole scene just, like, *beat*. I don't want to mention any bands—I'll probably get my ass kicked—but a lot of it was like the worst music ever," he says. "Everything that these people put out was always the sickest thing ever, no matter if it was or not. I found it seriously close-minded, like 'All I can listen to is the Exploited and GBH.' All they listen to is punk rock, especially new West Coast punk. That's not punk to me—it's jock rock. Nirvana is way more punk than any of those bands."

According to Gurewitz, connecting to music history is what made punk rock vital in the first place. "The first wave of punk rockers had *influences*," he says. "I mean, Joe Strummer was heavily influenced by Bob Dylan and Woody Guthrie; it's obvious that Steve Jones from the Sex Pistols had his own rock and roll heroes—everyone from Chuck Berry to Marc Bolan. Those guys were influenced by Muddy Waters and Howlin' Wolf."

It's inevitable that the bands that made up punk's original primordial ooze would continue to have major impact on multipierced ears today. The Sex Pistols' *Never Mind the Bollocks* is still so raw, so intense, so shocking, so expressive, that it sounds timeless even though it represents a very specific moment in music history. "If I had to choose one record to listen to, it would be *Never Mind the Bollocks*," Fat Mike writes on fatwreck.com. "That record changed my life."

"The reason why kids assimilate so much of this old music," Brody Dalle explains, "because it has that *truth*. When I heard X-ray Spex for the first time, I realized where Bikini Kill ripped off their whole vocal and musical style from. I thought it was a Bikini Kill record I'd never heard before—I'm dead serious."

Even the bands that go beyond *Dookie*, though, have made a classicism out of what most likely was meant to be an ephemeral expression of the time and place it came out of. Among many of the neo-punk bands, for example, a fetish has developed for the British punk bands of the second wave. Bands like Rancid, Dropkick Murphys, and the early Distillers in particular show the influence of U.K. post-1977 second-wavers like the Angelic Upstarts, Blitz, Discharge, G.B.H., U.K. Subs, and Cockney Rejects.

The connection between the U.K.'s second wave and neo-punk is symbiotic on some level. Obscure "oi!" bands like the Business, the 4 Skins, and the Last Resort are championed. Rancid namechecks the Last Resort in "The Ballad of Jimmy & Johnny" (and Lars Fredericksen wears a Last Resort T-shirt on the back cover photos on 2000's *Rancid*). The Dropkick Murphys, meanwhile, made a collaborative album with the Business. The Distillers even covered Blitz's classic hooligan anthem "Warriors" with bloodletting panache.

For the most part, the second wave of British punk was never a critical success—as good as some of those bands were, you don't hear the Angelic Upstarts, for example, typically mentioned in the same breath as the Clash. The second wave really represented punk's B team: this was music for diehards, and it hasn't aged well—therefore, when its influence shows up in neo-punk, it often results in a new, yet oddly dated, sound.

One of the best of the second-wave bands is Belfast, Ireland's Stiff Little Fingers, who mean quite a bit to some of neo-punk's greatest icons. In naming their hit "Roots Radicals," Rancid paid tribute to Stiff Little Fingers songs like "Roots, Radicals, Rockers, and Reggae," which, like Rancid, mixed West Indian *riddims* and loud, raucous guitars. "Stiff Little Fingers played as big a role in our musical upbringing as the Ramones, the Clash or any hardcore band," states the liner notes for the Dropkick Murphys' *Singles Collection, Volume 2—1998–2004: B-Sides, Covers, Comps & Other Crap*. There Dropkick Murphys cover "Nobody's Hero," their Irish forbears anthem of defiance, spitting out lines like "No one is a nobody—everyone is someone" with shambling ethnic pride. But Stiff Little Fingers, while good for the time, never escaped the stigma of being known as a second-hand version of the Clash.

Neo-punk insiders also bemoan neo-punk's stylistic rigidity. Dropkick Murphys' Matt Kelly notes how few bands of late embrace the iconoclastic yet inclusive innovations of groups like the New York Dolls, the Ramones, Black Flag, Minor Threat, Bad Brains, the Clash, the Damned, the Specials, and the Sex Pistols. "All those bands, in their own way, pushed the envelope," Kelly explains. "Nowadays, it seems more divided—everyone has their subscene niches. If you like garage, or straight-edge hardcore, you've got your place. There doesn't seem to be the mixture of subcultures at shows anymore."

"One time I was at Brody's house when she was married to Tim and I was watching a Cure video on MTV," says the Distillers' Tony Bevilacqua. "Tim was totally baffled by it and started goofing on me, like, 'Oh you're into *the Cure*, huh?' Like the Cure wasn't 'pure' punk like the Clash or something. I was like, 'Yeah, fuck you, I *am*.' Like, what are you, a fucking idiot? Grow up. I was so upset."

While many of the leading neo-punk bands stick to a rigid revivalist punk sound, there are exceptions to the rule that give the genre renewed vitality. "There have been a few bands that were good," Bevilacqua notes. "There were the Nerve Agents; they liked T.S.O.L, the good punk shit, you know—old stuff. I immediately thought F-Minus were fucking rad shit—just really fast and sick, with every song around just forty seconds long."

Often the bands whose legacy has lasted, however, are the ones that haven't always obeyed punk's loud, fast rules. "I've been listening to Black Flag since I was fourteen—they're a huge influence. But to me, Black Flag got really hot when they started playing really *slow*," Brody Dalle says. "I love that. That is like one of my favorite philosophies of Greg Ginn's: it doesn't have to be fast and all that shit for it to be punk."

Indeed, in the right hands, punk's basic formula can be innovated upon while keeping the form's vitality intact, if not enhanced. In their songs like "Helena" and in accompanying videos, New Jersey emo rockers My Chemical Romance, for example, bring the sweep and melodrama of musical theater to standard pop punk convention. MCR's epic results, with sound-expanding nuances like electronics and strings, suggests a punked-up version of Jim Steinman's mammoth productions for *Rocky Horror Picture Show* alumnus Meat Loaf in the 1970s. And I mean that in a good way. MCR's 2006 rock-opera-styled album *The Black Parade* is probably neo-punk's most sonically ambitious effort since *American Idiot*.

On *American Idiot*, Green Day triumphed not by rewriting the punk rule book so much as by expanding it. *American Idiot* remains as derivative as ever, but here Green Day either vary up their influences, or find a thrilling new context for old ones. Throughout the bombast of Queen has been ironically appropriated, and songs are boldly referential with surprising sources. "Holiday," for example, "borrows Iggy Pop's 'Passenger' riff like it's a P. Diddy sample," as I wrote in my review of the album for *Interview* magazine. And yes, while the album's anthemic title song still sounds like the Buzzcocks, its charged, utterly contemporary political subject matter gives it a new vividness.

In an interview with *Entertainment Weekly*, Green Day admit rummaging through unlikely, decidedly unpunk masterworks—David Bowie's faux-biography song cycle *The Rise and Fall of Ziggy Stardust and the Spiders from Mars*, the *West Side Story* soundtrack, the rock opera classic *Tommy* by the Who—for atypical yet appropriate songwriting stimuli. "We were getting our references straight," Armstrong said in the article. "The big challenge was, how do we do something that ambitious? I didn't want anyone to listen to *American Idiot* and think, Oh my God, this is so far removed from what Green Day is."

Rancid, probably the neo-punk band most lambasted by critics for its shameless borrowing of punk's past, also has unexpected nuances and influences that make its sound more stylistically dimensional than just mere pop punk. "In addition to reggae, dub, and ska, there's also rockabilly and rap in Rancid's sound," Brett Gurewitz says. "Rancid is even a little hip-hop."

Sometimes a lot, in fact. A Rancid song like "Rattlesnake" has hip-hop flow in its lyrics, with the faux-English-accented vocals sounding a little like Mike Skinner of U.K. rappers the Streets. Placing rap delivery over the Motörhead-style punk boogie of "Rattlesnake" takes Rancid's youth-culture signifiers on an intense game of Twister. And that's not Rancid's only sonic pop culture clusterfuck: Rancid front man Tim Armstrong collaborated with Cypress Hill on the stoner rap trio's single "What's Your Number," which goes even one step further by quoting the bass line from the Clash's "Guns of Brixton" in a rap context. Meanwhile, Armstrong's side project with Blink-182 drummer Travis Barker, the Transplants, features a manic punk-rapping M.C. named Skinhead Rob, alongside turntablist touches and collaborations with credible hip-hop artists like Cypress Hill and Dilated Peoples.

Punk's embrace of hip-hop isn't so surprising: both styles began organically as outspokenly defiant assaults both sonic and lyrical on the musical status quo. According to Bouncing Souls' Bryan Kienlen, it's the "same spirit, different aesthetic" that makes it a not-so-unlikely influence on today's punk. "Tupac is the greatest rapper ever," says Bert McCracken of the Used. "He's like the original 'emo' rapper: he just lets it hang out at all times."

Conversely, the punk aesthetic has had some crossover with underground rappers. "Guys like Atmosphere are making records on an MPC in their apartment bedroom, kicking it in the van, and putting it on tour," Brett Gurewitz says. "They're talking about real stuff from the heart, about their community, about the people. It's for real, and it has much more in common with punk rock as I know it than some rich suburban kid renting a rehearsal space on his allowance from his Christian parents who are putting him through private school so that he can go to Yale and work for Bush."

As well, since the early punk scene, musical virtuosity has been a dirty word in some circles. In the CBGB era, the jazzily expansive, guitar-solo heavy Television proved the historical exception, where the Ramones' basic four-chord attack still rules punk as the musical basis.

In recent years, however, punk-oriented music has made a tentative embrace of virtuosity to add dimensional heft to the genre's expected primitive ruckus. Bands like Motion City Soundtrack, for example, mix in idiosyncratic instrumentation like Moog synths with the melodic flair of classic pop-rock. "Motion City Soundtrack make music that's really innovative and just beautiful at the same time," says Brett Gurewitz, whose Epitaph releases Motion City's recorded efforts. "What they do gets me off musically. They're really, really talented, really earnest, and trying to take it to new places." On stage and record, meanwhile, Yellowcard have a full-time, classically trained violinist to open up the band's musical landscape. "Yellowcard having a violin shows they have more diverse influences," says Missy Suicide. "You don't start out playing punk rock on violin."

On the other hand, maybe neo-punk's slide into the aesthetics of conventional musical quality isn't such a good thing. Does Rise Against's ability to craft an effective, Dashboard Confessional–style ballad like "Swing Life Away" off their major label debut *Siren Song of the Counter Culture* represent musical progress—or just emo cheese? Is it musical advancement, or really the swan song for counterculture—for what made punk special in the first place? "I think Rise Against is amazing," says Fall Out Boy's Pete Wentz," but everything tastes better with sugar on top."

Some of the most interesting neo-punk explores both the roots of rock and roll and folk music tradition. "I've always loved blues piano, so I've learned a bit," says Bouncing Souls' Greg Attonitoi. "I'm not really that good and I can only vary off one trick, but I fucking love to play it." Sometimes neo-punk inadvertently displays its ties to rock's roots. The Distillers' song "Lordy, Lordy" reverberates with an Eddie Cochran–style twang, effortlessly bridging early rock and roll and country as if it's an immaculate conception. "I can write endless country songs all the time, dude," Brody Dalle says, "and I have no country background. I like Johnny Cash, sure, but I have no history with the music."

This roots emphasis is not unheard-of in punk: archetypal Los Angeles first-wave punk band X merged country, blues, folk, and early rock influences with the Doors' poetic mysticism and punk's ragged, hopped-up glory. In 2006, Bad Religion singer Greg Griffin released a solo album, *Cold As the Clay*, largely devoted to traditional folk songs. Dropkicks Murphys, meanwhile, have forged vital links with folk-oriented traditional music and instruments evoking roots-oriented Americana. From essaying a gnarled cover of classic roots rockers Creedence Clearwater Revival's anti-authority anthem "Fortunate Son" to incorporating Celtic folk instruments like bagpipes, mandolin, and tin whistle and collaborating with Shane Mac-Gowan of Irish ne'er do-wells the Pogues, the Dropkick Murphys have revitalized their sound beyond the pack mentality. They've shown not only that the hardest punk-influenced music can grow musically, but that the band knows its history, willfully putting themselves into the lineage of American protest music. And punk started as nothing but protest music.

Nowhere did this connection become more clear than when the descendents of famed folk singer-songwriter and activist Woody Guthrie asked Dropkick Murphys to set to music some of her father's previously unexhumed lyrics from his archive. It was a perfect match: Guthrie, the author of the classic American folk anthem "This Land Is Your Land," unwittingly influenced the Murphys in their shared interest in how the plight, pride, and poetry of America's unionized labor force have shaped history. "[Guthrie's granddaughter] contacted us, as her son is a big fan of the band," says Dropicks' Matt Kelly. "It was the most ridiculously high honor for the band to even be associated with that man's music, especially in light of the other people who've asked to get those lyrics. Punk is always protesting against what the band feels is a contemporary injustice, so it's pretty vital, I'd say."

If punk may be headed somewhere new and vital, the charge may be led by the culture swirling around bands like the Distillers, the Bronx, and the Icarus Line. Early on in the Distillers' career, the band's sound combined a healthy interest in speedy, metallic, liberty-spiked Brit punk like Discharge and GBH and the rollicking West Coast retro-punk sound epitomized by Rancid—both highly conventional neo-punk influences.

"There are pretty much two types of punks left in the world: those who act like it's 1977 and drape themselves in leather and studs—speaking vaguely of anarchy between sips of malt liquor—and those who won't wear leather at all, couldn't care less about 1970s punk rock and speak seriously about anarchy during vegan potlucks," Gordon Lamb writes in a review of the Distillers' 2002 sophomore album, *Sing Sing Death House*, for the Athens, Georgia, alternative weekly *Flagpole*. "The Distillers fall solidly into the first category." Yet even on the Distillers' earliest recordings there are signs that young Brody wanted to go in different, more expressive directions.

On the Distillers' eponymous first album, a yearning cover of Patti

Smith's "Ask the Angels" shows just how far Brody might take it: Dalle here sinks into Smith's insistent melody and revels in the song's pregnant religious imagery and complicated plea for redemption. It's a ballsy choice for a punk singer, one that requires equally large helpings of faith, *cojones*, and soul, like, say, attempting "Purple Rain" as your first-ever karaoke song.

In particular, it's a choice that stands out amid typical neo-punk aesthetics, connecting Brody to a greater tradition. Smith was a poetic iconoclast on the original punk scene; by covering her song Brody recasts herself a bit in that persona, in particular connecting to a like-minded independent female sensibility very different from the frequently macho West Coast punk vibe. "Brody has a very Patti Smith, bohemian vibe, an artistic side you don't see in most bands today. I think Brody would be just as easily influenced by a photography exhibition, or sculpture, or opera as she would be listening to old 'Oi!' albums," explains suicidegirls.com founder Missy Suicide.

"If you take from everything around you, you'll speak to something deeper in the soul than just partying or just 'rebelling against the man,'" Suicide continues. "Brody's releasing what's inside of her soul, just as Ian Mackaye uses his artistic side to get out a political agenda. Karen O from the Yeah Yeah Yeahs is the same kind of totally creative deal: they both touch on these moments that are universally applicable, but you don't know why."

Dalle's influences also are more varied than those within the conventional neo-punk canon. Give Dalle twenty minutes to talk about her musical tastes, and she'll rave on variously about mind-expanding, genre-exploding indie rock gods TV on the Radio to '60s psychedelic garage punk icons the 13th Floor Elevators, whose "You're Gonna Miss Me" the Distillers notoriously give a cathartic shredding in their live show; she admires, for example, the ragged yet subtle noise-blues guitar architecture of Thalia Zedek, leader of indie rockers Come. Dalle's also a devotee of proto-punk eccentric Captain Beefheart's 1969 skronk-rock classic *Trout Mask Replica,* a masterpiece of howling independence. On *Trout,* Beefheart reassembles evocative shards of bluesy jazzbo experimentalism into rock and roll. It's a test of deconstructionist endurance à la *Metal Machine Music,* but oozes tons more soul. Dalle discovered Beefheart's sonic brutalism as a small child.

"My parents had *Trout Mask Replica,*" Dalle recalls. "Such a weird record. I would always pull it out at night, you know; nine years later, it was a sweetheart. I was just fascinated by the cover photograph: in it, this man actually has a fish head! It's the most discombobulated music: Captain Beefheart would take the track from one song and the vocal from another and then just plop it together. I mean, that's what it sounds like to me—just madness."

Brody also favored local Australian acts making their own brand of sonic mayhem away from Europe and the States. Brody was an early supporter of Tumbleweed, a psychedelic stoner-rock combo from Woollongong, Australia, who are famed for opening Nirvana's only Oz-bound tour in 1992. Dalle was also a fan of Melbourne-based noise merchants Hunters & Collectors. A sort of Aussie Einsturzende Neubaten who, not inconsequently, borrowed their name from a Can song, Hunters & Collectors mixed machine-age funk with free jazz audacity, using junk metal as percussion. "Early on, they were so fucking bizarre and industrial," Dalle says today.

That Dalle grew up in Australia with a whole other set of cultural influences than your typical uber-Americanized O.C. punk puts a unique twist on the Distillers' sound. For one, there was the presence of the Saints, Aussie's most venerated export during punk rock's first explosion in the 1970s. "The Saints were to Australia what the Sex Pistols were to Britain, and the Ramones to America" notes a review of the Saints' first album (*I'm) Stranded*, by punk legend Jack Rabid of *Big Takeover* on allmusic.com. In fact, the Saints' 1976 debut single, also called "(I'm) Stranded," has long been considered one of the earliest seminal punk singles, arguably beating out efforts by the Damned and the Sex Pistols. Unlike their U.K. peers, the Saints incorporated horns and a bluesy, more soulful yet hard-rocking attack that was an Australian trademark (this is the birthplace of AC/DC we're talking about here). "The Saints was actually my first concert," Brody recalls. "My Uncle Frasier, who gave me my first guitar and taught me how to play it, took me. He was playing me punk records when I was eleven years old."

However, Dalle's musical education skipped a major stepping stone to canonical punkitude—maybe the biggest. "I was into the Clash later on for sure, but I was never that big of a Sex Pistols fan," she admits. "I listened to the Sex Pistols, but they never did that much for me; I'm really of a different generation. They didn't do the same thing that Nirvana did for me. That's one misconception about my generation. Bands like us and the Bronx, we play like the heart of punk rock, or a harder version of rock and roll. People categorize us as punk, but I started listening to the Sex Pistols when I was twenty-one. I never heard the Clash until I was nineteen. I discovered people way late, like I was in a coma."

When they jump-started grunge with their album *Nevermind*, Nirvana were the biggest band in the world, but nowhere more so than in

Australia—and nowhere more so than in the young Brody's heart. "We are the generation that was affected by Nirvana. That's my point of entry," Brody says. "We're influenced," she adds defiantly, "by *corporate rock!*"

For Brody, the Nirvana moment of epiphany proved that all corporate rock doesn't *entirely* still suck. "I just found Kurt and Nirvana quite different from anything I'd ever heard in my life," she says. "And it was just so cool, his structures, the way he goes over certain chords . . . I can't even describe it. I didn't know that he was taking stuff from the Beatles. Emotionally, it was just it made me sad and angry all at the same time, but really content. Like it filled some kind of hole, I think. Pardon the pun."

Nirvana's example led Dalle into the kind of punk rock that would inspire her to write and perform. "Through Nirvana, I discovered Flipper, I discovered Big Black, I discovered Black Flag," she says. She found a kindred Nirvana-obsessed soul in Distillers guitarist Tony Bevilacqua. "The first time I heard Nirvana it was like, 'Oh . . . my . . . God . . . This is the *best thing* I've ever heard,'" Bevilacqua says. "I was the first kid on my block to have *Nevermind*—I was! I went to a party at Melissa Wylie's house, popped it in the cassette player, and we listened to it all night."

"There is a rock element to the Distillers that's completely disregarded," Dalle continues. "I was *raised* on corporate rock! I've gone through my whole Discharge and GBH thing, but I love Swervedriver." "Swervedriver are amazing," Bevilacqua seconds of the unsung British group that bridged the gap between My Bloody Valentine–style shoegazing atmospherics, Sonic Youth's kaleidoscopic noise rock, and Seattle-style garage grunge. Bands like the Pixies especially affected the mature Distillers sound. The band even pays tribute to their golden era in their cover of Pixies leader Frank Black's angular outsider lament "I Want to Live on an Abstract Plain," and chose former Pixies producer Gil Norton to helm the sessions for 2003's *Coral Fang*. The Distillers were ecstatically honored, meanwhile, to be chosen as one of the opening bands for the Pixies' history-making comeback tour in 2004.

Indeed, the whole late '80s/early '90s wave of alternative music culture was what ultimately inspired the Distillers to make music. "The Pixies, Mudhoney, Dinosaur, Jr.—that was my 'punk rock,' know what I mean?" Bevilacqua continues. "It wasn't like the hair metal that was going around. When the whole alternative-Lollapalooza thing happened, that's immediately what I was into. Nine Inch Nails blowing up computers on-stage was like the coolest thing I'd ever heard or seen." He also rates everything from Los Angeles first-wave punkers X to 1990s noise-rock pranksters like Brainiac, the Jesus Lizard, Girls Against Boys, and Enon, all of whom were associated with Chicago's maverick Touch and Go label.

"That's the coolest shit ever—they all took the weirdest, most awful sounds and put them into a pop structure," he says.

That the Distillers consciously transcended out of neo-punk's stylistic shackles was made clear in the influences percolating through the band's controversial *Coral Fang* album, a rogue's gallery of idiosyncratic sonic avatars. The husky, complicated eroticism of PJ Harvey and, yes, Courtney Love shows up everywhere. Songs like "Drain the Blood" feature stuttering guitar lines that evoke a speedy revise on Iggy Pop's "The Passenger"; the charging beats and "whoa-whoas" in "Die on a Rope" evoke San Diego-based oddball post-punkers like Rocket from the Crypt and Drive Like Jehu. The droning, expert hooks on songs like "The Hunger" and "The Gallows Is God," however, make the Nirvana/Hole comparisons utterly tangible—if these tracks got any more *In Utero,* it'd still be in the womb connected to a placenta.

In fact, the only song on *Coral Fang* that wholeheartedly represents an umbilical cord tying the Distillers' to their neo-punk roots is album closer "Death Sex." Tht is, until "Death Sex" goes into a lengthy ten-minute-plus breakdown of punishing atonal squalor that recalls early Sonic Youth's like-minded hijinks. " 'Death Sex' is the one song on *Coral Fang* that was like our old records. It was originally supposed to be just the punk song in the vain of old Distillers music, but we were like, 'Let's make this *different,'* " Tony Bevilacqua says. "We didn't want it to seem like, 'Here's the song that sounds like the last record.' It almost turns into a 'fuck you' of sorts, like, 'Here's your punk song, but, oh, but you have to listen to fifty minutes of feedback."

For Tony Bevilacqua, knowing one's roots first gives a musician the power to take radical steps like "Death Sex." "You've got to learn the rules in order to break them. You've got to know where what your playing comes from," Bevilacqua explains. "It's great when people get turned onto a band like Nirvana and then go, 'Okay, where did *this* come from?' And then they discover the Melvins, and then go back a little further and discover the Wipers—that's awesome when that happens. The Wipers, X, and Wire, those are the kind of punk rock bands I like."

"[We] remembered that punk actually still is cool . . . as long as it only consists of Black Flag, the Ramones, the Circle Jerks, TSOL, the Stooges, Devo, and Creedence," former Distillers/Nerve Agents drummer Andy Granelli once wrote manifesto-style on the Distillers' Web site, "and has nothing to do with clothes, or bumming change, or gossip."

With bands like the Icarus Line, the Bronx, and the post-Rancid Distillers, neo-punk is starting to show renewed vision, with one foot in the genre's gritty golden age past and one in the go-for-broke future. Bands like the Bronx and the Icarus Line cull from classic punk influences, yet hotwire them through contemporary cultural existence for a hybrid that feels totally fresh and genuine. "Our musical influences range from all over the planet. However, the driving force behind the band has always been based on frustration with the current state of music," explains Matt Caughthran of the Bronx. "That is where the challenge comes from: to create something new and original, whether it is good or bad, just to say 'fuck you' to whatever formula musicians are supposed to fit into. It's a test of respect when people fuck with something you love. You either care or you don't care."

From the stage during Distillers' sets, Brody would shout out props to opener the Icarus Line at shows when they toured together, calling them the "new Stooges" due to their blistering, feedback-blasting, vanishing-point brio. And on the Bronx's amazing self-titled 2003 indie full-length debut, the Los Angeles-based band explores the primal missing links between Black Flag (an obvious influence), Drive Like Jehu's angular aggression, and the blues-anchored heft of AC/DC (check out the for-those-about-to-rock opening riff of an instant-classic Bronx bruiser like "White Tar" for proof).

Still, everybody has influences. But while the Offspring may pay homage to the Bad Brain's classic loping hardcore track "Reignition" on hits like "Self-Esteem," the result streamlines the original's intensity for mass consumption. That's not to say innovation and catchiness can't coexist within punk's aesthetic, however. Hooks abound in the sound created by the Bronx and Icarus Line, yes, but they don't make safe pop punk singalongs. No, the kind of hooks these mavericks traffic in are the ones that tear the flesh when they sink into you and draw blood. "Currently the punk scene is overrun with musical cowards: artists get stuck in this safety net of what keeps the money coming in. They get stuck in character," Matt Caughthran says. "They write the same songs over and over, year after year. Do not give them what *they* want, give them what *you* want. Bands that don't challenge their creative pattern get boring to their crowd—and most importantly, themselves. Constantly grow and evolve creative sperm until you drive yourself insane. I am fueled by weirdness, aggression, loneliness, and nature. It will always be different as long as I maintain my identity."

"The record company would send us bands they wanted us to tour with, like the Used, or Thursday, or Taking Back Sunday, Next Wednesday, or whatever; we'd be like, 'No, no, no.' You want to play with people that are of your caliber, if not better," Bevilacqua says. "When we got the Bronx record, we were like 'Fuck, it's like the new Black Flag.' The Bronx is a real punk rock band, but they turn very conventional songwriting inside out, making it stranger, more intense—and so fucking *sick*."

"We met up with the Distillers when they took us out as the opener for the U.S tour they did for the record *Coral Fang*," Matt Caughthran re-calls. "Headliner bands usually have a way of always belittling their open-ing acts. Whether it's cutting your rider or waiting for the last show of a three-month tour to introduce themselves, there is almost always some stupid ego trip. The Distillers had *no* ego trip: they welcomed us with open arms from the second we started the tour. When our van was smashed to hell by a drunk driver in Detroit and our bass player was nearly killed, the Distillers turned their tour bus around and drove four hours back to pick us up. We continued the tour on their bus—all of our gear, luggage, everything. Thanks again, guys."

What makes bands like the Bronx stand out is that they are bringing personality and character to a neo-punk scene that's increasingly anony-mous. "There are no front men anymore, but someone like [Icarus Line vocalist Joe Cardamone] is just up there singing," Bevilacqua states. "Meanwhile, [Bronx front man Matt Caughthran] will be out in the crowd with his shirt off, just daring people like crazy, swinging the mi-crophone stand around his head and flailing around on the ground. The kids were like kind of blown away by him. Bands like Icarus Line and the Bronx are just doing their own thing."

It's that renewed spirit of individualism that is perhaps neo-punk's best hope for renewed relevance. In an age where most so-called punk you hear on the radio or on MTV is as safe as milk, bands like the Distillers, the Bronx, and the Icarus Line are reasserting punk's capacity to shock and amaze—displaying the kind of provocative authenticity that made punk stand up and be counted in the first place. "Punk rock can never be new again," Kevin Hoper writes in a 2002 Distillers show preview for the *Albuquerque Journal*. "However, there are certain bands that do a very good job of carrying the torch of the old school, adding new ele-ments into the mix and holding their own against many of the originals."

The Distillers, the Bronx, the Icarus Line, Green Day, the Dropkick Murphys—all are acknowledging the past while remaking punk in their own image. In the process, punk's musical culture has regained some as-pect of its original spit-and-vinegar excitement. It's a sonic call-to-arms, a throwing-down of the gauntlet to shitty pop music everywhere—a musi-cal challenge stating that everything that society holds dear just may be wrong, the only antidote a guitar caterwaul so slashing it's scary.

Such vainglorious yet vanguard moves are made not necessarily to sell records or get on MTV—even if, as *American Idiot*'s multiplatinum suc-cess proves, they just might anyway. Thanks to such achievements, punk as a stylistic template just might have the potential for a future shock to the system. The time for rewriting the punk rock rule book is upon us—never has the necessity for another genre-smashing masterpiece like *London*

Calling or *Never Mind the Bollocks,* or a new revolution-starting band with the power of a Minor Threat or Black Flag, been so urgent.

For Tony Bevilacqua, that time just might be circa . . . *now.* "I think people will be more and more open to something weird coming out now," Bevilacqua says. "It's just a time factor. A kid that's into punk rock when they're eighteen, they're actually going to grow out of it. When they're twenty-one or twenty-two, they're listening to different bands—they're growing up." And punk just might grow right along with them.

6

PUNK, INC.: WHAT HAPPENED WHEN PUNK ROCK BECAME BIG BUSINESS

Almost any kind of music of a subversive nature that is in the spotlight has become commodified, sanitized, and packaged. They're little more than revenue-driven subcultures gone big-time, advertised by what clothes you wear.

—Matt Kelly, Dropkick Murphys

Is Business Killing Punk Rock?

—cover headline, *Maximum Rocknroll*, issue 276, May 2006

From "Cash from Chaos" to "Taste of Chaos": The Neo-Punk Entrepreneur Is Born

It took a visionary like Sex Pistols Svengali Malcolm McLaren to see that there was money in them there punk hills. For all the concern about "selling out" in the punk community, all its talk of revolution, punk's roots actually lie in McLaren's utterly capitalist desire to make money. In fact, McLaren's innovation was that, to him, revolution and the pursuit of filthy lucre remain intrinsically linked; the anarchist state the Sex Pistols fantasized about is really the purest free-market–driven, capitalist state possible—a place where forces of supply and demand have no checks and balances, no governmental regulation.

"The Sex Pistols were a commercial proposition and a cultural conspiracy, launched to change the music business and make money off the change," Greil Marcus writes in *Lipstick Traces*. In *England's Dreaming*, Jon Savage quotes influential '60s artist Richard Hamilton (incidentally the cover designer for the Beatles' masterpiece *Sgt. Pepper's Lonely Hearts Club Band*) on the definition of pop art: for Hamilton, the key elements to pop are "popular; transient; expendable; mass-produced; young; witty; sexy; gimmicky; glamorous; big business."

For both quotes, the key word is "business." Punk rock from the beginning was seen as commercially exploitable pop art; way back during punk's first wave, major labels were sure punk rock would be the next youth culture craze. They couldn't afford to miss out on a trend: punk might be the next heavy metal, the next folk rock, the next exploitable shift in the pop cultural universe. Who knew? What the music industry bigwigs *did* know was that punk had hype. After money, hype is the only other thing that the music industry is really capable of comprehending, and in some cases, there was thought to be a cause–effect relationship between the two. Malcolm McLaren made sure there was plenty of hype.

As the manager of the Sex Pistols, if McLaren wasn't punk's first real entrepreneur, he was definitely its most innovative and prophetic one. McLaren felt that the only way the Sex Pistols were to become successful was if he and the band engaged the music industry on its heaviest terms: approaching its biggest companies with the serious deal-making expected for an established star. Utilizing the media hype machine, McLaren wanted the majors to think the Sex Pistols were the de facto new-school replacement for Led Zeppelin. He figured if he kept them confused enough, they wouldn't be able to tell the difference anyway, and in the hubbub he could empty their wallets.

McLaren was right about most of it: he would sign the Sex Pistols to one major label after another, playing them like a piano. After each successive Sex Pistols–related media outrage, a major recording conglomerate like EMI would pay boom market prices for the privilege of releasing such bad boys from their contracts. This then freed up the Sex Pistols for an even bigger advance from the next company of suckers—and increased the hype nicely, too.

McLaren dubbed his provocateur business approach "cash from chaos." Here McLaren institutionalized into punk tradition the idea that when business is handled punk-style, on some level those transactions remain part of the art form: there should be an element of anti-authoritarianism in each of them. How one does business, in other words, expresses who one is, where one really stands, just as much as the music might.

The Malcolm McLarens dominating today's neo-punk world retain elements of original punk's innate antiauthority vibe, but twist it for a different time and place. The traditional—and nontraditional—music business has shifted postmillennium. The music industry today is rocked by an absence of superstars, escalating costs, and profit-eating Internet downloads. At the same time, non-major-label music entities are by their nature leaner, meaner, and more adaptable to changing times. These nonmajors are finding new, financially judicious, and meaningful ways to exploit Internet distribution, touring, and other aspects of the music industry that are in the midst of being revolutionized—or becoming obsolete for the majors. So how has the punk rock business model changed in the wake of punk going pop? Has the resulting punk rock business approach become distinct, or has it stayed the same as the mainstream music industry model?

"Major labels are signing most of the good punk bands," exclaims Fat Mike of NOFX and the Fat Wreck Chords label. "This is a generalization for sure, but it seems to me that bands who make it on majors are more about the image, and bands that make it on indies are more about the music. The problem is that a lot of bands want to make a lot of money, and going to a major is the fastest way to do that. The bands that want long careers and don't mind making *decent* amounts of money seem to stay on indie labels. The difference between punk bands now and in the '80s is that back then, there was no money *anywhere*. Money was not an option or even a dream. We all played and toured because we liked to and we were alcoholics and we had nothing better to do."

"Majors and indies are one and the same. 'Indie' no longer guarantees an alternative," says Matt Kelly of Dropkick Murphys, whose band releases records on Hellcat, an indie label collaboration between Rancid's Tim Armstrong and Epitaph Records. "Many of the same business practices are shared by both. Like any business, it's a few people getting rich off the hordes of youth."

Indeed, the true "Malcolm McLarens" of the new punk generation are two men: Kevin Lyman, the concert promoter best known for putting together the neo-punk traveling show package the Vans Warped Tour, and Brett Gurewitz, owner and founder of Epitaph Records and a founding member of Bad Religion. Lyman and Gurewitz are symbiotically linked via their punk-oriented business ventures. Inevitably, even though on some level they are competitors (Lyman owns a chunk of the indie label SideOneDummy), they use each other to cross-promote. Gurewitz needs Lyman's Warped Tour as an established platform through which to promote his Epitaph bands. Lyman simultaneously needs Gurewitz's Epitaph bands to fill his Warped lineups, giving them the Epitaph stamp of punk credibility.

"There's no [neo-punk] band of any significance that hasn't been exposed to or played Warped," Kevin Lyman claims, "or hasn't played a show with a band that's on Epitaph." Via Lyman's and Gurewitz' uncanny ability to channel punk's revolutionary ideology into the mainstream music industry, a whole new generation—the Warped generation—has followed in its wake, finding little contradiction in the commingling of punk and big-money business.

I'm with the Brand: How the Warped Tour Made Punk Rock Viable for Arenas

Another method of traditional punk promotion, the punk rock show, was about to undergo its own '90s-style innovation with Kevin Lyman's Warped tour. In a way, the success of Warped seemed an organic outgrowth from punk's nascent mainstream triumphs. That's because playing shows and touring have always been the real lifeblood of punk: before it had radio, before a single Green Day video was ever played on MTV, punk bands connected with their audience primarily by meeting them face-to-face and playing live. Ask any punk band, and they'll tell you that touring is the most important aspect of what they do. "Touring is the A-number-one reason for doing this shit," says Matt Kelly of the Dropkick Murphys.

"Touring for us was how we created our relationships with our audience and all the people we've met," says the Bouncing Souls' Greg Attonitoi. For the Bouncing Souls, playing live is a crucial litmus test of a band's true authenticity. "To be a successful band, yes, people have to see what you are really like," Attonitoi explains. "Especially today, when you don't have to actually play an instrument to make a decent-sounding recording."

The punk rock show became a sacred, churchlike institution, the community's town hall meeting. The punk rock tour proved to be the genre's Pony Express, taking news, sweat, and tears from town to town via tumbledown vehicles of dubious horsepower. The punk concert was even lionized in song—in their anthem "Punk Rawk Show," MxPx blithely declares they "ain't got no money to pay/[but] we'll get in anyway!" But as soon as Green Day got big, the ripple effect of their success began touching other institutions in the punk world; the beloved punk rock show would soon follow along in becoming a part of the mainstream pop experience. The punk rock show was about to get Warped out of recognition.

Pre-Warped, the venues the current generation of neo-punk came up in started with the improvised—rented Knights of Columbus halls, churches, even a rural pizza joint like Marty's Pizza in Mankato, Minnesota. For one, these venues had to be open to all ages and not just the drinking crowd, so a non-bar environment was key. "All ages" ended up fitting in perfectly with punk's DIY mode, training a generation in grassroots music industry guerrilla tactics.

"The all-ages aspect made you opt for different venues: V.F.W.s, warehouses, even basements. This put a lot of control into the hands of the kids, because, again, no one else was going to do it for you," says Matt Kelly. "Kids contacted the bands, did the advertising, collected money at the door—everything. Basically, the kids had to learn how to run a small business, whether they liked it or not. The phenomenon helped take punk out of the big cities where it started and reach disenfranchised kids out in the sticks, where it continued to grow and develop."

A key network of all-ages venues grew up around the scene as it grew, an echo of similar venues that birthed America's second wave of punk—all-ages places like Los Angeles' legendary Jabberjaw, Gilman St. of course, and Space Place in early-'80s Chicago.

"Ask any band and they'll tell you playing in small clubs is the best," Distillers' Tony Bevilacqua told the *Ventura Country Reporter* in 2003. Indeed, Southern California is lousy with all-ages punk venues, which extend in, out, and around the urban centers: there's the Smell in Los Angeles, the Glass House in Pomona, the Showcase Theatre in Corona, San Bernadino's Orange Pavillion, Chain Reaction in Anaheim, the Galaxy in Santa Ana, La Zona Rosa in San Pedro. These are the places where you'll see Darkest Hour, Mad Sin, the Silence, Underminded, the Burning Season—the next of the next waves—alongside punk "oldies" revival tours featuring the likes of the Dickies, Jody Foster's Army, and U.K. second-wavers like the Exploited and the Adicts.

"All-age venues mean everything," says Bouncing Souls' Bryan Kienlen. "It seems to have always been the 'kids,' usually 'underage,' who need shows most; the kids are who follow the music most closely. Younger people seem have always been the life's blood of the whole punk movement. I know this is some Socialist shit I'm getting into, but I believe kids should have a space they can go to and blow off steam, where they don't have to spend money to be there. To deny them entry to shows would be totally backward and destroy the scene."

The local all-ages venue typically becomes the totem, the divining rod, for any punk scene; often they become deeply cherished as symbolic of a more pure moment. For the Bouncing Souls, the key all-ages venue of their "scene" was City Gardens in Trenton, New Jersey; then, of course, the famous CBGB and Ritz in New York. When all else failed, there was always the band's backyard at their communal house at 174 Commercial Avenue in New Brunswick, New Jersey. "House parties became the live-show venue if there wasn't any other choice," says Bouncing Souls' Bryan Kienlen. One of the greatest, most vital of the all-ages neo-punk venues in any punker's book, though, is Chicago, Illinois's Fireside Bowl.

Windy City punkers Rise Against pay nostalgic homage to the Fireside in their punk power ballad "Swing Life Away," a song about loss of innocence. Fireside Bowl indeed is where many of today's biggest and/or greatest punk bands lost their punk rock virginity and entered national consciousness; Fireside was the place where one could see national touring acts before they got big, as well as the incubation of unsung Chi-town pop punk heroes the Smoking Popes and future pop punk stars Fall Out Boy and Alkaline Trio. "The Fireside was definitely extremely important to the bands I played in and play in," says Alkaline's Matt Skiba. "It was a great place where any band could play, and it was run by real punk rock kids." "The Fireside Bowl holds the warmest memories of my entire life," says Fall Out Boy's Pete Wentz. "It was a sanctuary, and it served its purpose perfectly."

Often oddball venues like the Fireside, a bowling alley, are located in seedier parts of the city, a fact that causes for some town-gown friction when punk's suburban faction drives up. Then again, that danger made for a big part of the clandestine fun of seeing a show in such an untraditional rock venue. These were not places built to last—the memories are stronger and last longer than some of the actual buildings themselves. "Fireside was a place where, if you parked your mom's Volvo in the wrong spot, chances are the windows and everything in it would be gone by the time the show was over," Skiba recalls. "I was sad to see it close, but it's almost a miracle it stayed open as long as it did."

Not everyone cherishes such legendary punk institutions like Gilman or Fireside—even the bands themselves who play them. For some, they become crucibles to re-create and marinate the "high school" politics of the scene. "As far as places with punk values, I feel like a lot of the clubs that are known for their classic punk ethics are actually just elitist," says Tsunami Bomb's Agent M.

And as punk became bigger, more mainstream, it needed a live music experience that wasn't so elitist, that could accommodate the growing amount of fans and help "grow" the scene by providing a promotional infrastructure for neo-punk. It would carry many of the values of the all-ages clubs circuit, but writ on a bigger scale. It would be untraditional and mainstream all at once. It would become what's known as the Vans Warped Tour, and most likely it's coming to a parking lot in your town this year. "Warped Tour has been an amazing tool for punk rock," says Agent M. "It's like a big showcase for punk listeners all over the country, which enables different types of punk bands to swap fans. It's almost like a traveling punk convention."

"Warped is a great idea because it brings a lot of music and ideas to people and places where they might not necessarily be otherwise exposed to them in their daily routine," says Bouncing Soul Bryan Kienlen. "Warped enables different types of bands to go places they wouldn't be able to go to alone, and then they can go back to them later. It's good for the 'scene' on every level."

More than anything, Warped has become a recognizable name in terms of marketing. One respected punk veteran I interviewed refused to be quoted on record about the "new punk." He was exasperated with where the genre was going, but he didn't want to be labeled as a bitter old fogy. His bile, though, couldn't be contained for long. "You know, the punk you hear on the radio proves that punk is no longer a movement," he grumbled. "It's become a *brand*."

As such, as the founder of the Vans Warped Tour, Kevin Lyman is the owner of neo-punk's most powerful brand name. Not surprisingly, Lyman shares with Malcolm McLaren a healthy interest in successful brand marketing of the unconventional; however, in many ways he has figured out far better than McLaren how to make and sustain real financial success over time, unlike early punk's spectacular flameouts.

Lyman, in fact, has an easy yardstick to measure punk rock success by. "If you go into the marketing, the bands that are remembered are the bands with the great logos," Lyman says. "Circle Jerks, Black Flag, Crass—they all had the greatest shirts. I heard a great story: Glenn Danzig gets six-figure checks every couple of months from the Misfits' 'skull' shirt selling at Hot Topic."

That punk can be reduced to a T-shirt for sale at a mall store like Hot Topic is a phenomenon that Kevin Lyman and the Warped Tour are partly responsible for. Whether or not that's a bad thing is up to the eye of the beholder. However, there's a particularly vocal contingent within the neo-punk scene that does think it's a bad thing. For them, someone like Kevin Lyman is responsible for the commodification (and subsequent weakening) of punk—for turning an irreverent, untamed youth subculture into a recognizable, and some would even say respectable, mainstream *brand*. "I was attacked by a guy at a club last year: he came up and head-butted me because he said I've ruined punk rock," Kevin Lyman admits. "I said, 'That's *your* opinion, and that's great.' I told him, 'We're getting older, dude—don't get bitter and old. Redefine yourself.' Somehow all this has changed."

The Vans Warped Tour™—as it's been officially trademarked in collaboration with its main sponsor, skate sneaker titan Vans—has developed into the umbrella for all the wayward genres and bands of the neo-punk era. Nearly every current punk band of any significance (and even a few with nil) has joined Lyman's rolling Warped caravan at some point.

Despite being trapped in the most severely depressed economic climate for live music in decades, Warped has flourished. 2004—the tour's most successful year yet, with over 650,000 tickets sold—marked Warped's tenth anniversary: that birthday earned it the honor of the longest-running festival-style package tour in pop music history, leaving more buzzed-about tours like the troubled Lollapalooza in the dust. Typical attendance at Warped in 2004 meant crowds 13,500 strong at each show; in its Detroit stop that year, Warped brought in 29,500 punk fans, setting a record for its biggest show to date. "It's like a big giant punk rock party, and once a year it happens in your town," Gurewitz explains.

At Warped, fans get to see some fifty-plus bands across eight stages over the course of a full day. It's an egalitarian circus—all bands play for just half an hour, regardless of their popularity, and the lineup's order gets reshuffled each day. "It's a little more action-packed than our regular show," Ryan Key of Yellowcard explains of his band's numerous Warped appearances. "It's shorter, but you have to fit it all in. We probably won't even talk—we'll just play seven songs straight through and say good-bye. But then we'll get out into the crowd and hang out at the merch stand all day."

Yellowcard is one of the most popular bands on the Warped circuit: in 2004 they were voted the band Warped attendees most wanted to see on warped.com. "It's hard for me to believe," Key says. "When we played Warped before, there were three hundred or so kids just rocking out at the Vans side stage. But to think the entire population of Warped wants to see our band makes it different from a typical Yellowcard show."

Key's key Warped tour advice: don't just hang out at the main stage for the superstars—check out the smaller Vans side stage, where the *real* discoveries happen. "That's where the smaller bands that only *you* know about play," Key explains. "It's the same kids watching the main stage all day, but at Vans the crowd changes with each band. A lot of the fun is watching the funny bands that come out. Some bands are out of their gourds, there to just put on a show: they'll wear full-on costumes, bang garbage cans, and play the craziest music you've ever heard. You find those bands, and you watch them every day."

Within neo-punk business institutions, traditional hierarchies are typically avoided so as to maintain a more egalitarian community. On the Warped Tour, the lineup changes every day—bands are given their set time fresh each morning. That means even punk icons like Rancid might find themselves opening for a less popular band. "Warped Tour is cool for the way it smashes the mystique of 'rock' bands," Fall Out Boy guru Pete Wentz. "It levels the playing field. I admire that."

"That idea comes from working on Lollapalooza. Rollins Band was the opening band. Henry Rollins would go on at one o'clock every day. There'd be some kids on the grass and some people sitting in seats; I know it played on his psyche," Kevin Lyman explains. "I always said if I ever do my own thing, I'm going to mix it up so every band is challenged by the other bands."

Lyman claims his approach helps keep quality up. It also means that kids tend to show up early just so they don't miss their favorite. "You never know whom you're going to play after," Lyman explains. "Bands get to be good live bands on Warped: by the end of the summer, you have to kick ass or kids are going to find something else to do. They're going to wander to another stage."

Over the past decade-plus, attending one's local summer Warped stop has become a rite of passage for the neo-punk generation. "I couldn't wait for summer and the Warped tour," Blink-182 rhapsodize on their hit "The Rock Show." In fact, many of neo-punk's best and brightest came to Warped before their bands became famous—or even before they had bands, period.

"In high school, I'd volunteer to work at Warped from six A.M. to six P.M., just to be a part of it," Yellowcard's Ryan Key recalls. "It was one of our biggest goals to ever be asked to be on Warped—when it happened, we were so excited. Being asked to be on the main stage is definitely mind-blowing."

And as the scene continues to grow nationally, insiders see the need for a sort of bellwether like Warped to keep things honest—as much as possible, anyway. "Warped has kept the punk rock movement inside the mainstream consciousness," Brett Gurewitz says. "Which is good—it's been good for me, it's been good for the punk bands, it's been good for the movement. It's kept some of the ideals, like fellowship and community, alive. Kids can go out once a year and see all the other kids that are like them, and have a big celebration of their shared culture."

As well, Warped offers a sweaty, one-day primer in the raging currents of the neo-punk moment; whether any of it sticks to the wall is up to the bands and the fans. "I don't think there is a typical 'Warped sound,'" says Bouncing Soul Greg Attonitoi. "The Warped tour is usually a cross-section of what's happening that summer. There are always regular Warped players alongside a 'flavor-of-the-month' band from out of nowhere that has some radio/MTV hit song. No one's ever heard of them the year before, and no one will care a year from now."

Warped's distinctive tenets—its philosophy of inclusion, a blending of the mainstream and the underground; the obstinate drive to create a market where the mainstream doesn't see one first—all come down to the tour's founder, Kevin Lyman. Lyman is so aligned with the ethos and image of the grimy, grinding punk rock tour machine that it's no surprise to find a Porta Potti in the front yard of his family's home in Los Angeles's Valley suburbs. Okay, he's not promoting a show in his backyard—the Porta Potti was there due to the construction of the house's new wing—but the presence of a portable washroom, that olfactorily resonant staple of outdoor festivals, remains a potent image regardless. The Porta Potti on the lawn serves as a symbolic reminder that Kevin Lyman lives and breathes every aspect of touring live music.

"I believe in the live-music experience," Lyman explains. "It went away for a while; it wasn't a *necessity*. It's about turning kids on to live music. That's what I love to know: that kids are into live music."

Nestled into his mid-forties, Lyman is no longer a kid himself, even if he acts like it. The Porta Potti is a sign of his success, too. His house is appropriately punk rock humble—it's nice, pretty big, Mediterranean-styled, but not opulent despite a fountain or two. It's unpretentiously like all the other nice houses dotting the not very busy, heavily wooded street in unassuming L.A. suburbia where Kevin Lyman lives with his wife and two children.

The giveaway that this is the home temple of the Warped Tour creator really is the Toyota SUV parked in the driveway, covered with stickers from punk bands, skater clothing lines like Hurley and Vans, and record label SideOne Dummy (of which Lyman is part owner). Even on a suburban soccer-mom traveling machine, Lyman keeps it real with the bumper stickers.

You may not be able to tell from the street, but this house is the nexus of all Vans Warped Tour activity. Lyman, an assistant, and the occasional intern all work out of a small, cluttered one-room office converted out of a garage in the backyard. A pink children's bike with training wheels and scattered Star Wars action figures fight for space with framed gold and platinum albums from bands like Blink-182 and the Used. The commemorative discs are made out to Lyman as thanks for his part in their success.

Kevin Lyman grew up even deeper in the Valley than where he lives today. To the relief of his conservative parents, he graduated high school in 1979 into adulthood and L.A.'s punk rock/New Wave scene practically simultaneously. Lyman at that point was a counterculture scavenger: he liked British second-wave punk like the Adicts, but was also into the neo-country rebel rock of Lone Justice and the scattered, silly ska punk of Fishbone. His first real job, however, would provide the cultural context for his sonic identity crisis.

"All of a sudden, through chance I found myself working for Goldenvoice," Lyman explains. Goldenvoice is a legendary Southern California concert promotions company started in the late '70s/early '80s. Run by its omnipresent founder Gary Tovar, Goldenvoice was the biggest of the promoters working during L.A. punk's 1980s golden age; as a result, Goldenvoice always proved controversial in Los Angeles scene reports in *Maximum Rocknroll*. Tovar has since left Goldenvoice, which has turned into a major company of late, having outgrown its punk roots: Goldenvoice is best known today as the driving force behind the internationally esteemed annual Coachella music festival, where bands like Radiohead, the Beastie Boys, Bloc Party, Coldplay, and the Pixies have all played. In the early days, however, punk ruled Goldenvoice's roost. And punk was Kevin Lyman's youthful epiphany.

"My Goldenvoice days are really when I got turned on to all the punk bands very quickly—working a Stiff Little Fingers or Adicts show, working GBH shows, working with Decry and D.R.I.," Lyman recalls. "Being around all these bands, I realized, 'Wow, this is the mindset I have, too.' I never thought I would fit into a traditional life."

Today, Lyman believes it was his early punk rock adventures that influenced him to create what is now known as the Warped experience. Back then, Warped was but a fleeting idea in Lyman's mind about a kind of traveling punk rock town hall meeting, a caravan of mosh-pit good vibes going fan to fan, town to town to build the brand—or brands, for that matter.

"I've always said from in the beginning, what if we all got together in the summertime and worked on our scene?" Lyman says. "That way, we can expose these kids to what we feel and care about—whether it's live music, or brands like Vans or record companies like Epitaph and SideOne Dummy. Sometimes we're business competitors in real life, but why not work together to build our scene? I don't think you see that attitude of shared responsibility in a lot of other businesses."

Kevin Lyman shares some of the entrepreneurial trail-blazing spirit of Jake Burton of Burton Snowboards. Well before snowboarding was a mainstream trend, Burton decided that if there was going to be an audience for his company, he had to create an audience for snowboarding itself; his company was as much about creating the snowboarding circuit as we know it as it was selling these newfangled, weird surfboards for the winter. Burton's quest was a long, gradual process heavy on the mistakes.

Similarly, Lyman started small and built the Vans Warped Tour slowly, learning from trial and error. Each year, he'd build his audience methodically, going to places deep on the American road to nowhere, and then returning again the next year; the crowd might've been small the first time, but it grew and grew with each annual pass. Now, Warped is a recognizable brand everywhere. Indeed, Lyman's afraid that if Warped hasn't yet outgrown its tartan bondage trousers, then it's still "hit a weird point of critical mass" in recent years.

"We did a half a million people two years ago," Lyman says, shaking his head. "Half a million to me is a lot of kids—but then we hit 652,000 this year. I'm always surprised. Then again, Warped Tour has always done good business. I used to do '$2 Tuesdays' at Citrus College, and it wasn't much different from what I do with Warped. It's still the same process: you have to get out there and promote and have a good product that makes people want to come out."

The annual announcement of the lineup for the latest edition of Warped has taken on for punk fans the equivalent anticipation of waiting in line overnight for Led Zeppelin the way their boomer parents might have. Where Warped lands and when has come to affect that utmost ritual of the nuclear family unit: the summer vacation. "I get e-mails from parents going 'I can't schedule the family vacation until you announce the dates. My kids want to go!' " laughs Lyman.

According to Lyman, Warped—which has extended into Canada and special dates in Japan—is now known as a dependable brand around the world. "Kids everywhere know about it by connecting through the Internet. We get international kids coming over here for vacations now who travel to see two or three shows. We're going to have a booth this year for all the British kids who come, so they can promote all the British bands in their scene. It makes me feel good, because people had stopped caring about live shows."

True to punk minimalist form, Warped remains a stripped-down existence. "I have always had a ton of fun on Warped," says Bouncing Soul Bryan Kienlen. "I like the whole camping aspect of it; it's either hot, cold, or raining all the time. We shower with these camping showers—basically, a bag of water with a little hose sticking out of it. Finding a decent toilet can be a whole adventure: you might find a pretty clean port-a-john if you're up early enough, but is there a real toilet anywhere?" According to Kienlen, as each Warped jaunt progresses deeper into the summer, the atmosphere becomes more primal. "The priorities in life become so simplified," he explains. " 'Body needs water.' 'Need to get clean.' 'Must take shit, but . . . *where?*' "

If neo-punk has any stories of *Almost Famous*–style rock and roll excess, most likely they happened in Warped's cozily claustrophobic sweatbox. According to Dropkick's Matt Kelly, Warped is "hot and dusty, like a two-month summer camp/frat party." Such a pressure-cooker environment subsequently results in suitably nutty behavior. "Crazy Warped Tour story case in point: this kid I know who worked on the tour drank twenty-seven beers with a beer bong in about fifteen minutes," Kelly claims.

"There are hundreds of Warped Tour stories," says Pete Wentz of Fall Out Boy, "but they are way too long, or incriminating."

"At night, I stay up late drinking; maybe I'll smoke a hit of weed—or whatever else is going down," Bouncing Soul Bryan Kienlen says of Warped's routine hedonism. "I'll walk around talking to different people all night, just watching it all. I'm the kind of guy that's up for any kind of trouble on tour to break up the monotony. I usually find it somewhere." Typically, trouble is easy to find, for on Warped, trouble has a name: Fletcher Dragge, guitarist for Pennywise. "Fletcher is the character everyone centers around on the Warped Tour," Kevin Lyman admits. "Fletcher from Pennywise losing five thousand dollars gambling? Yep, it happens every day on the Warped tour," says Bouncing Soul Greg Attonitoi.

Not everyone in the neo-punk universe is jazzed about the Warped experience, however—especially some of those who have endured it from the trenches. When asked if there is a typical Warped sound, Matt Skiba of Alkaline Trio replies, "Yeah. *Shitty.*" Tony Bevilacqua has no love lost for Warped himself. "Playing Warped sucked. I hated it—it's the worst," Bevilacqua says. "I'm so glad I don't have to ever go again on a Warped Tour with every crappy punk rock band and every mall-punk kid. It was just the worst thing *ever*, all jock shit where everything is 'bro' this and 'bro' that. There's so much fucking testosterone machismo, it's horrible. *Horrible!*"

Bevilacqua far preferred the more diverse climate of the established but troubled alternative rock tour Lollapalooza. In 2003 the Distillers appeared on Lollapalooza stages alongside the likes of the Donnas, Jurassic 5, Queens of the Stone Age, Audioslave, and the umpteenth Jane's Addiction reunion—which caused the band's die-hard punk fans to cry "sellout" at the abandonment of the likes of Warped. "Lollapalooza was great—it was just cool being on a tour that has different kinds of bands," Bevilacqua says. "We became friends with all those people. Whether or not you like those bands, I didn't care. I wanted to kiss Incubus because they're not a punk band."

Even Warped supporters have their criticisms. "Warped Tour is, like everything else in the world, both good and bad," says Alkaline's Matt Skiba. "Warped helped us out a lot, and is great for new bands to get heard. But by the time it's over, you never wanna see another band as long as you live. It's a blast, and I feel lucky to say I've done it, but I never wanna do it again."

Warped is actually more diverse than some critics actually give it credit for. In particular, Warped has built bridges between hip-hop and the neo-punk community, and hasn't shied away from more underground artists like Kool Keith, Sage Francis, and Atmosphere. "Artists like Jurassic 5 and Black Eyed Peas that are starting to show longevity on the hip-hop scene started on Warped and developed a fan base," Lyman says. In putting together his lineups, Lyman also has revealed a star-maker's eye: when I interviewed Lyman, he told me he had chosen My Chemical Romance and Fall Out Boy as headliners for Warped's 2005 trek. This was many *months* before either band had become mainstream superstars—months before it even seemed like a possibility. Lyman gambled presciently on these choices, and won. Now the Warped tour would forever be a key part of the legend of My Chemical Romance and Fall Out Boy's success, as well as the continuing mainstream success of pop punk.

According to Lyman, maintaining the proper balance of music that meets expectations and expands, however, is his hardest job. "Diversity's always there, but we have to be careful," he explains. "The year the kids got confused was when we had Eminem and Blink-182 as our focus bands. That kinda threw the audience—they were like, 'Is Warped becoming a hip-hop tour?' We've always had hip-hop, but first you have to have the bands that fall into that broad punk category—then you can fill in all the blanks. The audience ultimately appreciates the mix. It's a better show with diversity."

As Warped grows, however, so do expectations from bands and, more likely, their managers. "You've got these managers and other people in the music industry who are incessantly greedy, so they suspect everyone else is like that," Kevin Lyman explains. "U2's great because they've had one manager their whole life. Why does Bob Dylan have a pretty solid thirty-year career? Because he has one guy he's worked with his *whole life*. R.E.M.'s strongest part of their career, they had one guy," Lyman says. "Some of the people that come to punk rock as managers didn't grow up in the scene, and treat it like, 'How much money can I make in the shortest amount of time?'

"This one manager, Arthur Spivak, and I don't mind saying his name, he just sits there," Lyman continues. "It would great if a band like Finch did the Taste of Chaos tour [a Lyman-driven package tour spinoff from Warped]. Finch have been out of the picture for a while, so they should be there. Spivak manages Finch, and his perception is that we're making millions and millions and *millions* of dollars off Warped Tour."

The problem manifests when the need to feed what Lyman calls "the overhead machine" clouds the manager's ability to make useful decisions for his or her artists. "It's so funny: I have a nice home, I make a living, but Arthur Spivak should know I'm not rolling in it—not like he is, maybe," Lyman says. "These managers are out of touch—they all live in big homes in the Hollywood Hills, they all need their first-row seats at the Laker game. To them, bands are just a commodity, like a cow or a bag of wheat, just like how bands are treated by the majority of the music business. It's an interesting time for the industry right now."

(Arthur Spivak—who worked with bands like Saosin, Manic, Yellow-card, Three Days Grace, and Flyleaf as part of the powerhouse management company The Firm and on his own—has his own response to Lyman's criticisms. "Number one, Finch has broken up. I was frustrated myself at the time with the band. They had their own issues they were dealing with—they weren't listening to anybody from label to management. Number two, the decision to not to do Taste of Chaos was the band's decision, not management's—a decision that was made before we started managing them. I can't control the bands all the time; I wish I could," Spivak says. "If people want to generalize about managers, I understand that, but it's really not the case. Unfortunately, sometimes people's perception is that managers can force bands to do things they don't want to do. Artists do what they want—managers don't get up on stage and sing. I've never made a decision based on money: they're always based on career and longevity. I feel bands should grow organically and not go too fast, too soon." Ironically, Spivak-managed Saosin were one of the featured bands on the 2006 edition of the Warped Tour.)

That some bands and industry players are reluctant to jump on Lyman's punk behemoth is surprising, as Warped has also become a key element for any neo-punk band's plans to promote themselves and build an audience. Even the established icons need to hit Warped every so often to keep up with the younger pop-punk Joneses.

"The Offspring played in summer 2005, but they should've done it before," Lyman says. "A band like that has to suck it up and do Warped because it's going to expose them to 650,000 kids. If Brody and the Distillers had played Warped the summer they did Lollapalooza, it would've put her to the top level of people like Gwen Stefani and Courtney Love. Green Day has been smart about it—playing Warped in 2000 was the smartest thing they ever did. They went out, played thirty minutes of their hits, and just *killed it* live. They made the young bands go, 'Oh, man, I don't want to play after Green Day.' "

Undoubtedly, Green Day's 2000 Warped appearance solidified and expanded the band's core audience, adding crucially to the foundation Green Day would use to build the success of *American Idiot*. Lyman knows what bands get out of what he calls his "big umbrella." For Lyman, the greatest service Warped provides bands is *context*. It's the ultimate showcase for a band's promotion, giving them a viable platform with a national reputation and a built-in audience. In turn, the influx of labels and bands helps to, as he says, "reenergize the scene."

Sometimes what energizes a scene most, however, must come from the past. The showcase element of Warped, in fact, is classic music business acumen all the way, steeped in historical industry precedent. "Warped is like those old country fanfares and traveling road shows like Buddy Holly used to do," Lyman says. "Those guys used to go out and really promote that music. Warped is essentially a Motown revue. In them, you'd have eight or ten acts doing three songs each; a couple big-name artists would anchor all the young up-and-coming artists, who got support just from being associated. It's the same with Warped. The audience doesn't know who Anti-Flag is—they're coming to see Yellowcard, but they always discover three other new bands."

The smaller stages are, in fact, where canny Warped goers can see tomorrow's stars today; it's often the first place where neo-punk bands begin absorbing music biz lessons and bonding with their audience "New Found Glory began playing the local stage," Lyman says. "Even as a kid going to Warped as a fan, Bert from the Used says he learned things. He said, 'If I ever got on that stage, I'm going to jump off those speaker steps.' "

Smaller stages are also where younger bands go to work up what's known in the music industry as a fan base. According to Ryan Key, appearing for two years on the Warped Tour before the release of their breakthrough 2003 release *Ocean Avenue* "was really essential to the success of our record." According to Simple Plan's Chuck Comeau, the Warped tradition of having bands mingle offstage with the audience actually proved to be good business, helping to create one fan at a time.

"We do Warped every year—it's important for us," Comeau says. "The first year we played Warped as Simple Plan, it was a very big deal. We got to play for three weeks on the third or fourth stage, and we took it so seriously. Every day after I'd find out our stage time in the morning, I'd write it down on a piece of paper and then walk around the whole festival for four hours, talking to every kid with a Green Day T-shirt. I'd say 'Hey, what's up? I'm Chuck from Simple Plan and you should come watch our band at three P.M. on the Maurice stage.' We'd walk around with a Walkman and play kids our music, telling them, 'If you like Blink-182 or Green Day, then you'll love us.' We'd hang out at the merch tent and meet people, too."

The up-close-and-personal approach paid off for Simple Plan: with this hands-on approach, it's no surprise Simple Plan would eventually go on to be number-one in merchandise sales for whole tour. "Bands on the smaller stages typically have like twenty people there in the audience, but when we'd go on, we'd have two thousand kids, just from us walking around and introducing ourselves!" Comeau says. "It was so grassroots to get these kids to show up; I'd end up recognizing almost every face there I talked to that day in our crowd. That says a lot about how open Warped kids are to discovering new music, and how much we wanted it. It was the first time we felt we had a buzz—we had no radio, no MTV, but we could reach people one by one at Warped. Every show was important; we had to go play to get in the crowd's face and *convince* them."

Bands quickly discovered that their Warped exposure had a long-lasting effect on their careers even after the summer ended. "Warped has been really great for Tsunami Bomb: every show on Warped guarantees a bigger draw when we return," says Agent M. "It's also a great way for us to meet other bands that we could potentially tour with in the future."

Warped continues to get bigger when it returns every year, too, which only means its audience is expanding beyond the expected parameters. Lyman sees it as a passing of the punk torch from generation to generation, making Warped a truly "all-ages" experience. "The cool thing now is we're becoming the multigenerational tour," he says. "There are thirty-five-year-olds who've been coming to Warped since the beginning, and they're bringing their ten-year-old kids. *That's* what I think is cool."

Warped has had a ripple effect on associated businesses as well, keeping the tour industry going well after summer's over and school is back in session. "People thought, 'Hey, this market is going to get saturated in the fall,'" Lyman says. "So many bands went out this fall with Warped-related tour packages—Yellowcard, Story of the Year—and they all met in the Warped parking lot. I was in Philadelphia last week to see a Beastie Boys show and I talked to a promoter about it. He told me, 'Kevin, I'd take Warped Tour back. I thought we were going to have too many mini-Warped tours. But out of ten shows, I sold eight of them out. The other two were multiples of the same bands where we added a second night, and I still sold 90 percent of those tickets.'"

Taking Fugazi to the Masses, Warped Style

Warped has succeeded with a novel formula: keep costs down and quality high, punk style. Warped's commitment to low ticket prices comes from the example of an utterly independent-minded band Fugazi, headed by punk's living, breathing ethical conscience, Ian MacKaye. For years, Fugazi insisted on charging no more than five dollars per show. When those in charge of promoting a 1998 Fugazi tour stop at the University of Wisconsin at Eau Claire charged seven dollars for advance tickets, the band made them provide refunds.

Fugazi borrowed this fair-trade ethic from pioneering activist punk bands like the U.K.'s Crass. Crass felt that the information expressed at their shows was so important, it needed to be disseminated to whomever wanted to hear it. For similar reasons, the Clash kept album and ticket prices far below the mainstream's industry standard. Warped transfers such punk tenets of integrity to a big-business concept: held in humble stadium parking lots every year, Warped showcases dozens of bands, yet ticket prices are kept not much over thirty dollars (or below—Warped has been known to sometimes *decrease* ticket prices from year to year).

"Ticket prices have stayed roughly the same as costs have gone up," Lyman claims. "Warped's first year [in 1994], the ticket price was $15.50, and now we're up to $25. But the show is ten times as big. And the staff and crews want to get paid more. The insurance companies are definitely getting paid a lot more."

Kevin Lyman has transposed the Crass-Clash-Fugazi populist approach to a more traditionally pop-corporate tack. In other words, it's still capitalist business, but hopefully run with a little more conscience and soul. "If this business model works for Ian MacKaye, it'll work for a businessman," Lyman says. "Our business models are related. I think we appreciate each other in some ways. I know Ian, I've known him many, many years. Can he play at my show? No, because it's about integrity— what he's done doesn't fit. What *I've* done is just taken that example and tried to keep the price low."

"Kevin Lyman built an amazing tour—it's just smart," says Chuck Comeau of Simple Plan. "It gives you a chance to be up close to your fans. It's really cheap, but good value; it's cool, like what Fugazi does with keeping five-dollar ticket prices at five dollars. Now kids want value, a package that's worth their money. They have part-time jobs and earn money the hard way; it's about giving them something that's worth something."

Part of what keeps prices low at Warped is the presence of corporate sponsors, however—not something that Crass or Fugazi might approve of (although the odd Clash song or two has been known to appear on television as the soundtrack for ads). If you don't mind the incongruity of a little Samsung sandwiched between Pennywise and Fall Out Boy sets, then you'll have no ethical conflict with Warped Tour.

"We've been able to subsidize low ticket prices with the dollars we get from the sponsors of the tour," Lyman explains. "We've always been up front with that. It's a business model that *works*, and there are companies out there that understand. We're developing a great relationship with Samsung. All they're looking at is how can we help you promote your band, even though their ultimate goal is to sell phones. We're all going to have cell phones, every kid already has one—and there's not an indie cell phone company out there. It's like, 'Hey, I'm going to help the guy sell cell phones; that helps my scene and helps my music—why not?'"

"In terms of sponsors, we treat each situation individually as it comes, every time," Greg Attonitoi of Bouncing Souls explains. "We sold a song for use by Pepsi and iTunes for what I think are both good reasons and good money. Something like iTunes gets all kinds of music out there and makes it available to everybody; if Pepsi puts their money toward that, then I can support it."

"We use corporations to our advantage," Lyman says, sounding more than a bit like Malcolm McLaren during the "cash from chaos" Sex Pistols days. "They pay us a fee to be a sponsor on the tour, but there's all this side business that's done that's the band's choice—we don't force anyone to do it. If we can get Samsung and Cingular to buy one hundred thousand ringtones, we don't make that money on it—they're buying directly from, and helping to promote, the artist. But when bands do a signing for Samsung, they get a little extra money—and someone else is paying to help promote their career."

Lyman often sees the help that sponsors give bands ultimately outweighing the "sellout" jabs, especially when considering how it can affect a band's long-term career. "It means something when a band like Bouncing Souls are given the opportunity to have one hundred thousand posters and a ringtones promotion," Lyman says. "They've never had a big record, but they've been a great band for many years. Maybe us giving them that little push will help them later, when they're getting better royalties off their records. These days, people make more off ringtones than record sales."

Lyman knows, however, that it's not all about money, even when it is. He admits that juggling corporate sponsors and punk integrity can be a tricky balance to pull off, but he sees a solution to the volatile mix: if things are getting too corporate, just add social consciousness. Just not too loudly. "It's hard—we definitely try to balance [sponsors] out with support for nonprofits and environmental issues," he says. "Warped donates a lot to causes, but we don't run around with a flag saying, 'Hey, we donate to charity.' "

That Warped can be big business and support issues significant in the punk community comes from its DIY roots. The DIY template is indeed one aspect that has allowed something like the Vans Warped Tour to have such an impact on a national level. It's a tightly designed, efficient model of business and life, a moveable feast of punk rock community— anywhere where there's a parking lot, there can be a Warped tour. It's the audience that ultimately fills in the blanks. "What's punk is that I can set up a show in a parking lot and just do it with no rules, really," Kevin Lyman says. "Kids come and help, there's always participation—and no schedule. Then you pack it all up and go to the next city."

By keeping overhead low in the first place (in contrast to the major label system, which is saddled with immense international overhead and infrastructure), the punk entrepreneur is able to be more tenacious. With fewer costs, and communal thrift built into the aesthetic, it's easier to live outside the expectations and excesses of the mainstream and ride the waves of a music industry in constant flux. It's an approach similar to the maverick corporate lessons learned by say, Jet Blue or Toyota.

"The Japanese auto industry did it slowly and built up the market share. We've done it slowly, too," Lyman says. "The first-ever day of the Warped tour, eight hundred kids came and saw the show. It doesn't make me any happier to sell out; I just love the process of doing it."

In Pop Punk, Success Will Be Thine Epitaph

How music is released has long proved to be an important part of defining punk rock identity or identities. "I would go out to the stores and buy records based on the *labels alone*—even before I'd heard the music. That was back when pretty much every record on Epitaph and Fat Wreck Chords was *fucking amazing*," says Simple Plan's Chuck Comeau. "Every two weeks or so, Epitaph and Fat Wreck Chords would have a new record coming out: Bracket, No Use for a Name . . ." Comeau trails off wistfully before adding, "It was really cool—an exciting time."

"Indie labels are a vital part of the scene, and were seminal in getting the music out there to people in other towns, countries, and parts of the world," says Dropkick's Matt Kelly. "Listing vital indie labels could take up a whole page. Major labels never wanted to know when it came to small bands doing there own thing; majors are *businesses*, plain and simple. Why take a risk releasing a small-time band with an original sound . . . unless it can be marketed?"

Yet indies figured that "cool" could be marketed if they got it to the right people. Punk indies delivered "niche marketing" at its finest—then they found out that that "niche" could encompass eleven million Offspring fans, and create the foundation for an ongoing business relationship. "Like they did with Sire and SST, people buy records simply because they're on Epitaph," says Kevin Lyman.

For Brett Gurewitz, however, no matter how much money his Epitaph Records makes—and it has made a lot—he tries to avoid making what he sees as both the ethical violations and bad business moves of the major label wheeler-dealers. Gurewitz in fact sees what he does as an alternative to major label corporate culture, which he sees as a representative part of punk's legacy. "I'm not a teenager anymore and punk is music for teenagers, but I still run my business with those same ideals and the same

idealism," Gurewitz explains. "I try to have a life that's based on princi-
ples, and I try to run my business as an extension of that."

"Epitaph kind of existed in a parallel universe to Lookout!—it was far
more successful at developing a professionally run punk rock record label," claims Lawrence Livermore of Lookout! Records. "I personally just
didn't have the discipline or skill to do things on the level that Brett Gurewitz did, and he deserves a lot of credit for what he accomplished. They,
probably more than any other label at that time, helped define what punk
rock was going to become in the '90s and beyond."

It hasn't always been easy to keep running Epitaph according to punk
ethics, however—or to keep it running at all. Gurewitz experienced all of
this in that heady time when Green Day and then the Offspring exploded
within months of each other in 1994. The ripple effect was felt not just at
Epitaph, but across all punk-oriented indie labels, all of whom *just
might've* been home to the next Green Day. No one felt this transformation and the resulting feeding frenzy more than Green Day's former label,
Lookout! "We got very busy. Lookout! opened a record store, hired a full-
time publicist, and so on," Chris Appelgren explains. "Fundamentally, the
distinct line between major and indie labels became blurred."

Nothing contributed to that more than the out-of-left-field success of
the Offspring's *Smash*. *Smash* proved an embarassingly prophetic title:
what it did more than anything, however, was destroy music biz preju-
dices. With Offspring's breakthrough, Epitaph had done Michael Jackson
numbers totally autonomously, without any use of or interference from the
lugubrious and expensive major label promotional apparatus.

"I think it was kind of a good thing when Epitaph got so big because
it took some of the power from the majors," says Bouncing Soul Bryan
Kienlen. "It kind of fucked them up and shook them a little. It also got
a lot of regular people to become aware of the independent scene, too,
which is a good thing. It was great to see all that happen."

The Offspring's success with *Smash* is what will make ensure Epitaph's place in rock history. Yet it is the label's commitment to neo-punk
rock across the board that solidified the label's bond with genre aficionados. "Epitaph made a huge name for themselves with The Offspring,"
says Tsunami Bomb's Agent M. "After that, it seemed like any band on
Epitaph was considered cool. People still buy new releases just because
they're out on Epitaph and therefore assumed to be good."

For many nascent punk fans, Epitaph was a one-stop shop to discover a
nation of punk bands. It was a place where someone might recognize something in a band's scrappy basement-born energy and turn it into indie gold—
the Miramax Films of West Coast punk rock right after its *Pulp Fiction*

went supernova. The Epitaph universe provided a safe haven for a movement that had nowhere to go. "Epitaph released bands who wouldn't have had a chance with major labels," says Dropkick Murphys' Matt Kelly. "Hellcat gave us a chance when nobody else would have even cared."

Tracing the geographical location of Epitaph shows a direct correlation to its success. Epitaph began as a suburban bedroom operation, then moved by default to a tiny back room-cum-closet in Brett Gurewitz's already ramshackle recording studio, Westbeach Recorders. After that, Epitaph headquarters moved between a few locations in fairly sleazy Hollywood neighborhoods as the company grew, aided after the Offspring outbreak by a series of increasing-in-size warehouses barely holding the millions of *Smash* CDs being shipped around the world.

The company's current location belies the current identity of Epitaph—and Brett Gurewitz—to a T. Epitaph's base of operations is located in a big, vine-covered house on the farthest eastern stretch of Los Angeles's famed Sunset Boulevard. On the one hand, Epitaph's clubhouse lies smack dab in an urban center; on the other, it's also fairly removed, isolated, and hidden—the house seems to blend into the hill it adjoins. Epitaph is located on the fringe of the Silverlake neighborhood—where the fringe makes itself home anyway.

Caught somewhere between authentic and gentrified, Silverlake is Los Angeles's East Village, a gritty place turned hip, a minority-dominated neighborhood (Silverlake is a hotbed for Los Angeles's Latino community) overcome by indie rock musicians, the gay community, artists, poets, punk rockers, and anyone else who aspires to individuality in Los Angeles. It's a long way from Beverly Hills, and as close to raw youth culture as L.A. gets. In other words, it's a perfect home for the country's most beloved punk label, which fits into both the area's gentrification and rising property values and its very real urban-wasteland vibe, too.

Once buzzed into Epitaph's inner sanctum, the fruits of the label's success are immediately apparent, despite the building's self-consciously anonymous visage. The walls of the reception area are classic loft brick, on them hanging the spoils of Epitaph's success. There's a double-platinum Offspring album up there amid posters for label bands like Horrorpops, Converge, and From First to Last, which vie for wall space alongside one for one of the company's more unique signings, Tom Waits. A large framed poster of the cover for Bad Religion's latest album, *The Empire Strikes First*, dominates the room.

Epitaph's lobby also features the usual tasteful, modernist furniture of any successful record company. The room is distinguished, however, by the receptionist's enormous bespoke desk, which is fashioned in baroque style out of a custom hot-rod engine. The hot-rod desk is perfect: at once it's slightly dangerous and definitely "extra," a macho expression of California car culture that West Coast punk has adopted heartily. It's confrontational, yet it looks like it probably cost a bundle. In other words, it's the last thing you'd expect to see in, say, Sony's lobby, but the custom hot-rod desk is perfect for Epitaph—just what a lifelong punk rock kid would spend his money on after finally earning some disposable cash.

According to Brett Gurewitz, Epitaph's upscale-bohemian setting is a long way from where the company began. In person, Gurewitz evokes the ideal everypunk veering into middle age: still youthfully wiry, but intense and bespectacled. Gurewitz's dark hair is cut short and just fleckled with gray, his arms covered in punk tattoos that provide souvenirs of a wayward youth turned into profitable adulthood. He has the nerdy rebel charisma of, say, a physics professor gone wildly, horribly wrong.

"I started out by just wanting to make seven-inch vinyl singles for my band, Bad Religion," Gurewitz says. "I didn't have a business model of any kind other than kind of thinking it would be fun to press up some seven-inches and drive them around to record stores."

In the L.A.'s nascent embrace of punk, Gurewitz didn't have many places to sell his homemade Epitaph product. "I think it started with one record store, Middle Earth Records, which I think was in Downey— somewhere in the 714 area code," Gurewitz recalls. "For a long time, that was the only place selling local punk stuff. Then there was Zed's Records in Long Beach . . ."

By 1980, the year of Epitaph's first release, DIY startup SST Records had already made noise around the notoriety of Black Flag. Despite SST's precedent, Brett Gurewitz was working in a vacuum when it came to role models. "In 1980, I knew about Black Flag and everything, but I really wasn't aware of record labels," Gurewitz says. "I didn't think about it. In fact, I didn't even think I *was* a label; I just thought I was making a seven-inch and had to put some name on it."

Whatever business savvy Gurewitz brought to Epitaph most likely was genetically imparted, if anything. "I have a dad who's an entrepreneur— um, he makes fertilizer bags, stuff like that—so he gave me some advice: he said if I was gonna make any change off Epitaph, I should do what's called a 'doing business as,' or 'D.B.A.,'" Gurewitz says. "To do that, Epitaph had to have a name, an address, and a PO box. But it wasn't a business model; it wasn't a *plan*. It wasn't anything."

Epitaph's distinctively gloomy, tough moniker is an ideal punk brand name, but it came from a decidedly un-punk source: prog rock, the very thing the Sex Pistols was trying to abolish—and exactly what a brainy suburban high school kid would be freaking out to in his basement in the mid-'70s. "Before punk rock, there was prog," Gurewitz recalls wistfully. "Punk wasn't my first music, it wasn't what I was brought up on. I got 'epitaph' in fact from a line in a King Crimson song: 'Confusion shall be my epitaph.' It turned out to be a great 'punk name,' though."

Gurewitz soon discovered, however, that punk was something he could be an expert in. "It was something I knew about that was a niche, that I could occupy as a small business entrepreneur," he says. "And yeah, I love it." As his business progressed, Gurewitz decided his company was going to stand apart from traditional music industry practice in its *raison d'être*. Epitaph was going to be a true alternative to the industrial process that makes pop music so shitty when it comes from the major system. "I don't sign kids with computers who make music, but don't have a real band," he explains. "You know, I sign *real* bands. And I'm probably not gonna want to sign a band that just wants to be nothing."

By the time Epitaph had evolved into a viable business (circa the release of Bad Religion's 1988 comeback *Suffer*), a definite, individual, maverick business philosophy had evolved to drive the company and set it apart from the pack. "My model was simply this: a record company doesn't make records. *Bands* make records, musicians make records, not record companies," Gurewitz says. "So, in order not to confuse that, my paradigm was simply, 'I work for my bands. They don't work for me.' It's a simple rule, and if I remember it, I can't get anything wrong." Epitaph's modus operandi distinguished it from what Gurewitz calls the record industry's "plantation system." "The record label is the plantation owner, and then the artists work for the plantation," Gurewitz says. "And it's consistent that way."

For Gurewitz, the plantation is a very real metaphor—the way things are done in the mainstream music biz. "The different plantations trade their artists and decide what's best for them, and so on and so forth," he says. "It's pretty ridiculous when you think about it. Take a company like Nabisco They make and sell cookies; they don't need anybody else to make cookies for them. But Capitol Records didn't 'make' the Beatles records. The Beatles did; then they gave them to Capitol, who then has the *privilege* of selling them. You see, it's the opposite paradigm. But Capitol Records doesn't think of itself as a service provider to the Beatles, right? But that's mainly what they are, because without the Beatles, they cannot exist. They cannot possibly make a Beatles record without the Beatles. Basically, this is a fancy way of saying that I determined that I wanted to have an artist-friendly record label."

Being artist-friendly for Gurewitz is like how some view enforcing environmentally friendly business practice as good business sense: it pays off in the long haul. Also, Gurewitz feels that Epitaph's inclusive approach abets and complements the creative process that gets records made in the first place.

"Let's say you're Picasso, right?" Gurewitz says by way of example. "You don't want to be bothered with the business side of selling your paintings, 'cause you're *fucking Picasso*. So you hire an agent, who works for you. What you say to him is, 'Hey, man, if you help me sell my paintings, then I'll give you a little taste every time you sell one. But remember, they're *my* paintings, and I call the shots creatively. If you ever have an opinion on my paintings, you're fired.' That's what my bands get to say to me. They don't work for me; *we* work for the bands."

Gurewitz's approach has paid off. Under his watch, in addition to the Offspring's tens of millions of units sold, Epitaph has moved millions more in its twenty-five-year history. Epitaph has that all-sustaining thing in the music industry—a catalog library of consistently selling releases—and its catalog is not just deep, but moves in big numbers. NOFX has moved the most individual product, with 3.1 million releases sold in total. Epitaph has sold roughly 2.5 million cumulatively with Rancid, and did about as many Bad Religion albums. Pennywise have sold almost two million records, the Dropkick Murphys close to 700,000. At worst, bands like the Transplants, Matchbook Romance, and Epitaph's rap signing Atmosphere can expect to sell around a couple hundred thousand copies, all on budgets that wouldn't pay for the catering on a major release. Gurewitz has also perfected the art of marketing punk compilations: Epitaph's *Punk-O-Rama* series, along with various editions of affiliated label Hellcat's *Give 'Em the Boot*, provide standard-issue documentation of what's going on in neo-punk at a fair price. They're the ideal starters for a peek into Epitaph's culture, from the graphics to the variety of bands anthologized.

Even Epitaph's nonpunk releases, through its specialized subsidiary imprint, Anti, have done well. Under Anti's banner, Gurewitz has sold about 700,000 Tom Waits albums, while Elliott Smith has posthumously moved 200,000 units. Gurewitz's ability to sell records while creating a brand loyalty relationship with his customers—where the consumer recognizes the Epitaph name as representative of a certain quality and sound—has made Epitaph a lucrative property. Despite a business approach contrary to their own, major music industry conglomerates have attempted to purchase Epitaph outright, or some chunk thereof.

"I've had offers," Gurewitz admits. "My first offer for half of the business was fifty million dollars, which I think came from Polygram; I turned it down. And then I almost did a deal that was worth a hundred million dollars, but I'm not gonna name names." The deal didn't happen—Epitaph is still 100 percent privately owned by Gurewitz and independent as ever—but rumors persist that Epitaph has secretly become a subsidiary of Warner Bros.

"Yeah, it's not—*I* own Epitaph," he says. "People told me they'd seen something to that effect on music industry gossip Web sites, but it's not true."

Ironically, Epitaph's success could have killed the label. Often, DIY indie operations run by artists can't sustain the pressure, let alone the financial and infrastructure needs, created by a surprise hit record. The returned units alone on a hit record—often in the high thousands—can debilitate a company without the cash flow reserves a diversified multi-national conglomerate offers. "Do you remember Delicious Vinyl?" Gurewitz offers by way of example. "Well, success destroyed them."

In the late 1980s, Delicious Vinyl was an indie rap label whose massive mainstream successes and number one hits posited it as a successor to the likes of Def Jam before they imploded when demand outstripped their resources. "They had 'Wild Thing' and 'Funky Cold Medina' by Tone-Lōc, they had 'Bust a Move' by Young MC," Gurewitz says, "and then the next moment it was all *gone*. It's hard: what you have to do is grow, but in a way that allows you to contract when you need to, and still not lose your essence."

Gurewitz admits Epitaph was barely able to handle demand for their big Offspring record: he had to mortgage out his house, take out bank loans, and relapse back into heroin addiction to get it done. Most punk indies aren't set up for that kind of hit, even the bigger ones.

"You set up indie record labels, and they get better at it," Kevin Lyman explains. "They can start carrying a record at two or three hundred thousand records. I'm involved with SideOne Dummy Records, and they're set up in the system to do that many, but not *all at once*. An indie doesn't typically know how to do that. It's not set up for that: if your record stops selling, you get these massive returns. The market's been flooded with a half a million records or something, and if it comes back it'll put an independent label out of business. It's about knowing your resources and what you're good at. Offspring sold something like twelve million records worldwide: if that thing had already stopped and there were a million returns, it would've clobbered Epitaph at that point."

Tony Bevilacqua of the Distillers actually worked at Epitaph during its most troubled moment, when the chaos of success threatened to ruin everything Gurewitz had built up to that point. "I started interning there," Bevilacqua says. "I just used to go there and work for free for *hours*—photocopying a thousand flyers, then stuffing the new NOFX record into manila envelopes and then mailing them to record stores. It was mindless."

When Bevilacqua started at Epitaph, Gurewitz was in fact in rehab, kicking his relapsed heroin addiction. "Yeah, I never got to know him," Bevilacqua says. "He wasn't there, wasn't involved—Epitaph was run for him by the people that I worked with. Just when he started coming back,

Epitaph gave me a real job, and I still didn't really get to know him well. I got introduced to him like, five times; five minutes later after he'd met me, he couldn't remember who I was. He would see me in the hallway and be like, 'Why are you here?' It was that kind of thing."

Those lost days thankfully remain behind Epitaph for the moment. But on any indie label, however, another crossroads is always just around the corner. Epitaph's sales are no longer what they were at their peak. Of the current punk acts signed to Epitaph, the biggest seller is Motion City Soundtrack with 200,000 albums sold—respectable and, indeed, fantastic for an underground band, but chicken feed compared to Offspring's landmark eleven million. Meanwhile, the label's flagship acts, NOFX and Rancid, have left the label: Rancid departed for Warner Bros. in 2003, while NOFX is opting for the moment to put out their future releases on their own label, Fat Wreck Chords.

The future of Epitaph may lay outside of punk, in fact. While as committed as ever to Epitaph (and its Hellcat subsidiary that he runs with Rancid's Tim Armstrong), Gurewitz has also set up Anti, a label for musicians that don't fit in with the main label's punk aesthetic sonically. Anti's not Gurewitz's only stylistic diversion—he has had a business involvement with the upstart Mississippi blues label Fat Possum (which has since fallen apart into a nasty, mud-slinging divorce).

Attitudewise, however, Anti's lineup of full of incredible, iconoclastic mavericks, from Australian post-punk gloom-monger Nick Cave to trip-hop troublemaker Tricky and gravel-voiced, unclassifiable genius Tom Waits. Also on Anti are roots-rock anticlassicists like Daniel Lanois and Joe Henry alongside similarly hard-to-pigeonhole Americana siren Neko Case, country outlaw innovator Merle Haggard, and honky-blues noisemakers the Black Keys. Adding to the stylistic insanity are releases from left-field hip-hoppers like Muggs (of Cypress Hill fame), cross-dressing British comedian Eddie Izzard, '60s icon and heroin survivor Marianne Faithfull, soul shouter Solomon Burke, neo-troubadour martyr Elliott Smith, and emo kings the Promise Ring.

Anti's diversifying begs the question, when does an indie label become a major? Is there a butterflylike transformation, or does one just "know"? If Epitaph's corporate culture ends up with the lineup and size of a major label, what would most likely set it apart would be Gurewitz's hands-on aesthetic and taste. Either way, he doesn't see Epitaph's expansion into nonpunk waters as selling out, but as essential to serving the label's vision. "I saw that I had to diversify," Gurewitz explains, "if I want to not just survive, but remain viable and alive."

At the same time, industry insiders insist that Epitaph's brand identification within the neo-punk community remains necessary to keep vital.

"They have to protect the Epitaph brand," Kevin Lyman says. "They started confusing their audience a little bit by putting out hip-hop like Atmosphere and diversifying. But they put it into Anti and Hellcat, and kept Epitaph what it's always been. They've learned."

Dig the New Breed: The Children of Epitaph

As role models, Gurewitz and Lyman have spawned a legion of similarly inclined neo-punk entrepreneurs. Ironically, while his band was signed to Epitaph, Fat Mike of NOFX ended up spawning Epitaph's greatest compatriot and competitor, Fat Wreck Chords. Fat Wreck is now home to many of neo-punk's strongest bands—Bracket, Lagwagon, No Use for a Name, Strung Out, Avail—as well as simpatico older-school faves like the Descendents, Sick of It All, Screeching Weasel, and Subhumans.

"Epitaph helped create and promulgate a whole lifestyle around the baggy-shorts-and-wallet-chain aesthetic, something that Fat picked up on and ran with," sats Lawrence Livermore. "Lookout! was almost deliberately unprofessional and amateurish, which appealed very much to a certain category of punk rockers, especially the younger ones who were at a very idealistic phase in life, whereas Epitaph was more about producing a very good and consistent musical product. Fat didn't appear on the picture until both Lookout! and Epitaph were well established, but you might say that they benefited from the experience and mistakes of both those earlier labels. To some extent, Fat formed kind of a synthesis of both styles. And where Epitaph and Lookout! began branching out and exploring other varieties of music, Fat always stuck very close to its basic style and core audience—and prospered greatly as a result."

Fat Wreck has become almost too successful, often unwittingly serving as an inadvertent breeding ground for the major labels; both Chicago punks Rise Against and Virginia-based political rockers Anti-Flag recently left Fat Wreck for Geffen and RCA, respectively. Conversely, Fat Wreck also provides a welcome return haven for bands like Face to Face and Less Than Jake who were less than thrilled by their own major label experiences. "Bands on Fat Wreck Chords like the fact that they are not a commodity that would be dropped if sales were bad or they weren't cool anymore," Fat Mike explains. " 'Fat' bands know that they are part of a family, and whether they break up or leave the label, they will always be part of that family."

Another success story is Victory Records and its charismatic owner, Tony Brummell. Victory has proven ubersuccessful, cutting a wide swath through the punk and metal-associated scenes with emo acts like Thursday, Taking Back Sunday, and Hawthorne Heights and more metallic acts like Atreyu—all of whom are, naturally, Warped Tour favorites in the neo-punk big happy family. Victory has done so well of late that *Billboard* magazine called it "the No. 2 independent rock label in the United States," behind only TVT Records, famed as the label that "discovered" Nine Inch Nails through its current status as home of Li'l Jon's "crunk" revolution.

Victory has such a devoted following that there is a cult trend of fans having Victory's bulldog logo tattooed onto their skin; that's not just viral marketing, but epidermal to boot. Major labels, on the other hand, have developed little consumer identity of late, which wasn't always the case. In the 1960s, a band like the Rolling Stones was interested in signing to Atlantic Records, spawning ground for the likes of Ray Charles and Aretha Franklin, because of the label's significance to the birth of rhythm and blues. Today, however, if a fan buys a record on Sony, it's because of the artist, not because it's on Sony. Independent punk labels like Victory, Epitaph, and Fat Wreck Chords, on the other hand, reverse that equation to create the exact opposite relationship with their consumers: the neo-punk customer understands that he or she will get a certain quality, a certain genre sound, and support a certain ethical business attitude outside of the mainstream if they purchase, say, a Fat Wreck release.

Labels like Victory and Fat Wreck survive alone on the perception that they're an authentic voice of the community they represent, with profits coming second. However, the profits are definitely there, placing these labels into capitalism's world of filthy lucre, even as they fight against it.

"I can't deny that Fat Wreck Chords makes a bunch of dough, but the difference between Fat Wreck and corporate America is that we don't exploit or take advantage of anybody," Fat Mike writes on Fat Wreck's Web site. "We don't fool anyone into buying something they don't want, and we don't rip anybody off. The bands don't get ripped off, our employees don't get ripped off, and the kids who buy our music don't get ripped off. Everybody in the equation is happy. Also, our CDs are made in America, not some sweatshop in China, and the CD booklets are made in Canada. No one gets exploited. Not only that, but at the end of every year, if Fat had a good year, we give big bonuses to all our employees and more importantly to all the bands (something that is unheard-of in the music industry). Fat might be doing well, but so are a lot of bands and people involved with it."

Indie versus Major: Neo-Punk's Celebrity Deathmatch

This "indie versus major" debate has been swimming in punk rock's genes since its inception. "It's arguable that the major labels started punk,"

Brett Gurewitz notes. He lists the Ramones (Sire/Warner Bros.), the Sex Pistols (Virgin/Warner Bros.), Television (Elektra), and the Clash (Epic) as proof. Patti Smith was a favorite cause of and muse to her megamogul label head, Arista Records founder Clive Davis, a titanic of the music industry establishment who's played a crucial Svengali role in the legendary careers of everyone from Janis Joplin, the Eurythmics, and Whitney Houston to OutKast and Puff Daddy. Yet the limited major label attention span for hard-to-format, unconventional music with small sales forced punk's subsequent waves to fend for themselves. "Independent labels were born out of a need for them," says Bryan Kienlen of the Bouncing Souls. "When the entire record industry consisted of a handful of major labels holding so much power and influence, something had to give."

"Without indie labels, I don't think there would be much choice in music today," says Alkaline Trio's Matt Skiba. "They provide an outlet for things less 'marketable,' which often times is the best shit out there. Without indie labels, I wouldn't be able to pay my rent."

According to Brody Dalle, it's not about indie versus major as much as "what kind of deal you make. There's good and bad on all sides—you can be screwed over just as badly by an indie as you can by a major." On the one hand, the major label issue isn't such a problem in terms of alienating fans, as neo-punk major label bands like Green Day and Yellowcard are selling more than they ever have in their career, but once a punk band crosses that line (or rather, signs on a contract's dotted one), the major label stigma becomes a permanent topic. And punk bands making the indie-to-major move find it has variable effects on their career.

Rancid courted controversy—and may have lost fans—when they signed with Warner Bros. after a decade-plus as Epitaph's premier band. The Distillers were selling around a quarter-million or so on indie Epitaph; when they moved to Sire/Warner Bros., they sold roughly the same number of albums, but with massively increased costs and expenses for videos, studio time, and so on—all charged as recoupable expenses to the band. According to Kevin Lyman, if your band signs to a major label, chances are you'll have to reach platinum sales just to break even. "For a major label record with a big push, you're a million records into the deal before you're seeing more money," says Kevin Lyman. "There's the $200,000 video; then you have to buy your way onto radio via independent radio promotion—which is no more than payola, really. The base amount to get a record on the radio is $300,000, and it doesn't even hold it. If you're a flabby cow and don't get a hit, you'll get sent to the hamburger mill; eventually, you're going to get slaughtered. Record sales will go down, and all of a sudden you're not that valuable to someone's 'system.'"

"My stance on punk bands going to majors is this: if an indie is no longer able to handle a band's capacity of fans, it only makes sense to move up," explains Agent M, whose band Tsunami Bomb is signed to indie Kung-Fu. "If it seems that an indie has done all it can to promote and help a band with their available budget, the only other place the band can go is to a major."

Different bands have different, individual reasons for signing to a major: both the Distillers and Simple Plan are signed to labels within the Warner group, but are completely different bands. Still, the major label experience provides an odd common ground. "We wanted to take things a little further," former Distillers drummer Andy "Outbreak" Granelli told *Chord* magazine soon after the release of the Distillers' major label debut, *Coral Fang*. "Nothing against Hellcat [the band's former label], but we wanted more freedom to step it up a little. We wanted more time and support to record the album we always wanted to make."

According to Chuck Comeau, Simple Plan "wanted to sign to a major because we came from an indie scene where we saw the limitations of being on an indie label. An indie label can't break you in Australia, and they can't support you the way Atlantic-Warner supports us right now. We're using the Atlantic label to bring our music all over the world. We go to Singapore, Indonesia, Thailand—people know us and there's a big reaction. We're going to South Africa and South America, where the band is huge."

The major versus indie debate has proven neo-punk's line in the sand, with two opposing views. "The music biz has always tried to do anything it can to sell as many records as possible," Bouncing Souls' Greg Attonitoi explains for the indie side. "They just package up trends and market them on a large scale. Independents work their own way and majors don't know what the hell they are doing anymore because of the Internet and the technology that is available to record music for so little money."

"People have a warped perception that you sign to a major label and you're an instant millionaire and can sit on your ass," says Simple Plan's Chuck Comeau, from his perspective being in a major label band. "In fact, the amount of work we have to put in compared to how much money we make is huge: it's not all easy and manufactured. You don't start a band because you want to get rich—there's a lot easier paths to that."

"Personally, I haven't really been tempted to go the major route," says Agent M. "We wanted to sign with a label that had at least some footing in the punk community, and Kung-Fu seemed like it would fit well with us. Kung-Fu is a small/midsized indie label that is constantly striving to become more established. They're still in certain experimental stages, but I think that Kung-Fu has a lot of potential and room to grow in the scene. It's evolved into a better-functioning business over time." Then again, for

Agent M and others on the neo-punk scene, a successful punk indie like Epitaph or Victory might not seem all that different ultimately from their bigger-business brethren. "I think that indies and majors are becoming more alike. They all want to make money off their bands, and punk bands are more marketable now," says Agent M. "So the indies that previously just signed punk bands for their underground talent are now just signing them for their widespread appeal, possibly hoping they can develop bands to sell to majors."

Indeed, Victory Records, who have indeed "upstreamed" for profit bands like Thursday and Taking Back Sunday to major labels, are now fully competing as equals with the majors as each lays claim to who has pole position on the *Billboard* charts. This was made clear when Victory Records sent out a seminotorious press release to journalists touting the first-week sales and radio airplay of Victory breakout band Hawthorne Heights' second album, 2006's *If Only You Were Lonely*. In particular, by comparing Hawthorne Heights' performance in the marketplace to more commercial, major-label acts like Def Jam/Universal R&B act Ne-Yo and Interscope's Pussycat Dolls (as well as pop-punk peers like Fall Out Boy and Simple Plan), Victory's press release aimed to show the difference between perception and reality—that an indie label like Victory and an underdog band like Hawthorne Heights could, in fact, be more popular than whatever the major label was shoving down the public's throat at that moment. The press release demonstrated how punk rock's solvency as a business has become part of the narrative, a true point of pride, a declaration of independence—that being successful and selling out are actually . . . cool. Here's the release:

Music Lovers,

I have some very interesting numbers for you regarding spins vs. sales. Today Hawthorne Heights is in stores. We are going head to head with Universal's Ne-Yo. Ne-Yo has 160,000 radio spins on his current single. Hawthorne Heights has 3,800 radio spins on their current single. Their sophomore album comes out tomorrow. Their debut album was released 20 months ago and has shipped 1,000,000 copies.

Best,
Heather

Sales Per Spin (Units being sold as a function of airplay) for Comparable Artists

Weezer—3.28 Sales Per Spin
Green Day—5.13 Sales Per Spin
FOB [Fall Out Boy]—6.94 Sales Per Spin

AAR [All-American Rejects]—7.76 Sales Per Spin

Simple Plan—8.56 Sales Per Spin

Death Cab [For Cutie]—12.32 Sales Per Spin

Good Charlotte—15.83 Sales Per Spin

MCR [My Chemical Romance]—20.3 Sales Per Spin

HH [Hawthorne Heights]—59.4 Sales Per Spin (using 771,785 units sold and 12,999 spins*)

As a corollary simply of spins, Hawthorne Sales Per Spin is out performing these artists:

Beating Weezer by 1550%

Beating Green Day by 1157%

Beating FOB by 853%

Beating All American Rejects by 765%

Beating Simple Plan by 692%

Beating Death Cab by 481%

Beating Good Charlotte by 375%

Beating MCR by 292%

Sales Per Spin (Units being sold as a function of airplay) for Mainstream Artists

Pussycat Dolls—2.64 Sales Per Spin

Ashlee Simpson—11.17 Sales Per Spin

HH—59.4 Sales Per Spin (using 771,785 units sold and 12,999 spins*)

As a corollary simply of spins, Hawthorne Sales Per Spin is out performing these artists:

Beating Pussycat Dolls by 2242%

Beating Ashlee Simpson by 532%

*36% of all HH Spins are on overnight rotation

This was neopunkonomics, a competitive blood sport being played out on the scale of the majors' playing field. Others, however, have created a hybrid approach by splitting the difference between major and indie. This mode combines both the long-tentacled global resources of the former with the niche-marketing TLC of the latter. Alkaline Trio, for example, are signed to Vagrant, which began as a DIY punk indie before becoming a subsidiary of supermajor Interscope Records, home of U2, Dr. Dre, Eminem, and so on. "Vagrant is half-owned by Interscope Records, so I guess in some regard we're already on a major," says Alkaline Trio's Matt Skiba. "We've been lucky that we've been afforded the luxuries of a major label without any of the pitfalls."

"The label thing is something you are never really going to fully control. You just have to guess who's not lying and focus on your music." So says Matt Caughthran of the Bronx, who independently self-released their raw self-titled 2003 album debut before signing with Island/Def Jam after a bloody bidding war. "You will get fucked by major-label machine whores and you will get fucked by the cute little indie label in some nerd's kitchen," Caughthran adds. "Just remember, the more money you take, the more money they want. At the time, I could not believe we were going to sign a record deal with Island/Def Jam. But the more labels you meet with, the more you are able to cross-analyze through all the bullshit. So far, so good."

As well, many bands have started indie labels of their own while enjoying the big time on a major, combining their own experience as artists in the indie realm with that of greater success in the corporate realm. The Offspring have their Nitro imprint, which released seminal recordings by bands like AFI, as well as providing a home for revered old-schoolers like the Damned and T.S.O.L. Blink-182 drummer Travis Barker has his own label, LaSalle, which released the second album from the Transplants, his collaborative project with Rancid's Tim Armstrong, in conjunction with major label Atlantic in 2005. Even Good Charlotte has their own vanity boutique label, DC Flag.

It's not so surprising: within even the most commercially successful aspects of the neo-punk community, from the biggest record labels to the most popular bands, one often finds some embrace or link to punk's original DIY spirit. Many successful neo-punk businesses were formed out of necessity, with no thought of them turning into ongoing, wealth-enhancing concerns. Brett Gurewitz formed Epitaph in 1980 simply to release Bad Religion's early seven-inch efforts; Tony Brummel started Victory in 1989 out of his Chicago-area bedroom, spending a budget of just $800 to release his first single, by California thrashers Inner Strength.

"When this bullshit record industry turned its back on an entire sound, bands had to release and sell their own records themselves; it's that simple," explains Bouncing Souls' Bryan Kienlen, who knows of what he speaks: Bouncing Souls now release their own records through Epitaph, but their first recorded efforts were released on their own small, grassroots label Chunksaah. Since then, however, the label has grown along with the Bouncing Souls' career; since its beginnings, Chunksaah has come to release music from everyone from obscure pop punk bands to ska punk heroes the Mighty Mighty Bosstones. "That's our story with Chunksaah Records," Kienlen explains. "We started that label because no one else would put out our records, so we had to do it ourselves."

Proving the cliché true, necessity has proven to be the mother of invention for punk rock business approaches. It's the glue, the commonality that links the punk rock nation all over the world. "Indie labels are important because they are created by the artists . . . in theory, " says Greg Attonitoi of Bouncing Souls. "Epitaph has been a great unifier—they really brought together a sort of *world scene*. But the best thing about indie labels is there are tons of 'em, with all their little scenes everywhere documenting people creating and doing their thing."

World domination, however, was typically the last thing on the minds of those unwittingly blazing neo-punk's trail to success. "Prior to Green Day and the Offspring, very few people working with independent labels had any serious expectations of making a lot of money or having a significant impact on mainstream culture," says Lawrence Livermore of Lookout! Records. "It was extremely amateurish when we started—being 'professional' was considered the antithesis of punk. No one ever expected for there to be any money to worry about. Green Day were already big stars by our standards long before they went to Reprise: we'd sold over fifty thousand, of each of their albums, and Operation Ivy were even bigger, having sold over seventy-five thousand."

Considering the meager resources Lookout! began with, those numbers already felt like success enough. "We'd started with a total investment of $4,000 to make four seven-inch EPs, so it never occurred to us that we were a small or struggling little label, and in fact we weren't," Livermore says. "True, we weren't making a lot of money, but it was enough to get by on. We knew that there were bigger labels out there who might not take us seriously, but that just didn't matter, because there was no doubt in our minds that we had the best bands and the best scene of any in America. I tried to foster an attitude with our bands and employees that what we were doing was important and deserved to be taken seriously: the music we were working with was clearly superior to almost everything on the radio or in the record shops, so there was no reason that someday we shouldn't make money from it."

Instead, entrepreneurs like Gurewitz, Lyman, et al. rose up organically by creating new, innovative business models from punk's DIY approach. Those that did DIY releases learned on the job, having to be creative by managing limited budgets and handmade, often improvised marketing campaigns—if they even knew what marketing was. But the band-driven label definitely knows its audience better than anyone, and typically is committed to capturing the artist's vision in an undiluted form.

"If you release your records yourself," says Dropkick Murphys' Matt Kelly, "*you* call the shots. You don't feel like you're working for a label or company." Brett Gurewitz has long discussed how he works for his bands—that record companies don't make music, bands do, and labels can't exist without the music makers. This is the root of the unusual hierarchy he works from in his business—one that's the direct inverse of typical major label practice. Undoubtedly, this approach stems from Gurewitz's dual experience as musician and label owner.

Learning how to run a business from the ground up in the DIY mode, however, can have its pitfalls. Indeed, blazing a trail can often lead to unexpected minefields. "There weren't many role models for running a label when Lookout! first started aside from Dischord, SST, and possibly Touch & Go," says Lookout co-owner Chris Appelgren. "But as Lookout! seemed to grow each year, and the popularity of our artists seemed to be blossoming naturally, we spent more time making friendly fun of peers as opposed to taking cues or lessons."

When Lookout! began in the late 1980s to put out Operation Ivy's music, well before Green Day would leave for greener major-label pastures and explode in 1994, the mission was simple, according to Appelgren: "Put out good records, take out ads in *Flipside* and *Maximum Rocknroll*, and send one hundred copies of each release to college radio stations. Fill mail orders. Stuff seven inches." Repeat that simple model times a nation of millions, and the organic success of punk's innate grassroots business model becomes clear.

Many of punk's greatest indie labels were formed initially to document regional punk scenes—Dischord, home of Minor Threat, Rites of Spring, and Fugazi, only puts out music rooted in its Washington, D.C., environment. "My model for Lookout! was primarily the Dischord label," says Lookout! founder Lawrence Livermore. "Dischord focused on its local scene. They kept record prices low, treated its bands well, and took itself seriously, but not too seriously."

But as punk began to grow in popularity, the punk indie's focus often went national, and in some cases, international (Epitaph Records has a partnership deal with Swedish punk label Burning Hearts, for example, a pairing that has produced the triumphant likes of the Hives and Refused). "Initially, Lookout! was created to document the East Bay/Gilman punk scene," Chris Appelgren explains. "As bands from the Berkeley/Oakland area began to tour nationally, our scope reflected new friendships between bands and like individuals from other cities."

Even the most popular, biggest-selling, commercial pop punk has its roots in the indie value system. For example, Simple Plan's aw-shucks pop punk and cute, girl-friendly image is often derided as the worst kind of manufactured major label music; the band is often mentioned in the same breath as artificial 'N Sync-styled "boy bands" assembled by managers and executives. Yet Simple Plan's success is in fact largely self-built, with the band still using lessons learned in the DIY trenches in the sharky big business world of the majors and MTV.

"The DIY approach is a huge part of Simple Plan. We learned to be a band on our own—we made every single decision," says Simple Plan's Chuck Comeau. "It's still like that, and it comes straight from that world. After fifteen years, this band still wants to control everything we do: it comes from all those years of booking our own shows—from waking up every day and thinking, 'What can I do to make this band go further?'"

By learning the DIY way, Simple Plan knew how to develop their whole aesthetic, down to the T-shirts and packaging, before they ever signed with a major. When they did sign with Atlantic, they were better prepared and in more control than a typical novice signing. They already spoke the language, and couldn't be fooled.

"When we started out, we had to find printers and design our own merchandise," Comeau says. "We carry that on today—in our world, we're one of the only bands that doesn't have a merch deal. All our merchandise is designed by one of our best friends. We know him because he was in a band that used to tour with Reset; now he does all our merch designs. That way, we keep it tight and under our control."

Radio Babylon: Punk Hits the Airwaves

One of the hardest areas to control in the music industry is radio, whether they play punk rock or not. "Radio generally sucks," says Bouncing Souls' Bryan Kienlen, "whether they play Green Day or not." Yet it was Green Day that provided the shock of hearing something that resembled punk rock on Top 40 pop radio for the first time, really. Yes, there had been some Clash singles that broke through, but those hits like "Rock the Casbah" felt like novelties that had slipped through the cracks, not defiant expressions of punk's sonic manifesto.

But Green Day looked and played the part. It was the coup de grâce, the second shoe-drop moment after Nirvana broke through on the airwaves. And it was the support of a major alternative rock station, Los Angeles's KROQ, the kind that broke Nirvana, that provided the spark to the Offspring's platinum punk nitro. It was strange to hear the aesthetics of speedy chords, inadequate vocals, and a specific brand of lyrical alienation in such a commercial housing. Punk was supposed to be radio's unpassable stage of sonic dissonance. Yet radio proved to be the final straw in the breaking of neo-punk: along with MTV, radio and broadcast media were what finally brought neo-punk to the masses and turned it into big business—just like any other pop trend. Once kids could see and hear punk in their living room without too much mediation, they saw themselves in it. The revolution was televised, and someone was actually tuning in.

Punk promotion before punk actually was played on the radio was typically more laissez-faire. A punk band might be "serviced" to college radio, for example, or the label might get more creative with song placement: the Offspring might, say, place a song on a snowboard video that hopefully someone might overhear while it played in the dorm TV room. But commercial radio was something else. Naturally, the community had something to say about punk rock on the radio.

"We wrote this song, it's not too short, not too long/It's got backup vocals in just the right places," Fat Mike croons over the incredibly catchy pop-rock of "Please Play This Song on the Radio." It's an ace parody of alt-rock's sheeplike mentality (and the kind of music that actually gets on the radio). At the same time, "Please Play . . ." is also a devious trick— after NOFX sucks the listener (and radio programmer) in with a hooky melody and slick production, Fat Mike lets fly with a rash of expletives that definitely *cannot* be played on the radio—enough to make "the FCC take a shit on your head!" Tsunami Bomb also tackles the topic on "Top 40 Hit," taking a swipe at corporate powers who "have their hands over your ears/[so] you'll never hear the sounds that matter."

" 'Top 40 Hit' isn't so much about major labels as it is about mainstream radio sucking real bad," says Tsunami Bomb's Agent M. "It makes me angry that radio stations have the capability to make bands huge and help the music scene so much, yet they only play the same fifteen songs over and over again because of corporate decisions and payoffs."

The Internet, of course, is the latest minefield of punk rock music and information distribution. "The best thing is, any band can record a song and put it online," say Fall Out Boy's Pete Wentz. "The worst is, you can get music everywhere." The Internet is where the ideological fanzine battles of the past are now played out on a far grander scale; it's where illegal downloading both coincides nicely with punk's anti-authoritarian (and cheap) spirit, and conflicts with its no-ripoffs policy. Punknews.org is the home-grown world-wide-webbed CNN of neo-punk, and of course there's the (legal) download site punkdownload.com.

Naturally, the punk rock world has produced an appropriately spiky reaction to the Internet. "Rush out and get your copy of *Coral Fang*—and don't steal it off the Internet you little assholes": so reads the band-sanctioned copy from the Distillers' press announcement announcing the official release of 2003's *Coral Fang*. None has been more mischievous, and almost Dada-esque, about the Internet than Offspring, for example. After Offspring took the top spot on *Rolling Stone*'s Top Pirated Internet Songs chart for the twenty-two million illegal downloads their hit "Pretty Fly (for a White Guy)" enjoyed in 1998, the gloves came off.

The Offspring realized that taking the po' faced, fan-punishing Metal-

lica approach to Internet downloads wasn't going to work. No, it re-
quired a more creative, irreverent attack. First, in 2000 the Offspring began selling T-shirts of notorious peer-to-peer network Napster's
distinctive headphones-wearing cat logo on its official band Web site.
When Offspring received a cease-and-desist order from Napster, the band
feigned confusion, claiming they were only "sharing the logo with fans."

Later that year, Offspring used the Internet again to tweak the music
industry in an almost Malcolm McLaren-esque show of cyber grandstanding and manipulation. Not only did the Offspring offer their latest album
at the time, 2000's *Conspiracy of One*, as a free download on their Web
site well before it hit stores, they turned the whole cyberpirate process into
a contest: whoever downloaded the album in advance would be registered
for a contest where the band would give the winner one million dollars live
on MTV on the day of *Conspiracy of One*'s legal release to stores.

Offspring's international conglomerate label, Sony, wasn't so happy
about the Offspring's Internet antics, however, and threatened legal action. The band backed down, but the point was made: the old ways aren't
working, and if you don't take action, the punks will take matters into
their own hands.

The Big Sellout

But even if a band like the Offspring can act in a nonconformist manner while signed to a major label, have they sold out so far in advance that
such counterculture moves no longer carry the same power? The Warped
Tour has no problem selling out tickets, but are bands that play those
tours selling out to, say, the corporate sponsors? Are bands signed to Epitaph really punk anymore? Do "real" punk bands play Warped?

These notions of selling out remain key accusations whenever a punk
musician does anything that smacks remotely of careerism, even in one's
love life: Bert McCracken of the Used was accused of selling out when he
started dating Kelly Osbourne. "Just like any other band who has enjoyed
even a mild amount of success, of course we've been accused of selling
out," says Dropkick Murphys' Matt Kelly.

"That shit comes from fans of a band becoming almost sort of jealous
of their little secret being shared with a bigger audience," says Bryan
Kienlen of Bouncing Souls. "They hold onto a golden moment, not wanting anything to change. The problem is, things always change."

"I have to tell people, 'Hey, don't piss where you may be sitting in a
year,'" Kevin Lyman says. "These backlashes are just bandwagon-jumping.
The younger bands that start having success, they're just looking at their

own shadows with alcohol-fueled boldness. Good Charlotte was getting a little flack from a band like Yellowcard on Warped this past summer. I was trying to tell Yellowcard, 'What are you doing? You may end up there, too.' Starting that kind of talk can backfire and accelerate the Web sites to start bagging on you next."

In the Internet age especially, accusations of selling out multiply exponentially, doing greater harm with little repercussion for accountability. "The term *'sellout'* is usually thrown out there in usually the most cowardly way: from sitting behind a computer in the anonymous safety of their home on some message board," Bryan Kienlen notes.

For Gurewitz, adding the Internet to the equation creates a hypocrisy of just who is selling out who in the punk world: "Today, the kids who are screaming sellout are in peer-to-peer file-sharing networks. They don't think bands should be paid anything, so fuck them. If you want to get paid for doing work, you're not a sellout; being extremely successful and getting paid extremely well, that doesn't necessarily make you a sellout, either. It hurts my feelings, but I don't seek it out."

"Selling out means selling out your ideals. But that means different things to different people," Gurewitz adds. "The Offspring were accused of it; Green Day suffered from that a lot. I suffer from it—people accuse me of selling out punk rock. I think it's a lot of ado about nothing, especially in the digital era."

Musicians aren't the only ones susceptible to the sellout charge in the punk-oriented world. Missy Suicide learned that lesson the hard way when suicidegirls.com courted controversy. The "punk erotica" Web site partnered on a business venture with *Playboy*, whose airbrushed, surgically enhanced, heterosexual-male-driven ideal of beauty seemed to contradict the Suicide Girls' freedom-of-expression-through-nudity stance.

Soon after tattooed and pierced Suicide Girls began appearing on playboy.com as the "Suicide Girl of the Week," hateration about suicidegirls.com and its business practices began appearing cyberside. "It's different working with *Playboy* when they're talking *to* you," Missy Suicide explains. "Working *for* white-haired old men is different from working *with* them. It's a whole different ballpark: *Playboy* came to *us*, so they're going to listen to and respect what we have to say. We definitely want to uphold a certain value and not sell out in certain ways."

For Suicide Girl Bee, hitching up with *Playboy* fulfills an aspect of the populist mission of suicidegirls.com. After all, it's not as if these women are posing nude on the Internet so nobody will see them, and reaching a more mass audience just may spread suicidegirls' alternative message even farther beyond the already converted. "If they were like, 'Hey, you're 'Suicide Girl of the Month' on playboy.com,' I'd be like, 'Fuck, yeah!' "

Bee explains. "It just means I hit more people. I don't see suicidegirls losing sight of what it stands for." Bee also knows that if suicidegirls were sellouts, they wouldn't put their money where their mouth is and share the wealth. "I know suicidegirls isn't selling out," she adds, "because when *they* make more money, we the models also make more money."

For the Bouncing Souls, it comes down to creative autonomy. "The Bouncing Souls have built our own world. It's a world where *we* make all the decisions on an individual basis regarding our music and our lives," Bryan Kienlen says. "We make our own rules, but the only rule is how we feel in our hearts. This is our cornerstone, upon which we have never wavered—and will never waver. To do something that felt really wrong in my heart, that would be selling out."

As much as major corporations are blamed for their sellout incentive, according to Attonitoi some of the worst pressure to compromise one's art can come from pressure created from within the artists themselves. "The part of being in a band that made me miserable was when I started *trying* to fit in," he says. "Instead of developing my own individuality, as the band developed I retreated into an image to hide away in."

Lyman wishes that when talk turns to selling out, those involved, be they band or fan, would pause for perspective and put things into relative terms: in an era where often the big choice kids are left with is between Britney Spears' bubblegum and Warped-style punk, well, the choice is perfectly clear. And this isn't just business talk—this time it's personal. "We're the antithesis to Ashlee Simpson," Lyman states. "All I care about is turning kids on to live music. Kids are getting into Warped Tour bands at nine, ten, eleven years old. Those same kids have to make a decision: am I going to go to Britney Spears' concert or the Warped Tour this summer?"

The Offspring of Epitaph and Warped

Leading punktrepreneurs like Kevin Lyman, Fat Mike, and Brett Gurewitz have by example spawned, either directly or indirectly, depending on whom you're speaking with, a new breed of punk-influenced and -bred businesspeople: label owners, managers, booking agents, publishers, Web site developers, and so on. It's a class that stands on its own and does things their own way, which is the only way most of them can operate. If you've fought to make things happen when nobody cared, it's hard to change your MO when suddenly they do.

When asked who defines the soul of neo-punk business today, Kevin Lyman states, "There's not one heart and soul to it, but a lot of hearts." In particular, Lyman namechecks Andrew Ellis as a new-school punk businessperson to watch. Ellis presides over Ellis Industries, one of neo-punk's most esteemed booking agencies, whose bands include bands like Brand New and New Found Glory. "As an agent, Andrew has a smart, smart way of dealing with these bands," Lyman says. "He's focused on a group of artists that are like-minded in some ways, and he's built a nice model for those bands. They're all working and successful."

Another luminary involved in the running of the neo-punk machine are Steve Martin, founder of the publicity firm Nasty Little Man. Martin is a veteran of New York's hardcore scene (he was a guitarist for a spell with Agnostic Front) before he fell into flackery. Over the years Martin has done press duties not only for, say, Radiohead and the Beastie Boys but also Rancid, AFI, Alkaline Trio, Civ, At the Drive-In, Jimmy Eat World, and Coheed & Cambria; he was also the publicist for the first Warped Tour.

Manager Jim Guerinot, meanwhile, has built an empire with his Rebel Waltz company—named, appropriately, after a Clash song. Guerinot has a long history in the music industry (in the mid-1990s he was general manager of A&M Records). He and his team currently manage the careers of everyone from Social Distortion and the Offspring to Gwen Stefani and No Doubt, Rancid's Tim Armstrong, and even neo-punk superstar session drummer Josh Freese. Guerinot's punk ethics make him appealing to more than just punks, however: he recently took on Nine Inch Nails's Trent Reznor after Reznor's previous management allegedly took the industrial Goth star to the cleaners.

Stormy Shepherd, meanwhile, remains one of neo-punk's most beloved figureheads; many consider her name a synonym for integrity. "Stormy is like the den mother to all those punk rock bands," Brody Dalle explains. "I have a lot of respect for her." Shepherd runs the Salt Lake City, Utah–based Leave Home Booking (named, naturally, after a favorite Ramones album), which is nominated for—and wins—many industry awards. A practicing Mormon, Shepherd started booking tours for punk bands well before neo-punk hit big and Shepherd's clients started becoming big stars; today she handles the likes of the Offspring, Rancid, AFI, NOFX, Tiger Army, Sick of It All, lesser-known bands like Form of Rocket and the Aquabats, the occasional old-school punk icons (the Adolescents), and even some graying U.K. punk/oi! first- and second-wavers (the Business, the Toy Dolls, the Damned). Many of Shepherd's longtime clients have stayed with her even as they've found big success. Conversely, despite her big-time status, Shepherd still books smaller bands with equal vigor; she doesn't ignore all-ages and untraditional venues, either.

In addition to Epitaph, meanwhile, numerous independent punk labels have sprung up to document the varying strands and bands of the neo-punk experience: Victory, Drive Thru, Vagrant, Hopeless, Trustkill, Ferret, the Militia Group, Sub City, Kung Fu, Revelation, SideOneDummy, Jade Tree, Tarantulas, Fiddler, and so on. Some of these labels make deals within the major-label system; others keep it totally independent. Many of these newfangled record companies are simple mom-and-pop operations (if a kid has a band, see, it's not so hard for him to have a label, too); others maintain numerous staff. It all depends on what segment of the neo-punk world each individual company is built to capitalize on.

These days, the line between major and indpendent remains blurred, a sometimes symbiotic but often hostile arrangement. On the one hand, someone like Tony Brummel of Victory can make a lot of money grooming a band like Thursday to then sell to the majors (Thursday now records for Island-Def Jam, part of the Universal group). On the other hand, when Brummel sold a stake of Victory to MCA for multimillions, it didn't work out. Ultimately Brummel felt that he and MCA were in different businesses, and he returned the money, which he'd kept in escrow. Victory's example shows that even when they want to stay independent, neo-punk's savviest business minds still have the resources to throw the dice right alongside the major-label big boys.

"You've got all these strong pieces that do not depend on one Epitaph— and even Epitaph is having a resurgence," Lyman says. "The thing is, if you can't get paid by your distributors, you'll go out of business. And they have better distribution than they ever have."

Neo-punk's simultaneous rise in popularity and business acumen has resulted in its own media network as well, outside the traditional national music and general-interest press that is the grail of most major music industry marketing. Web sites like punknews.org and magazines like *Alternative Press* have built a significant niche out of neo-punk. *Alternative Press*, by becoming the print bible for the neo-punk community, has in the process not only found an audience at a time when most mags are struggling; it's defined itself as an even more relevant conduit to youth culture than it ever has been in its nearly two-decade history.

"I don't live or die whether *Rolling Stone* or *The New York Times* covers Warped," Kevin Lyman says. "It's the fanzines, it's the kids—*that's* who I want to get to. I take it more personally when someone says shit about me on a Web site like punkrock.net than if someone wrote about me in *Rolling Stone*. I'm just focusing on my niche, and that niche is growing."

Affiliations between complementary businesses like Warped and Alternative Press, meanwhile, prove mutually beneficial. "I told *Alternative Press*, 'Who cares if other magazines are at Warped? If you're the best magazine, you're going to raise your subscription base by ten thousand people this summer,'" Kevin Lyman explains. "That's a nice jump. They're the only people catering to the niche. These kids are really passionate about this—if *SPIN*'s out there, who cares? We give them *choices*."

Neo-punk's independently minded business practice has also expanded choices in the area of music-based television. "The Warped Tour's role in the blowing up of punk isn't nearly as big as MTV's," says Bouncing Soul Bryan Kienlen. "Ironically, it seems like MTV has mostly ignored the Warped Tour, never really covering it properly. Chalk up one "punk point" for the Warped Tour."

Instead of established youth culture media outlets like MTV, many of neo-punk's luminaries have cultivated relationships with newer, edgier music broadcast entities. Warped has recently partnered frequently with MTV's primary rival on cable television, the Canadian-based Fuse network. In a way, Fuse and Warped's partnership is more about cultivating and maintaining their own audience, rather than trying to steal MTV's. And Lyman has found that when things get big enough organically, MTV snaps right back around like a boomerang anyway.

"It was a fight when we did a deal with Fuse television," Kevin Lyman says. "Everyone, all these traditional people, said, 'Oh my God, you're going against MTV.' But we created a fuckin' avenue over there where they were starting to play bands and videos which previously had no chance. Then those bands turned it right around and went over to MTV, and you know what? They got a push—all of a sudden, MTV was paying attention to Warped Tour–style bands, and they hadn't in ages. So are we changing the business model? In some ways, I think we are."

The key difference with the neo-punk business model as opposed to the majors? *Identity.* When fans tattoo the Victory Records bulldog logo on their arms, they're not representing a band per se, but their belonging to a cultural unit, a *tribe*: Victory is down for them, and vice versa. That the Offspring can achieve sales on the scale of, say, a Michael Jackson is mind-boggling, and perhaps the future of the music business, as the Internet allows ears to be educated and find their place much faster. Even in its most crass, commercial state, Punk, Inc., offers more integrity and authenticity than anything comparable on the pure pop side.

For one, there's still too many checks and balances, even on the bullshit. What Punk, Inc., does right, the rest of music industry typically does wrong: a supercommercial, internationally popular, multiplatinum band like Simple Plan ultimately has more control over their career because of their knowledge and experience of punk rock business ideas than just another alternative rock band formed out of nothing. Even at its most debased and submerged, there's always a tension, as punk's maverick spirit remains hidden, looming; it's like a dormant volcano that could go off at any time.

"We've been accused of selling out on several occasions—no matter what you do, someone's going to be pissed about it," says Alkaline Trio's Matt Skiba. "I wouldn't be a very good punk rocker if I gave a flying fuck about what people think. If you don't like it, start your own band and do it the way *you* think it should be done."

That maverick, individualist spirit, however tangential it may be after all these years, is still what links like minds like Gurewitz, Lyman, Fat Mike, Stormy Shepherd, and Tony Brummel to the Malcolm McLarens who paved the way in decades previous for a future generation of punk rock businesspeople. There will most certainly be new McClarens popping up whom we'll be writing about in a few years' time. More than likely, despite the divisions within punk, a lot of the new McLarens will be working together off the same page to fight the opposition, which is an approach of the moment they might've learned from adversarial quarters. It's like the Republican Party putting aside differences and bonding together like ideological superglue during an election: in their minds, the right side winning is all that matters, and by any means necessary.

And winning isn't always an option: in summer 2005, Lookout! Records was significantly reduced as a business when Green Day reclaimed the rights to their pre-*Dookie* albums due to a dispute over nonpayment of royalties. "We got behind in payments as money that was due to artists was used to maintain our business or in some cases fund new releases," Chris Appelgren wrote in an open letter posted on lookoutrecords.com. ". . . It was high time to make some hard decisions about how Lookout will exist in the future. The changes we looked at were not because Lookout would no longer have Green Day's first two albums but had to happen because our business was not healthy. Green Day's decision was a result of our internal problems not a cause." Even in punk rock, money remains the great divider. Further complicating matters, of late Lookout! hadn't yet found a band as culturally relevant as Green Day (or even Screeching Weasel), and sales suffered. "To be honest, I'm not that impressed with any of the bands Lookout! has put out in recent years," admits Lawrence Livermore, who had sold his stake in Lookout! long before Green Day pulled the plug. "Fat Wreck Chords stuck close to its roots, whereas Lookout!, especially today, has very little connection to the scene it originally set out to document. I think that goes a long way toward explaining why Fat is thriving and Lookout! is now floundering."

Despite the occasional speed bump on the business highway, neo-punk knows it's fighting the good fight. The idea that alternative rock might provide any kind of "alternative" above cliché is now considered ridiculous; still, even at its most banal, neo-punk needs to define itself as a real alternative to the mainstream music industry it tentatively embraces. And it's a group effort.

"I'd like to help change the business model—I hope we're all changing the business model in some way," Kevin Lyman says. "Hopefully, we're getting these bands to go out and build careers on live touring, making them not so dependent on a radio hit or a label. In terms of labels, bands really have to do the work themselves. That said, I never knew that what we were doing was going to be this . . . *bridge*."

Or this big. "Green Day changed things massively and forever," Lawrence Livermore recalls. "Although they'll always be one of my favorite bands, if not my very favorite, I must admit to having a bit of regret: once they became so massive, it would probably never again be possible to do the kind of thing that Lookout! did—i.e., go from a tiny bedroom label to being a major cultural force in punk rock without all the big-money guys noticing and moving in the first time we had even a moderately successful record. They'd be lucky to get their first LP out without a bidding war erupting."

"Today, the cynic might say that there's very little difference between the punk rock and mainstream music business," Livermore concludes somewhat wistfully. "Where there is a difference, it's usually that punk rock labels can try and excuse their incompetence or dishonesty by saying, 'Hey, it's punk rock!' "

7

There's no revolution anymore/On the edge of tomorrow, what are we fighting for?

—The Explosion, "No Revolution"

If you're going to mainstream any sort of punk rock politics, I don't think the Sex Pistols is going to be it.

—Missy Suicide

Green Day's Grammy performance of *American Idiot* was the first moment a modern-day punk artist was shown standing up to the establishment in a long time—and being rewarded for it in spades by the music-biz establisment. So, then, what is the political significance of Green Day performing an anti-Bush punk song at the Grammy—and on stages in countries across the world? Is it a "Dylan going electric" moment? Only time will tell.

Perhaps Green Day's Grammy honor was both a tacit acknowledgment and endorsement of *American Idiot*'s politics by the most conservative wing of the music industry. Indeed, many Grammy voters are baby-boomer children of the 1960s who may in fact be excited by Green Day's activist-populist bent. Now that they're highly compensated CEOs, it's likely a relief to see that someone has picked up the torch of protest that they dropped when they left behind their hippie/yippie cultural apparatus to join the corporate world.

Either way, *American Idiot* more than anything seemed like a tightening of the tether between mainstream punk and the explosive, uncompromising politics the genre has been associated with from its inception—"a return to punk's outspoken, politically volatile roots," Cole Haddon wrote in a 2005 *East Bay Express* article entitled "Burning Bush: Green Day replaced *Dookie*'s idiocy with *American Idiot*'s insurgency. Will the kids follow?" "There was an element of danger to pretty much anything the Clash or the [Sex] Pistols were saying," longtime Green Day producer Rob Cavallo is quoted in Haddon's piece. "But if you look at the last five or six years, you'll see there's been no danger, or real statement that talked to kids directly: 'What's your government doing? What is your news telling you at six o'clock on Channel 4? Why do you have to believe that?'" "Often you need overly political bands to serve as a slap across people's faces," says Fall Out Boy's Pete Wentz. "Green Day's *American Idiot* was just that."

From the beginning, it was always assumed that punk rock had revolution on its maverick mind. "Anarchy in the U.K.," "God Save the Queen," "I'm So Bored with the U.S.A."—classic punk rock song titles were often little more than agitprop pop sloganeering: if it looked good rendered in spray paint on the wall of a government building, it would probably work well as a song title. A band like the Ramones featured conflicting political viewpoints, none of them representing the mainstream, which added an electric tension: singer Joey Ramone was Jewish and liberal-minded, but sang songs redolent with controversial Nazi imagery courtesy of his less-enlightened bandmates.

For a bohemian like Patti Smith, the mere act of *existing* as a contrary voice was political. The political aspect is what gave original punk some measure of its real charge: the English punk community was always supportive of causes like the Campaign for Nuclear Disarmanent and Amnesty International. The group Crass, in particular, was less a band than a collective espousing the most radical, anarchist, vegan politics ever: Crass released albums, yes, but those served more as manifestoes for the underground, never intended for chart entry. The Crass logo remains one of the most meaningful ever—probably the greatest expression of punk graphic design after Jamie Reid's famous cut-and-paste Sex Pistols images. Wearing the Crass logo on a T-shirt or patch signified that you were down for the cause in the most radical way.

Even more mainstream bands like the Clash were infamous for living up to their moral, ethical, and political stances, expressed in album titles like *Sandinista* and pointed songs like "Spanish Bombs" and "Straight to Hell." The Clash famously billed themselves as "The only band that matters," backing up their tough talk with action like playing antiracism benefits and keeping album prices down at a direct loss of profit to *them*. If a song was deemed too commercial, it would be left unlisted as a bonus track; in fact, of the band's three hits, two of them, "Train in Vain" and

"Should I Stay or Should I Go?," were intended only as bonus tracks on *London Calling* and *Combat Rock*, respectively. The band didn't want to look like it was shilling for radio play, God forbid.

"I invented that phrase, 'the only band that matters,' for the Clash," claims former Captain Beefheart and Jeff Buckley collaborator Gary Lucas. "I came up with it while I was working in the creative services department for CBS Records. But it was true: they were the only band that mattered. We believed in what they were singing about, because they sang about what was really going on in the world. It was exciting."

Some of the most heartfelt and engaging songs by Rancid are their more topical efforts—sometimes even more so than their more obviously personal lyrics. Sometimes it's down to the band's performance: Rancid's anti-authority song "Antennas" remains fairly generalized punk raging against the machine, but the band's sweaty intensity provides the alchemical touch, transforms it into something powerful. However, "Rwanda," the key track off 2000's *Rancid*, is probably the band's greatest song. With its insanely catchy refrain "Rwanda, won't you be strong like a lion?," Rancid find more passion and poetry in this song about genocide in a distant land than Tim Armstrong's more familiar struggles with his own demons. Punks sing about anarchy, but a place like Rwanda is really the closest thing we have to anarchy in the contemporary world; Rancid understands this parallel and finds the heartbreak in it. In "Rwanda's" insistent minute and twenty seconds of spit and vinegar, Rancid comes as close in their career to inheriting the legacy of the Clash, while sounding nothing like them for once. "Rwanda" indeed remains one of Rancid's most interesting and fluid musical moments.

The Distillers, meanwhile, write some of neo-punk's best political lyrics because of how Brody Dalle both mines history for literary metaphor and doesn't shy away from the rich complexity in the dichotomy between past and present. Dalle's lyrics truly represent someone who trawls through history looking for truth and roots, for a better way to understand what's happening around us today. A Distillers song like "Red Carpet and Rebellion" from 2002's *Sing Sing Death House* wittily contrasts turn-of-the-century peasant uprisings in St. Petersburg, Russia, with contemporary ideas about fame and marginalization. An early Distillers song like "The Blackest Years" uses the Berlin Wall as a metaphor that could represent either the personal or the political: "Oh, Berlin, your heart has been drawn and quartered again." Inspired by Ken Burns's Civil War documentaries, Dalle crafted the *Sing Sing* standout "Seneca Falls," which name-drops Susan B. Anthony and Elizabeth Cady in praise of woman's suffrage—not the names you think might pop up in an artfully hooky neo-punk song. "Colossus U.S.A.," meanwhile, explores how the relativity of suffering can result in hypocritical absurdity: "I met a man on the street, he said this is poverty/Downtown on Broadway!" Dalle intones incredulously. "It's weird shit," Tony Bevilacqua says. "People don't really write about stuff like that."

"Sick of It All," meanwhile, bluntly confronts the issue of "cutting"— the pathological self-mutilation that haunts many punk/alternative kids, and Brody Dalle herself. "I used to cut a lot," Dalle admitted in a 2002 interview for soundcheck.net. "It's about self-hate and control."

Like, say, "Lost in the Supermarket" and "Clampdown" by the Clash, the more socially oriented Distillers songs suggest there's a bigger, realer world out there—putting the political, personal, and pragmatic all into perspective. "I'm not really educated or well-versed in economics or politics and [I] wouldn't be able to sit down and have a serious conversation about what's wrong with the world," Dalle told *New Music Monthly* in November 2003. "But what I see on the news and read in newspapers and see from other people's stories are gonna come out of me. My music's more about injustice than real politics. I'm not a victim, and I ain't no martyr . . ."

In the contemporary punk world, however, politics remain a cloudy topic—a potential minefield that many would rather avoid. It's surprising because of how the social unrest of the 1960s so inspired a generation to stand up and express itself through pop culture. Despite its antihippie rhetoric, music as revolutionary forum is the legacy punk inherited from flower power. Despite its radical bloodline, much of today's punk remains apolitical, despite the massive turbulence in postmillennial society—the world is just too scary a place to deal with (or risk commercial failure in). Yet apathy, in many ways, can provoke controversy almost as much as outspokenness. "Without naming names, there are a couple of bands that—especially with how Clash-influenced they are—I'm really surprised have basically come out and said, 'We're not political,' " Green Day's Billie Joe Armstrong told *Threat* magazine. "And, well, that kind of sucks."

But just how important, really, are politics to the generation of punk rockers weaned on *Dookie*? On their song "No Revolution," neo-punk's other Clash revivalists the Explosion bemoan the apathetic state of punk rock today, especially considering the genre's history of protest. "We look to the past and ask for nothing more," goes a typical, bittersweet line in "No Revolution" 's lyric; here, from within the neo-punk world, the Explosion fully acknowledge how the post–Green Day scene has bit the style, but not the substance, of its punk ancestors. Indeed, within its own DNA, neo-punk initially didn't take punk's pledge of allegiance to protest. It's hard to imagine after *American Idiot*'s polemics, but back in 1994 even Green Day felt the pull of apathy (then again, they did name themselves after a day spent on a pot bender). "It was a little hipper to be apathetic [when the band first started]," Billie Joe Armstrong said in an interview with the Associated Press. "Right now, it's more about facing danger . . . That's what growing up is all about."

For many coming up in the neo-punk community, however, growing up meant letting go of the knee-jerk dogma of youth. When Canadian hardcore band Reset evolved into pop punk superstars Simple Plan in 1999, they let go of Reset's commitment to polemical politics. "Lyrically, at the time with Reset, I was really into politics and social issues. We thought that would be a cool songwriting direction," says Reset/Simple Plan drummer Chuck Comeau. "Reset's lyrics were simple but militant—not in a Rage Against the Machine way, but more in a mix of personal and social. We'd go to the newspaper and look for stories. With Simple Plan, however, all our songs come from *life*. We made a decision to write about more personal issues than Reset was writing about: social lyrics are cool, but sometimes they're a little abstract."

Naturally, the decision to forgo Reset's politics in Simple Plan's songwriting was one of the first things to get Simple Plan tagged as sellouts. If Simple Plan's lyrics were political, suggested the voices nagging away in cyberspace, maybe they wouldn't get played so much on Disney Radio, perhaps? Those questioning Internet voices resumed such chatter like a Greek chorus in the wake of emo, where lyrical navel-gazing about girlfriends greatly reduced topical diatribe in the lyric-producing aspect of the equation. However, on some level, neo-punk isn't as completely apolitical as it may appear.

In recent American political elections, the punk community had largely united to attempt the unseating of incumbent president George W. Bush; as well, there has always been an authentic antiwar voice within neo-punk. Even in the most establishment neo-punk institution like the Warped Tour, political causes of all stripes find a place to pitch their ideological tents. Meanwhile, community groups like punkvoter.com have worked alongside and taken inspiration from populist voter empowerment movements like moveon.org. "Punkvoter.com plays a big role in politics in punk," explains Agent M of Tsunami Bomb. "Punkvoter.com is somehow associated with Fat Wreck Chords. They basically worked really hard to get punk kids to vote in the 2004 elections so Bush wouldn't be president again."

Indeed, punkvoter.com remains defiantly partisan; if there is any commonplace tendency in punk politics, it's that unless one has no political opinion at all (still, yes, a surprisingly popular choice), then one shall doggedly defend their dogma of choice. Once a punk chooses a side, there's typically not a lot of gray area left to swim in. On the Web site that defined a movement, punkvoter.com defines itself as "a grassroots coalition of punk bands, punk labels, and most importantly, punk fans coming together to form a united front in opposition to the dangerous, deadly and destructive policies of George Bush, Jr. . . . Punkvoter.com seeks to inform, inspire, enrage and help turn millions of punk fans into a political force to be reckoned with." The enemy? An administration that spends "billions on a disastrous, preemptive war in Iraq, passing hundreds of billions of dollars in debt on to a future generation [in other words: US!]." The prey? A right-wing political culture "waging an unprecedented attack on civil rights and personal freedoms."

Indeed, despite its anti-establishment view, punkvoter.com realizes what top cards it carries in terms of economic and demographic impact and uses them, not unlike a classic lobbying organization. "We got the numbers," its home page boasts, "so sign up!" What gives punkvoter.com the capital of power, however, is that it is driven by a driven demographic. "Passion Is a Fashion" was the title of a recent Clash biography, and today's punk activism shows that passion is still in style.

"Punk bands, musicians, and record labels have built a coalition to educate, register and mobilize progressive voters," goes the official copy in punkvoter.com's Web site manifesto. "Something needs to be done to unite the youth vote and bring real activism back into our society. Punk rock has always been on the edge and in the forefront of politics. It is time to energize the majority of today's disenfranchised youth movement and punk rockers to make change a reality."

Punkvoter.com's mission—and that of many within the punk community that resides comfortably in the music industry mainstream—has calmed from '77 punk's original nation-toppling fire, however. For one, the bomb-tossing incendiary rhetoric of early punk just doesn't fly post-9/11; it looks, sounds and walks too much like terrorism to the unironic, untrained eye (and it probably was, in some cases—Joe Strummer sure liked wearing his inflammatory *Brigade Rosse* shirts when the Clash played).

According to Agent M, the biggest neo-punk artists involved politically "are probably Fat Mike and NOFX, and Green Day"—all really representing the older school of punk's resurgence. Bad Religion remains the *eminence grise* of neo-punk both sonically and as its liberal-radical political conscience, but Fat Mike of NOFX is neo-punk's political go-to guy of the moment, the Jello Biafra of his generation.

Fat Mike for president? It may not be so far-fetched—or far off. Working with organizations like punkvoter.com and moveon.org, Fat Mike spearheaded the release of two *Rock Against Bush* compilation albums. The *Rock Against Bush* series is the *Let Them Eat Jellybeans* of its day: it featured, not surprisingly, politically charged bands like Anti-Flag, Rise Against, and Bad Religion and outspoken old-schoolers like Jello Biafra, D.O.A., and the Descendents. More surprisingly, some of pop punk's biggest stars like Yellowcard, Sum 41, the Offspring, Rancid, and Green Day make appearances, as well as alt-rock bigshots like Ministry and the Foo Fighters; even indie rockers Sleater-Kinney contribute a track.

There are limits to how radical *Rock Against Bush* was supposedly willing to go, however. The politically radical Canadian punk band Propagandhi (who also spawned the acclaimed Weakerthans, another socially conscious punk band of the new school) chose not to appear on the compilation after Fat Mike decided that Propagandhi's song and liner notes dissing billionaire activist George Soros—who has worked closely with moveon.org and supported anti-Bush efforts across the country—didn't smell like team spirit. The result was an Internet outcry of censorship that revealed the *Rock Against Bush* team's greater interest in working for change *within* the system, as opposed to dismantling the state entirely, as some punkers might prefer.

"This is not really the message I am trying to convey because I believe Democrats are a bit better than Republicans, and I think Bush is fucking the world worse than anyone possibly could," Fat Mike said in a statement following the Propagandhi controversy published on Propagandhi's Web site. While he acknowledges the fact that some of George Soros's fortune comes from weapon sales ("that sucks"), he admits he "didn't want an anti-Soros message on the first *Rock Against Bush* comp, because I don't want to make enemies within our movement." (Fat Mike also caused a similar controversy on the Internet when he altered the cover of an Anti-Flag album so it could be sold comfortably at Wal-Mart.)

For many in the neo-punk community, Fat Mike's political moves are hardly surprising. "I guess there are a few groups representing the Republican side of things, but punk seems to have always leaned more toward democracy, if not anarchy," says Agent M of Tsunami Bomb. "Classically, punk seemed to be about chaos and rebellion, but punks nowadays are using their influence to promote the lesser of two evils—i.e., liberalism—instead of dreaming of anarchy."

Just as no one even today can decide on a single definition of what punk is, seemingly no one can figure out exactly what role politics should play in punk, either. "I was just listening to Dicky Barrett from the Mighty Mighty Bosstones on his radio show here in L.A.," says Greg Attonitoi. "A guy who said he was a Republican military man called in and said he loved the show but he didn't agree with the guest Dicky had on the show the day before. The guest was a former soldier who joined the army in the wake of 9/11, wanting to protect his country. In his experience he became disillusioned with the government and their choices. The caller discredited this man's military experience and complained that while he loved Dicky's show and rock music, he wanted to keep politics out of his music. Dicky's answer to him was, 'Everything is political.' I'm going to agree with Dicky on this one. Everything you do and say is making a political statement every moment of your day. Personal and political are not separate."

"If punk is a movement of the mind," adds Attonitoi's bandmate Bryan Kienlen, "an endeavor of young people to change what they are not content with, to find themselves through self-expression, then it is a positive movement and a political movement. The way the Bouncing Souls have chosen to live our lives is our political statement."

Many of the Warped generation still remain active activists, even after signing to major labels. For example, in 2006 Sony issued a "media advisory" about Sony-signed band Anti-Flag's protest activity: "On March 24th, 2006, members of Anti-Flag and Congressman Jim McDermott (D-WA), the legislative leader on Depleted Uranium, will hold a News Conference about the military's use of Depleted Uranium in combat zones, including Iraq, and launch a petition drive. The musicians worked with the congressman on their new song, 'Depleted Uranium Is a War Crime' and premiered it with a congressional action on After Downing Street Coalition's Web site. . . ."

That Anti-Flag collaborated with a politician on a song might produce some scary artistic dividends, but at the least it's not an obvious move for a band in their position. As well, such commitment indicates that Anti-Flag is willing to put their money where their mouth is—that their positions aren't just another aspect of the marketing campaign. Some of Anti-Flag's peers, however, find that living the life of a typical rock star takes precedence over political action, as Kevin Lyman has seen over many a Warped Tour. For Lyman, the environment that today's successful punk band is in encourages bad behavior—another unintended echo of the "hair metal" years. "When I used to work in clubs back then in L.A., there was sex and gangs and people would fight, but now bands are younger," Lyman says. "A lot of them are getting success kinda young and not handling it—instead, they're being juvenile in their behavior. Immediately, they're getting into that juvenile rock phase, like metal bands like Warrant."

Then again, it was maturity that allowed Green Day to write corrosively pointed lyrics like "*Sieg heil* to President Gasman" (from *American Idiot*'s hit "Holiday") and open concerts by saying "Fuck you" to George W. Bush. No, there are still some in punk, even at the top of the food chain, who aren't afraid of any Dixie Chicks–style backlash. "It's just important to be really outspoken," Billie Joe Armstrong told *Entertainment Weekly*.

As such, the punk community remains most fans' gateway into Beltway politics—and beyond into global concerns. In punk rock, knowing who Noam Chomsky is remains a badge of honor; if anything, Chomsky isn't radical enough to withstand the constant questioning of underground punk culture. "I've gotten most of my education through music whether it's the Dead Kennedys or Clash records or just something like the Replacements," Billie Joe Armstrong told the Associated Press. "Music can make a difference in people's lives. It's not just there for entertainment."

Indeed, of all the subcultures, punk rock encourages reading and cultural literacy more than most popular youth movements. Often the political leaning of a city will influence the corresponding punk scene. "D.C. punk was so much more political given the nature of it being the base of politics," says Missy Suicide. "I wouldn't trade my teen years in D.C. for anything because it made me grow up with this ethic of creating music that you want to," says Andrew Black of the Explosion. "It wasn't about creating music for the sake of just playing music, making money, or dictating fashion. It kept me humble."

It's not surprising, then, that D.C. icon Ian MacKaye, frontman for Minor Threat and Fugazi, sees punk rock in revolutionary terms. For MacKaye, punk is the real CNN for the young and not-so-useless.

"For me, what was good about punk rock and what continues to be good about punk rock was that the music was a currency that a lot of people exchanged, and those people were able to be exposed to radically different ideas about, obviously, music, but also about philosophy, lifestyles, sexuality, theology, everything," MacKaye noted in an interview with punrockacademy.com.

MacKaye also founded Dischord Records, which is venerated as one of punk's great record labels of integrity, an independent as divorced as possible from the values and practices of a corrupt music industry (and consequently, from the politics of an even more corrupt society). Yet even the most successful business ventures in the current punk rock world stand as attempts to mix successful, more mass-appeal business approaches with more community-oriented punk values and practice. Epitaph, for one, relishes its totally independent status, free of major label ethical conflicts that come with being a conglomerate. "I run Epitaph based on my ideals," Gurewitz states. "My ideals are about, you know, rebelling against authority, skepticism, individuality, integrity, freedom, and compassion." On his Web site, Fat Mike notes that he, Fat Wreck Chords, and NOFX contribute "tens of thousands of dollars to PETA, Food Not Bombs, and other charities. So, yeah, I make a lot of money, but I don't consider myself a Capitalist in the traditional sense."

Punk's tradition of social consciousness—and legions of devoted fans—has finally made believers out of some icons of contemporary political activism. "Amnesty International didn't want to come [to Warped Tour] at first. Then after they checked it out, they wrote me a letter that was like, 'Oh my God!'" Kevin Lyman says. "They've been to enough U2 shows. The Warped tour is dirty, crazy, and not real focused for them, but if I get fifteen thousand kids a day, they get seven hundred kids signing up. The youth are there: kids are willing to learn more and expose themselves."

Indeed, punk today has an ideology for everyone to find themselves in; sometimes these ideologies evolve and mutate into each other. Still going strong is the straight-edge movement originated in the '80s by Minor Threat and their ilk. "Straight edge is about finding something that you can identify with—something that will give you the answers," says Missy Suicide, who notes there are even straight-edgers among the nude models on suicidegirls.com. "When you're in that adolescent stage and you need some structure, some guidance, it provides that. It's probably more healthy than organized religion."

In fact, the original straight-edge movement and organized religion have made for interesting bedfellows of late. Like everything in punk, the straight-edge faction split into faction upon faction. It shouldn't have been a surprise, but Christian punks have found kinship in straight edge's personal pledge to sobriety and chastity. "Wow, I never would have thought of it until I saw it . . . Christian punk," says Greg Attonitoi of Bouncing Souls. "Why not? Freedom of expression should have no boundaries. Yes, there is room for all." Faith-based bands like Washington State pop-punkers MxPx—beloved by both religious and nonreligious fans alike—began popping up to sate this audience's needs.

"The MxPx guys were vegan, straight-edge Christian punk rockers," says Missy Suicide. "They felt comfortable having boundaries—rules for how they should live their life. Maybe the people that question more are still trying to figure that out."

MxPx first recorded for the label Tooth and Nail, which has become a hugely successful Christian-punk imprint. In fact, Christianity has so pervaded current punk rock that there are numerous bands of the faith that don't advertise their religion directly in song; sometimes you find the Lord working within even neo-punk's most profane, juvenile outfits, like Blink-182. "I'm a believer in Jesus Christ," *Rolling Stone* quotes Blink-182's Tom Delonge for a 2000 cover story on the band. In the same story, Blink bassist Mark Hoppus admits, "I pray before I go onstage, and I pray at night." In a *Threat* magazine interview, Joel Madden of Good Charlotte clarifies his "real relationship with the Creator." At the same time, not all

Christian-identified punk musicians want to be stuck in a pigeonhole so laden with expectations and stigma. "Hey, church is on Sunday, and it's free," MxPx guitarist Tom Wisniewski told the *Las Vegas Weekly* in 2000. "Nobody needs to hear that stuff from us."

Punk and religion have always enjoyed a sometimes confrontational, but almost always contradictory, relationship—typified by that '70s punk moment when Jewish Sex Pistols manager Malcolm McClaren started putting swastikas on T-shirts. At the same time, there's something appropriately, punkishly defiant and shocking about claiming Christian punk solidarity, and yet it's also even more conformist. It's like a two-party system: believe in punk rock and Jesus, ignore the gray area on the way out—or revel in it. "There are definitely some things that are in opposition in Christianity and punk rock, like abortion," says Missy Suicide. "Ninety-nine percent of punk rockers would stand for a woman's right to choose. I'm shocked every day—there's pro-life suicide girls. I don't understand their mentality, but they can be who they wanna be."

"It's evolved," adds Kevin Lyman. "Punk started as a rebellion, anti-establishment, anti-people in power, but it's been twenty-five, thirty years. Now people are just standing up for their individual scenes—standing up for what they believe in. They feel that strongly about it. It's about the energy, the music: you have kids that like rock *and* gospel, and want to espouse their religion." It's not just Christianity, either, as other religions have created safe havens in punk rock for their beliefs. "It's the same reason you see the Hare Krishnas at the Warped Tour," Kevin Lyman says. "The Hare Krishnas have always been an outlet for the street, gutter-punk kid. They've given them families they've never had."

Not surprisingly, however, as faith-based culture becomes more prevalent in America, Christianity remains the biggest elephant in the mosh pit. Indeed, not everyone in neo-punk has jumped on the Christian bandwagon, however, even those coming from religious backgrounds. "I am and most of the band is Catholic, but religious themes in punk are a bit much," says Matt Kelly of the Dropkick Murphys. "I don't really think it's a good idea."

"I really try to refrain from judging everybody and try mostly to concern myself with my own path. Everyone has their own experience of punk and I have mine," Bouncing Souls' Bryan Kienlen explains. "Mine is not, and has never been, 'Christian punk.' My answer is that dogma is the enemy of true freedom."

Religion is really punk's ideological litmus test; what's interesting is finding those who in fact see the shades of gray—who are able to explore the metaphors of religion while maybe protesting some aspect of it. The Distillers have been pretty harsh on religion in songs like "Old Scratch"

("They sell you a religous escapade/You join the church and they take your life away!") or the title track from *Sing Sing Death House* ("I am agnostic but I hang on a cross/Faithless, saintless, my sin stabs"). At the same time, former Catholic schoolgirl Brody Dalle's lyrics are steeped in religious imagery yet also confrontationally critical of faith, producing a provocative, beguiling paradox. More than anything, Dalle's lyrics touch on how religion has lost its spiritual aspect. "Religion is sick—talk about the perils of the world!" Dalle says. "That is the root of all evil as far as I'm concerned. I'm not talking about spirituality; I'm talking about *patriarchal* religion based on lies and corruption. Religion started with a great scripture that has just been corrected, conformed and raped, basically."

For some, the anti-authoritarian, resolute-in-his-beliefs Jesus in many ways could be the original punk. "I started a band called Bad Religion and all, so I don't want this to turn into some you know, Christian-bashing thing," says Brett Gurewitz, who was raised in Judaism. "Personally, I'm not anti-Christian at all. In fact, for the record, I think Christianity is a beautiful thing. Christ was probably one of the most revolutionary progressive liberals in history. There's nothing he wanted to do more than fight and tear down the power. The problem is not with Christ's teachings—the problem is with the fanatics, and the establishment."

Neo-punk's embrace of Christianity suggests, in fact, that punk now mirrors cultural trends and social mores more than it necessarily critiques them. In this way, the punk scene has become a microcosm of society rather than a subcultural response to it. "These Christian punk bands and these Web sites of conservative punk are a function of a grassroots, conservative groundswell in America," Gurewitz explains. "There are even patriotic oi! bands out there. I think it's a scary kind of America right now: the political pendulum is swinging to the right, hopefully about as far right as it can get."

Gurewitz holds a surprising take on the zeitgeist circa now: in his eyes, it is paradoxically the conservatives, and not punk rockers, who are most showing the birthright of 1960s revolutionary politics. "What the country's going through is a conservative revolution that's akin to the progressive revolution that happened in the '60s. Little conservative kids buy records in Christian bookstores with the approval of their parents, who go to big rallies with other Christians, to hear evangelical preachers and evangelical rock bands, filling places like Dodger Stadium. It's a genuine, organic, grassroots conservative movement; I'm not necessarily comparing Christians to Hitler—that isn't the case at all—but the Nazis and Hitler Youth were coming from the same thing. That's what scares me so much."

Indeed, Gurewitz's example demonstrates that there are limits to punk tolerance. "I won't sign a punk band if they're evangelical Christians who are rallying for George Bush," he says. Yet the conservative movement has encroached on pop culture in its omnipresence. Through television icons like Bill O'Reilly, Bush-supporting celebrities like Bruce Willis and accidental politician Arnold Schwarzenegger, the all-consuming media saturation of the Iraq war, and the phenomenon of Mel Gibson's *Passion of the Christ*, conservative culture has *become* pop culture, competing with the likes of Madonna and Brad Pitt in the tabloid's column inches.

The Offspring even have a song, "Neocon," that deals with the conservative phase America has been in for some time. A blunt, Ramonesian first-person look into the mind of a power-mad conservative, "Neocon" ends with multiple repetitions of "We will never lose to you!" Such a cultural mash-up is what inspired Green Day, in fact, to create *American Idiot*—to take action in the aftermath. "Reality television meets news and war . . . tanks going into Baghad with splashes of Viagra commercials in between. I was just so confused about what was going on," Billie Joe Armstrong told the Associated Press. "[*American Idiot*] comes from that standpoint. It's unavoidable, being in the United States right now [with] what's been going on in the past couple years . . ."

Recent events in the world, however, make some in the neo-punk world feel that the situation is beyond the analytical abilities of the typical punk musician. The result is an awkward combination of apathy and awareness. "My beliefs about politics are that I don't really want to get involved, and especially not with music. I've never been a political person, and I don't feel like I should start just because I sing in a band," says Tsunami Bomb's Agent M. "Me personally being involved in politics is like a dentist being involved in filmmaking. I don't really want to have anything to do with politics."

Agent M's aware that just by saying this, she could be causing another ideological Internet punk meltdown. "That stance might not go over well with people who work with punkvoter.com, because they want influential people to help communicate with the kids. I understand that," she says. "I think it's great that punkvoter gets people involved, but I'm just not one of those people. A lot of people may think that's a really crappy stance, but I am honest about it."

As well, an anti-p.c. element within punk rock has begun to unwittingly resemble conservative thinking, even if those making such statements would never label themselves conservative. "There is a sense of political correctness which almost becomes strangling after a while. A lady sued McDonald's because she spilled hot coffee on herself; it's getting to the point where you're going to have to put a sign on the window that says 'Don't jump out of this window' when you're in a hotel," says the Offspring's Dexter Holland. "They're just going to put iron bars up because they'll be afraid of the liability. That sense of trying to protect, and being p.c., ends up inhibiting your freedom more."

More controversial, however—and interesting—are the actual conservative punks: Joe Escalante, drummer of the Vandals and owner of Kung-Fu Records, is infamous as the fulcrum for West Coast punk rock's politically conservative elite. Not surprisingly, however, Escalante doesn't hold the momentum that power liberalism still maintains in punk rock. "Warped went out with punkvoter.com because Fat Mike believes in that," Kevin Lyman says. "Joe Escalante has different political views: if he was really as passionate, he should've organized conservative punkers on that level. They would've been welcome."

In fact, Lyman claims that the Warped Tour has become an equal opportunity "sounding board" for the various political currents zapping through the neo-punk scene. Well, almost equal. "Everyone's opposing views are there—that's why we've had problems," Lyman says. "I let the Marines come in. Up to a certain point, I have no problems with the Marines because they've been an outlet for kids: a lot of people I knew in the L.A. punk scene went into the service and came back and were able to go to school and get an education. I may have a problem, however, with where our leader sends our Marines. The only ones I wouldn't allow at the shows were those with straight racist views. I couldn't do it; I keep my political views out of it, but that's one thing I couldn't do. We were actually contacted by the John Birch Society; they wanted to come out to Warped Tour, but I said no."

In the 1980s, a punk band called themselves Reagan Youth, putting an ironic yet pointed twist on Hitler youth. Now, however, we're dealing with the real children of the Reagan revolution; since many of today's punk fans and band members were born in the midst of the Reagan era, they have often known nothing different, especially if their parents vote Republican. And because many can only trace their punk-rock lineage back to the more apolitical Green Day of the mid-'90s, the idea that radicalized politics even remains in punk's gene pool was a faint concept until the most recent U.S. election. "I voted for Bush in 2000," Yellowcard's Ryan Key admitted to *Rolling Stone* in a special 2004 election piece. "I was fresh out of high school. That's the way my parents were voting, so I just voted that way." Key's confession indicates that, thanks to immersion in punk's more open-minded world, he'd seen the error of his ways. "If I could take it back," Key concludes, "I would."

"Kids are starting to care again. Everything was so easy for so long," Kevin Lyman explains. "Your first election, ninety percent of people vote like their parents. My dad and mom were Republicans; I was a registered

Republican until last year. I didn't vote that way ever, but I finally switched it over just because it was convenient at that moment. People make choices as they mature. We have to become more involved. Maybe we *can* make a little change."

Perhaps where change is most needed remains in the area of race. Punk rock has always had a tentative relationship to racial politics that, on the one hand, has produced some of punk's most exciting, vital commentaries that convey just how electric this issue remains in society. The Clash's "White Man in Hammersmith Palais," one of the greatest punk anthems ever, describes the racial incongruity of attending a London reggae concert and realizing you're the only Caucasian in the crowd. The Clash's "White Riot," on the other hand, stems from an altercation witnessed by Clash members between black British youth and the police at London's annual Carnival street party. "White Riot" 's sentiment is that whites need to study the passion of oppressed minorities and have "a riot of [their] own." "White Minority" by Black Flag, on the other hand, is a potent satire brutally depicting an inevitable transition in power: the tables-turning moment when those who have been downtrodden as the minority now enjoy the power of majority rule. That "White Minority" was originally sung by a Mexican-American gives it even greater *frisson*.

Minor Threat's "Guilty of Being White," meanwhile, confronts head-on the potentially politically incorrect thoughts even an open-minded individual could feel about race. "Guilty . . ." describes Minor Threat singer Ian MacKaye's frustration at getting beaten up at his school in the largely African-American Washington, D.C., area every time *Roots* was shown on television—a situation due entirely to the fact that, just because MacKaye's white, he's considered part of a "racist plan," regardless of his actual beliefs or participation. In other words, the day after *Roots'* brutal scenes of shameful history are televised, MacKaye's skin color symbolizes "slave owner" all the more vividly, even though he was born long after slavery ended. This reverse racism confuses MacKaye, yet the result is powerful: "Guilty of Being White" is the cathartic sound of someone struggling with the gaps their belief system, however open-minded, didn't provide for.

"Guilty of Being White" is Minor Threat at its most scathingly personal *and* political. At the same time, punk rock songs about race walk a hazardous ideological tightrope. Such songs are typically misunderstood by those incapable of irony and prone to violence; without an irony dividing rod, songs like "White Minority" and "Guilty of Being White" can become unwitting anthems of hate in the wrong ears—ears that hear what they want to hear in a song, regardless of artistic intent.

Racism has long been on the punk rock radar, from the times when the

Clash played antiracism gigs and a drunken Elvis Costello called Ray Charles a "blind, ignorant nigger" in public earshot, a screwup he hasn't entirely ever lived down. Punk rock's complicated relationship with racism in fact gave the scene a tension, an edge of real-life urban danger and urbane irony: primordial punk group the London S.S. took its name from National Socialism, yet was founded by a Jew, future Clash guitarist Mick Jones. One of the greatest essays to come out of the earlier punk subculture was Lester Bangs's 1979 piece "The White Noise Supremacists," which cut a deep swath through punk's contradictory racist attitudes.

In more contemporary punk, artists like NOFX tweak racial attitudes with album titles like 1992's *White Trash, Two Heebs and a Bean*, which spells out the band's ethnic makeup in the most offensive way possible. NOFX songs like "Kill All the White Man" and "Don't Call Me White" build on the satirical provocateur tradition of punk songs like Black Flag's "White Minority"; they're defiantly anti-p.c., equal opportunity offenders.

"The only thing I ever remember being anything close to 'rules' within the punk scene were rules against racism, sexism, homophobia," says Bouncing Soul Bryan Kienlen. "But intolerance also kills." According to Missy Suicide, the volatile righteousness and potential for violence surrounding ideological debate in punk rock gave it a heightened, adolescent melodrama. "You had a clear-cut enemy—you were either a Jet or a S.H.A.R.P.!," Missy Suicide says of the *West Side Story*-style divisions in the punk scene, each of whom only saw the world in their vision of literal black or white. (S.H.A.R.P. stands for "Skinheads Against Racial Prejudice," a group that felt it was justifiably open season to beat up anyone with racist beliefs.) "You had that one team you were against," Suicide continues. "Everything you stood for was clear-cut good and evil!"

For actual minorities, however, their relationship is anything *but* clear-cut within the punk scene. The early punk world on both sides of the Atlantic was not necessarily a bastion of racial tolerance, yet it was openly indebted to black music. The Clash and the Sex Pistols were both huge reggae fans, and helped introduce a largely white audience to West Indian roots music. The Clash also revered American black music titans like Screamin' Jay Hawkins, Chuck Berry, and Bo Diddley. Don Letts, a black Briton of West Indian descent, was a crucial part of the Clash's entourage: as band videographer, he helped define the Clash's visual image, and later collaborated with Mick Jones in Jones's post-Clash group Big Audio Dynamite. Letts is most famed in punk history, however, for playing reggae music as the DJ for famed London punk club the Roxy, turning on a whole generation of innovative musicians to a punky reggae party.

And in early New York punk, African-American Ivan Julian played a key role in expanding the genre's sonic vocabulary as one-half of the innovative guitar team driving Richard Hell and the Voidoids. The Ramones and Blondie also were heavily influenced by Motown's girl-group soul of the 1960s, adapting its anachronistic sound into their decidedly contemporary attack.

Outside New York, over in Washington, D.C., the Bad Brains, one of the most brilliant bands of the hardcore movement regardless of their racial makeup, made punk rock black music, whether it chose to be or not. At their peak, the Bad Brains took no prisoners. Their best moments highlighted the band's mind-numbing live intensity, jazzy but rarely self-indulgent virtuousity, volatile group interplay, and a spiritual, political, and sonic embrace of the group's West Indian roots. As a result, the Bad Brains at their height might just knock out their hometown followers Minor Threat out of competition for the honor of greatest American hardcore band ever.

Bands like Rancid have followed their Clash influence into their own healthy interest in reggae and bluebeat. Rancid have in fact recorded in Jamaica and collaborated with contemporary dancehall stars like Buju Banton. Today, however, there aren't that many persons of color working as punk musicians in nationally scaled bands: Yellowcard drummer Longineu Parsons, who has played with George Clinton and studied jazz under icons like Max Roach, is African-American, and his virtuosity plays a crucial part in the Yellowcard sound. However, Parsons's example is rare.

"Punk has always been a male, white-dominated subculture for some reason. I think other races have cultural frameworks and identifying roles to attach themselves to, whereas the typical American white male doesn't. So he attaches himself to punk," says Dropkick Murphys' Matt Kelly. "With the welcoming, all-for-one sentiment in punk, I'd think it'd be more racially diverse. In some places, it obviously is, but all in all, it's very white male dominated."

For underground African-American rapper Murs, who spent many weeks on the Warped Tour as "hype man" to white "emo rap" group Atmosphere, being a minority within the neo-punk community can become a sort of "White Man in Hammersmith Palais" in reverse. "I had this conversation with Slug from Atmosphere, who's one of my best friends in the industry," Murs explains. "On the Warped Tour, we had the time of our lives, but he was happy for different reasons. I had a great time because I was experiencing a new culture, but it wasn't because I was living out my dream. If I was a white kid into drinking beer every night with tattooed white girls, I would've made it. Right now, it's bad to be a black underground rapper."

At the same time, there are new groups that challenge the conventional white male stereotype of neo-punk. Go Betty Go, a quartet of young Latinas from the Los Angeles valley suburb of Glendale, California, have created quite a stir on the neo-punk scene. Singing in both English and Spanish, Go Betty Go make pop punk that's as catchy as it is surprisingly vulnerable and unpretentious. Go Betty Go transcend their more juvenile peers, however, through documentary—by capturing exactly the mood of their environment: what it must feel like to be a young urban woman between cultures just trying to live. There's a message behind Go Betty Go, but it never devolves into didacticism.

The band Whole Wheat Bread, meanwhile, tweaks any number of punk's racial stereotypes—and beyond. A trio of African-Americans from Jacksonville, Florida, Whole Wheat Bread flips expectations by making hooky, basic pop punk that's more the province of young white males while looking more like of gangsta rappers; in the case of Whole Wheat Bread bassist Nicholas Largen, Whole Wheat Bread also have a prison/crime background someone like 50 Cent could spin whole albums out of (Largen spent a year in prison, and has a rap sheet that includes over seventeen felonies). "Being in a band with my brother is great," states Nicholas Largen's brother Joe, who plays drums for Whole Wheat Bread, in a press release. "Someone has to be there to keep him out of prison!"

The band's name in fact belies their uniqueness: if "white bread" is the racially coded standard for "generic" and "soulless," then "whole wheat bread" must be the opposite, right? Regardless of whether they fit the genre's racial archetypes, Whole Wheat Bread make totally credible neo-punk. Their indie 2005, debut, *Minority Rules*, is produced in appropriately crude fashion by neo-punk studio vet Darian Rundall (who's worked with biggies like Yellowcard and Pennywise). Still, despite the band's 'core genre cred, it's still an eyebrow-raising experience to hear a pop punk band sing about getting "busted for possession" and dropping lines charged with racial identity conflict like "It ain't because I'm black, it's because I don't have a thing/I'm nineteen years old and broke as fuck." Indeed, it's disconcerting to hear words dripping inner-city blues like "Mr. Police Officer, we're not doing nothing wrong/Take your damn hands off of us or we're not gonna get along," sung as in the same aesthetic as a Blink-182 love song.

At the same time as they play punk under their "real" names, Whole Wheat Bread incorporate surprisingly credible hardcore hip-hop into their act, the members even maintaining separate gangsta rap personas with ironic street aliases like Nasty Nigga Fleetwood, DJ Dirtee Skeet, and Mr. Whitefolks. It's a cultural contradiction that Whole Wheat Bread revels in; at some point, in the future, it most likely won't be the contradiction, but, in fact, the norm. Bands like Whole White Bread won't be crashing the party anymore—they *will* be the party.

"People joke about us looking like NWA but sounding like Green Day," says Aaron Abraham in the band's official bio. "I'd say we live our lives naturally somewhere in-between . . . edgy, but full of emotion. I got into Green Day at a young age, which was exactly the same time I started playing guitar."

The ethnic, racial, and gender makeup of punk bands definitely affects one's unconscious perception and embrace of that band's outlook. The Dropkick Murphys, for example, exude a special vitality due to the embrace of their Irish heritage and all that means politically and culturally. Meanwhile, a band like the Distillers holds a unique kind of political charge in the contemporary punk scene simply because they're fronted by a strong, independent, outspoken woman. In terms of politics, however, the Distillers stand out because of Brody Dalle's complex, literary songwriting on the topic.

Typically, the majority of neo-punk bands verge on the generic, simplistic, or at worst nostalgic when approaching political topics; Pennywise's "American Dream" comes to mind. There are exceptions, however, to punk's time-tested-into-cliché political tropes. For Brody Dalle, the universe is bigger than punk rock, and we can't ever forget it. Her songs are a cry for substance in a genre where moaning about one's girlfriend troubles has become neo-punk's all-too-typical lyrical template. They're not so much in the protest tradition as they are analytical and impressionistic. Reading the Distillers' lyrics, one doesn't find any easy answers—just the pregnant, evocative problems and questions that make life strange, dangerous, and vital.

"I think there's always a place you can draw from and it's usually the human condition," Dalle told the Seattle alt-weekly *The Stranger* in 2003. "It's something we struggle with constantly. Trying to unravel the human spirit and figure stuff out, it's what it's all about. It's not all roses and candy. You don't have to look too far to see that."

Ultimately, the power of music trumps politics, even when they're seemingly intertwined. "From a musical standpoint, [*American Idiot*] is just incredible. I can't stop playing it. The politics don't bug me that much," says Nick Rizzuto, co-founder of the online forum conservativepunk.com, in an *Entertainment Weekly* article on Green Day. Rizzuto's stance isn't surprising. Since the dawn of the original punks, the world's political spectrum has expanded. The old enemies have been replaced. This not-so-brave new world is ultimately a more complicated place, with grayer areas between good and evil, right and wrong, black and white. While dogmatic factions within punk certainly still exist, the manifold options and opinions more likely result in an iPod approach to choosing one's ideological stance in the community. Straight-edge and Christian? Why not? Pro-choice and pro-Iraq war? Okay. Anti-abortion and anti-Republican? It happens. Voted for Bush and sing in a punk rock band? Not unlikely.

Punk's ideological melting pot remains a relevant prism through which to see today's world and process the traumatic events of contemporary life. The 1977-vintage "White Man in Hammersmith Palais" by the Clash features a line—"If Adolph Hitler were here today, they'd send a limousine anyway"—that seems oddly prescient: the song, while almost thirty years old, could be describing the contemporary mindset in just that one line. "It's so much easier to sample bits of culture—that's more prevalent these days," says Missy Suicide. "I don't think that anybody subscribes to that John Hughes mentality where everybody has to be compartmentalized. Everybody takes from what is relevant to them—and everyone has a different perspective on life; different things speak to them on different levels."

Defining oneself against the tension among radical, conservative, and radically conservative as the Clash do in "White Man in Hammersmith Palais" is one way that punk has remained relevant through the years, even in its most defanged, chart-friendly state. Yet ultimately what is most political and threatening about punk is its embrace of the concept of freedom and liberation.

For some in punk, freedom means living by rules; for others, freedom is defined by the rejection of rules and boundaries. Some punks see freedom in communist manfestoes or anarchist graffiti, some in Jesus. Others never want to move out of their parents' basement—and the suburban mentality. A wave-loving band like Pennywise is naturally going to be attracted to causes like the Surfrider Foundation, a self-proclaimed "nonprofit environmental organization working to preserve our oceans, waves & beaches" that allows for thinking both globally and locally. Even cute, party-hardy MTV faves Sum 41 have been forced to define what freedom really means to them: they found their social consciousness woken from its slumber when confronted with the deadly reality of global politics. Sum 41 in fact named their 2004 album *Chuck* after the U.N. worker who whisked the group to safety when they came under fire during a humanitarian awareness stop in Africa's Congo, a state perennially thrashed by violent civil war.

Punk continues to embody all these concepts, and probably a few more, in the individual's conception of freedom. As a result, in oppressed countries from Europe to the Middle East and beyond, punk still stands as the freedom aesthetic—in the very places where embracing such a concept is against the law. "What's so great about America is the concept of freedom. I believe in personal freedom to the utmost," explains the Offspring's Dexter Holland. "The flip side of that is that you have to have the utmost personal responsibility—you can't just blame other people if you fuck up."

"You know, writing a line like 'Maybe I'm the faggot America/I'm not a part of the redneck agenda'—it was such a release to write it," Billie Joe Armstrong recently told *Threat* magazine. "And then, afterward, when we were listening to it, I was like, 'Does anybody mind if I'm saying that?' And Mike [Dirnt, Green Day's bassist] was like, 'You can say anything you want.'"

Saying anything you want—now *that's* punk!

PUNK IS: *the personal expression of uniqueness that comes from the experiences of growing up in touch with our human ability to reason and ask questions . . . PUNK IS: a movement that serves to refute social attitudes that have been perpetuated through willful ignorance of human nature. . . . a process of questioning and commitment to understanding that results in self-progress, and by extrapolation, could lead to social progress . . . [It is] a belief that this world is what we make of it, truth comes from our understanding of the way things are, not from the blind adherence to prescriptions about the way things should be.*

—*Greg Graffin,* "A Punk Manifesto"

8

... That the objection of indelicacy and impropriety, which is so often brought against woman when she addresses a public audience, comes with a very ill-grace from those who encourage, by their attendance, her appearance on the stage, in the concert.

—Elizabeth Cady Stanton,
the Seneca Falls Declaration of 1848

Women on display at Suicide Girls look a lot like the indie-rock chicks you'd expect to see at a Strokes show but never thought you'd get to see naked. . . . Suddenly, Suicide Girls starts to look less like regular porn, and more like—well, more like porn for people who cry to the Smiths but ain't gonna let that get in the way of a little sumpin' sumpin'.

—Nick Phillips, "Cynical, Bitter, Jaded as Hell.
Also Naked," *City Pages*, November 27, 2002

In 2003, Brody Dalle was asked to be a "suicide girl"—the online punk equivalent of *Playboy*, a "punk erotica" Web site that has become a media-hype sensation. Brody's response? "I was like hell no—are they crazy?," she says. "No fucking *way*, dude."

Brody is a big deal on suicidegirls.com, where she and her band, the

207

Distillers, remain a constant subject of threads and the site's online groups. One of the SGs (as the young women who pose nude and maintain their own personal blog pages on the site are called) is named "Sphinx" (on suicidegirls.com, the models have just one name only, and it's almost always fake, like a stripper's stage moniker). Sphinx in particular appears to have a heavy Brody/Distillers fixation. In her starkers photo sets, this twenty-year-old Canadian (who shares her astrological sign, Capricorn, with Dalle) twists her hair into liberty spikes that pay exact homage to one of Brody's numerous radical hair phases. In the "gets me hot" section in the biographical section of her page on suicidegirls.com, Sphinx lists both Brody Dalle and the Distillers, separately.

It's not a surprise that Brody gets Suicide Girls hot and bothered—or that the Web site asked her to model (although probably not at the regular rate of $200 to $400 a "set," as most suicidegirls get). To the SGs, Brody fits the suicide girls' visual and ideological stereotype.

Like many SGs, Brody has embroidered her flesh with piercings and not-so-subtle tattoos—an Asiatic line drawing on one bicep, the words "Fuck you" on the other, an unfortunate "punx" scribble on her hand. Brody's hair color and style changes with her moods, and she's moody. Her clothes are aggressive and sexy, but on her terms, expressing what her idea of sexy is (think death, by sexy). She's no girly-girl, but Brody's definitely a woman, tough, but no tomboy—and attractive enough conventionally to be listed among Maxim's hottest babes of 2004 (albeit at number ninety-five!). Brody's style and sexuality are aggressive and individual, yet her appeal both beyond the fringe and to it belies a tug between traditional feminine ideals and unconventionality. This paradox was defined most clearly in an August 2004 Q&A between Brody and her pal, Garbage's Shirley Manson, in *Interview* magazine.

"All I want to do is nest and have babies right now; I don't want to fucking be on tour," Dalle confesses to Manson. "[Domesticity] becomes an extreme desire, huh? Like, yes, I want a garden, and I want to get my nails dirty. . . . All I can think about right now is fucking being pregnant and cooking dinner."

The image of a mumu-sporting barefoot and pregnant Brody Dalle on hands and knees in the garden deeply conflicts with the staunchly independent woman rocker persona Dalle has presented in both the media and song. Or does it? Reality often doesn't conform to persona. On January 17, 2006, Brody hit the gossip pages and message boards again: on that day, Dalle gave birth to a daughter, Camille Homme (Camille takes her last name from her father, Josh Homme of Queens of the Stone Age).

"There's no reason why you can't be both," says Missy Suicide. "A lot of women felt like they needed to repress their femininity and their natural instincts in order to be perceived as hard or punk rock. There's no reason you can't have a kid and enjoy being a mother. The ability to have kids is one of the gifts of being a woman. Yeah, that is really punk rock!"

For Brody Dalle, strong maternal figures have been crucial figureheads in her life: "I love the women who raised me. I'm very close to my mother. It wasn't until I was about seventeen years old and moved back home that I started to have an incredible respect for her."

Brody's seemingly contradictory qualities are in fact not so surprising. Exploring sexuality and gender identity in punk rock makes for a strange journey wherever one enters into the equation. When punk began, it had a pansexual edge to it. Conventional sexuality was mocked by in-your-face S&M elements. The homoerotic irony of straight ragamuffin boys sporting leather and studs, all bouncing into each other in hot, sweaty punk clubs with their shirts off, was not lost on many.

For women, punk added extra dimensions of gender identity. On one level, punk was glamour with a revolutionary mandate. One aspect of punk style advocated the use of makeup as war paint, grotesquely exaggerating the beautifying role of makeup for women in society by turning it into something garish and grotesque. Androgyny, in all its Sapphic and butch undertones, was celebrated; the transgressive, adored. For the early punks, sexuality was worn openly like a badge, but it was an ambiguous, perhaps mixed message. To early punks, sex represented everything real about the dark amphetamine comedown of supposedly groovy '70s carnal knowledge.

Punk sexuality always typically represented underground currents. But as the neo-punk phenomenon hit the mainstream, however, punk style and all its semiotic signifiers changed in the process. What was taboo before was now available at the mall for $19.99—even body modification like a nipple pierce.

On the one hand, punk style and sexuality entering the mainstream is a potentially good thing: it opens up the conventional idea of beauty to a greater range of expression and individuality. But it also encourages conformity to a punk "look" that's now all too easily assembled at Hot Topic. What was once truly shocking to see on a punk—a Mohawk, studded belt, big, mean boots—is now conventional high-street, low-rent fashion. Even Janet Jackson has a nipple adornment, as football fans and Justin Timberlake discovered one fateful Super Bowl Sunday in 2004.

This new ideal of beauty and sexuality is intrinsically tied to shifting ideas of female empowerment and all its attendant ironies. When *The Beauty Myth* was first published in 1991, the irony was that its author,

Naomi Wolf, was so conventionally attractive; critics sniped that only an attractive woman could become a superstar author writing about how beauty has enslaved our society. Around the same time, punk rock had become even more male-dominated and macho (and unwittingly homoerotic) as it began to marinate in mainstream waters. This isn't so surprising: the establishment has never been a bastion of radical female empowerment; instead, it's typically driven by the most conventional, white male culture possible—a group most glacially resistant to change. Once punk rock started making big money, it not surprisingly took on more macho establishment characteristics. What sexuality exists in commercial neo-punk, for example, tends toward the cartoon juvenilia of a band like Blink-182, which has more in common with frat boys' ideas of women than, say, Siouxsie Sioux's or Bikini Kill's. Even more shocking is when one sometimes notices in neo-punk the absence of anything resembling sexuality at all: it's clean-shaven and buff like a frat boy, and sometimes even straight-edge celibate.

Some factions of neo-punk represent a retro sexuality for a millennial era: safe, comfortable, and far from the dangerous, naughty S&M culture of the Sex Pistols. In this meltdown of conventional gender roles and today's alternative lifestyles, where do the women of the neo-punk movement fit in? Or even those who don't fit the current manifestation of the genre's conventional heterosexual dude orthodoxy?

Brody Dalle: The Ultimate Suicide Girl?

In the eyes of some SGs, in many ways Brody Dalle is a sort of ultimate Suicide Girl, the one who made it—she's famous but has her integrity, is valued for her creativity, *and* hooks up with supercool creative (and hot) anti-authority icons like Rancid's Tim Armstrong and Queens of the Stone Age's Josh Homme. She is the aspiration, the dream, the ideal of a generation of young, nude counterculture femmes: if her contrary bad self can make it on her own terms, then maybe one of them will, too.

"Being a Suicide Girl and all that, we do focus on Brody because she's a total symbol for everything that we stand for," explains "Bee Suicide," a model on the SG Web site and an active part of its community. "She's just very open, and not about bullshit or what other people think. It's all about finding your own ideals within yourself and becoming that, instead of relying on conditioning. Brody's the truth—and the whole band portrays that."

According to Missy Suicide, Brody Dalle is "definitely a suicide girl, if you're using it as an adjective." "She does what she wants to do, and doesn't let her creativity be stifled by anybody," Suicide continues. "She embraces who she is even though she's not stereotypical. She's beautiful but she's not Gwen Stefani: she doesn't capitalize or market herself as just a pretty face. Brody has the perception of being in control in a band that's all men. Her gender has never affected her street cred—she expresses herself unashamedly, and always is whoever she wants to be. She uses her femininity, but not as a crutch, and is honest about her experiences and shares her life. It doesn't matter if she's woman or man: she is who she is. It's hard to be a role model. You can't deny your nature."

According to Missy Suicide, that, ultimately, is the message of suicidegirls.com. "You have to be true to yourself," Suicide says. "You can't try to be any one thing. For me, changing hair color and piercings and tattoos are very personal choices to express yourself. If you have all these options, why limit yourself to one? Appearance is the first way people perceive you, and Suicide Girls have more room to play with that."

Missy claims that, in fact, there is no stereotype to the SGs despite some fairly common signifiers. Just because these are live nude girls doesn't mean they're dumb ones. "SGs are going to fuck with your perception," she says. "One of the girls on the site just got her doctorate in math—in, like, string theory. It's a subtle fuck you to stereotypes, like, 'I can be a doctoral candidate mom with pink hair who goes to punk rock shows and poses nude. I can do whatever the fuck I want to.'"

For Missy Suicide, when choosing a potential Suicide Girl, it all comes down to one thing: attitude. "All the girls are comfortable and confident in who they are, and uncompromising. The same characteristics can be found in Brody," Suicide says. "An SG that, say, lives in the middle-of-nowhere Michigan, of the thirty people in her town, she'll be the fiercely independent one. Suicide Girls give those people someone who they can relate to, who lets them know they're not freaks."

"Rae," as this petite, beautiful Filipina-American model is known on SG's Web site, initially discovered Brody and the Distillers via an online discussion thread on suicidegirls.com. "I've been intrigued by her," Rae says. "It seems like Brody's a really strong person. I like how she does what she wants to do and doesn't care about anybody else. I really admire her for that."

For Rae, Brody's appeal is simultaneously visual, sexual, and ideological: "The way she looks—her makeup, 'body mods,' tattoos—all that is obviously very us, but it's her attitude toward life that's *really* like Suicide Girls. Suicide girls do what they wanna do in life, whether someone else wants them to or not."

To that end, Rae is particularly impressed by Brody's prominent "Fuck Off" tattoo. "Not a lot of people will get a 'fuck off' tattoo—that's really ballsy," Rae notes. In fact, Rae once planned to get a tattoo inspired by the Distillers' song "City of Angels" and its haunted images of angels with "dead wings." "I wanted the tattoo to be an angel, but her wings are torn into pieces across my back and her boobs are scarred," Rae explains. "She's really torn, but the way she stands to be strong. That's basically what Brody, the Suicide Girls, and I all have in common—we stand strong even though people judge us."

According to Missy Suicide, Suicide Girls' aesthetic definitely evolved out of "the punk rock ethic." It's a discipline, a code those on the inside recognize. "The punk rock aesthetic definitely appeals to most of the girls," she explains. "That aesthetic takes from Debbie Harry to Siouxsie Sioux through Peaches. There's a total package that goes into it."

That package captures the whole range of female beauty ideals, tying it up in a postmodern package that raggedly samples and tweaks the style from various eras for their iconic power. "On SG, there will be throwbacks to old glamour, too, like Audrey Hepburn's classic 'cat-eye' style," Suicide explains. "Everyone's kind of a collage artist—they just take what appeals to them and put it all into a package that speaks to them."

The House That Suicide Built

Today, the Suicide Girls operation works out of an airy, tasteful bungalow-style Los Angeles house set up amid the trees of the Hollywood Hills. Suicide Girls HQ actually lies directly in the shadow of the Hollywood sign, which looms ominously in the background every time one of the SG faithful wanders out for a cigarette break.

Inside, the SG environment hums along with an almost entirely feminine milieu, from the shy, kohl-eyed beauties in pulled-up hoodies and Converse high tops hovering studiously over Apple computers to the pneumatic Vargas pinups hanging on the soft peach walls. It's an utterly serene, quiet, nurturing working environment, but appearances deceive: with its eight busy employees, the SG house is a real place of serious, nose-to-the-grindstone business. The SG's promise of unalloyed hedonism isn't going to be found here: cranking out epic amounts of punk erotica to be consumed online every day takes *work*.

Viewing the SG's work scene—the boxes stuffed with officially SG-branded panties overflowing out of the corners, the muted intensity amid tangled wires and servers—one realizes how much it recalls the era of the dot-com boom. The environment makes clear just how much suicide-girls.com is really just another Internet startup company, but with a twist that might actually let it survive. Unlike most of those ultimately doomed startups, suicidegirls.com fills a void in the culture, and makes money off it—"turning rebellion into money," as the Clash sang in "White Man in Hammersmith Palais."

The SG phenomenon, started, however, a few years earlier in Portland, Oregon, where Missy Suicide grew up. The SG aesthetic comes directly out of Portland's open-minded counterculture. "In Portland, nobody messes with one another," Suicide explains. "1977-style punk rock kids share the same space peacefully with 1969 burnout hippies."

Suicide notes that before Nike and Intel came to Portland and Seattle got Boeing and Microsoft, the Pacific Northwest was not known as a center of industry. "Logging doesn't necessarily breed the most educated people in the world," she shrugs, admitting that she eventually had to move the SG business out to Los Angeles for better access to the entertainment industry. But that the concept evolved in Portland was crucial in SG's development. Being in a liberal backwater away from the media glare allowed Missy and her art school pals to foster their own local microbrew variation on youth subculture.

"Everybody was exposed to different countercultures—and feminism," Suicide explains of her hometown's uniquely volatile cultural mix. "Most of the riot grrls' mothers were more feminist than your typical Midwestern soccer mom. But there's a biker mentality and a white trash element, too, mixed in with Portland's very big history of protest, rebellion, and activism. It's kind of a melting pot of all those things."

Portland kids would accordingly synthesize various youth culture styles according to local taste. In the process, the area's communal, hippie-activist roots got spiked by its new urban renegades. The scene became more female-driven—and sexually independent—than those in many other cities. The Pacific Northwest region, lest we forget, managed to nurture both Courtney Love and Kathleen Hanna into the cultural touchstones they are today to the SGs.

"Growing up in Portland, there were two very distinct factions: the 'all men are rapists' riot-grrl punks and then the whole Courtney Love thing—the powerful little girl in a baby-doll dress," Suicide recalls. "I don't think the riot grrls were so into nudity so much. But then there's the whole strip-club culture—and it's definitely a culture. There's not a lot of other places where you can be tattooed and pierced and still get a job."

Suicide Girls made up the sum of all those parts and more: looking like the tattooed punk rock betty cheerleaders in Nirvana's "Smells Like Teen Spirit" video, the members of the SG movement hung around Portland's city center and generally made a scene out of their urban survivalist alternative lifestyle. Novelist Chuck Palahniuk (*Fight Club*) unwittingly gave the SG style a name thanks to some particularly expressive imagery.

in his book, *Survivor*, which struck a nerve. " 'The suicide girls calling with hair wet down in the rain in a public telephone booth' was the phrase," Palahniuk noted in an interview on suicidegirls.com with Daniel Robert Epstein. "[The 'suicide girls'] were young women in distress."

Their distress was real, as was their sexual-identity crisis. For Missy Suicide, if there was going to be a SG revolution, it had to start first by retrofitting that most basic of instincts. "I was repressed and didn't express my sexuality," Suicide says. "I had an inner embarrassment about enjoying sex. I'm trying to show with suicidegirls that they shouldn't be embarrassed of their sexuality."

The key innovation of SG's aesthetic was to find the place where the egalitarian punk inclusiveness of indie-activist bands could coexist with a complex, independent, and active version of female sexuality. "Even the most pious Christians get laid," Suicide says. "They didn't have to have bodies like Tyra Banks or Cindy Crawford—they could be proud of their bodies."

The SG phenomenon in many ways recalls a return to the art school influence that distilled the ideology of punk bands like the Sex Pistols and the Clash into a recognizable, wearable aesthetic. Missy Suicide is very much a product of her local public school system's emphasis on creativity: growing up "solidly middle class," she took up photography in junior high, later went to art school in Portland, and still is the main photographer of the SG models.

The art school aesthetic figures deeply into the environments each SG creates themselves to shoot their "sets" in: there's a homemade, Andy-Warhol-via-John-Waters outcast spirit about the whole SG enterprise that makes up a lot of its charm. In one of Bee's featured SG photo sets, entitled "Pancake," the waifish pixie goes all out in all her nude, nipple-studded glory, making a solo erotic mess in the kitchen with pancake batter. "That set shows that it's okay to like cooking pancakes naked and wanting to get down with them," Bee explains. "I have no problem with it!

"There's not many venues where one can get these things out," Bee says by way of explanation. "Like where can I go where I can take lots of erotic photos that depict the way I believe sexuality should be in my mind? To me personally, I want everyone to see it, and if they want to comment on it, that's *awesome*. I like to get any kind of my sexual fantasies or frustrations—or even perversions—out on film. Sharing is just about helping other people learn that it's not a problem, but in fact it's *okay* to like high-heeled shoes inside your mouth. It's okay to think that's *hot*."

Amazingly, suicidegirls.com is a unique junction. It's a place where the ideology behind Fugazi's cheap ticket prices and those who think sticking high-heeled shoes inside your mouth is hot can meet cute, reflected in SG's inexpensive monthly subscription fee. "I believe in those values where you don't jack up the prices just to make a buck," Bee says. "You make something affordable so almost everyone can experience it. Subscribing to suicidegirls.com costs just four bucks a month. Yeah, we need money to keep it up and going. But there's a point to where you're capitalizing on it."

However, since Missy Suicide—by then a veteran of music Web site operations from the likes of Ticketmaster—and her co-creator Sean launched suicidegirls.com in 2001, there's been quite a bit to capitalize on. According to the site's own numbers, SG's Web site is visited by 500,000 to 1 million unique viewers a week, resulting in 24 million pageviews per month.

The overwhelming majority of the SG audience cranking out those pageviews lies somewhere between the marketing demographer's preferred age group of eighteen-to-twenty-six-year-olds. As such, the company has done promotional collaborations with major record labels like Interscope, Island-Def Jam, and Capitol, punk labels like Vagrant, bands like the Dandy Warhols, and, of course, the Warped tour. There's already a SG DVD, a coffee table art/photo book, and a popular touring SG punk-burlesque revue, which has even toured as a support act for the likes of Courtney Love.

Indeed, the SG phenomenon has been embraced by numerous alternative and punk music notables like Dave Navarro and Nirvana drummer and chief Foo Fighter Dave Grohl, who hired a crew of SGs for the promo video for his heavy metal side project Probot. Warped Tour's fave hip-hop act Atmosphere wrote a tribute song entitled "Suicide Girls." In addition, many well-known underground musicians represent as SG fans, wearing the clothes or stickers in videos; some are even hired as celebrity photographers to shoot sets of their favorite Suicide Girls. "Dave Grohl was funny, really nice," Rae says. "I've met [AFI frontman] Davey Havok at a club. He was cool—he knows about suicidegirls. I actually met him at a suicidegirls event, actually."

It's no surprise that there are, er, warm relations between rock stars and the SGs, as many of the girls overlap into the music scene. "We're not just women who want to get naked and get paid for it," Bee explains. "I do fashion, and a lot of Suicide Girls have their bands." And, as SG tour-revue veteran Pearl points out in her page on the site, "Suicide Girls party like rock stars!" so if all else fails, they have that in common.

As such, Missy Suicide's empire is extending its lithe, inked arms into all areas of mainstream counterculture. A Suicide Girls photo book has been published. The Suicide Girls now have their own radio show on tastemaker Los Angeles radio station Indie 103.1. Epitaph honcho Brett Gurewitz has also embraced the SG mojo: his label has begun releasing Suicide Girl–branded DVD and audio projects. "I'm just a fan and wanted to do something with them," Gurewitz says. "I like punk chicks, so I especially like, you know, pictures of *naked* punk chicks."

Indeed, suicidegirls.com has reached a level of media hype saturation that may indicate it has peaked—although the phenomenon keeps growing, with one to three new SGs added daily along with many new members. Since SG has blown up, the Suicide Girl has become a cultural paradigm, an easily recognizable (and reproducible) subset of youth culture to both belong to and express one's individuality in. "Eight months ago, if someone found out I was a Suicide Girl, they'd be like, 'How can you respect yourself? How dare you?'," Bee says. "Now, it's become cool: that same person would be like, 'I accept that.' Now girls come up to be and are like, 'I want to be a suicide girl . . . *how?*' "

For many, SG is a new mode of identity through which members define themselves and meet other like-minded (and likely pierced and tattooed) souls. "It's like a little subculture already," Rae says. "You have members checking the site every day. You'd never think a Web site would do this: it defines who people are."

And it defines them on an international scale as well. Suicidegirls.com is now a global phenomenon, with model-members hailing from all corners of the Earth. "Oh my God, there's girls from everywhere—Taiwan, Singapore, Brazil, Japan, England," says Missy. "They come from all over the world, identifying closely with subgenres, but they're all who they are. They're not the outsider anymore; they just want to be accepted for being themselves, not just for looking weird and kooky."

Rae herself experienced how SG "exploded" recently. "A *lot* of people know about Suicide Girls," she says. "I'm a bartender, and people I don't know recognize me from the site, which is funny. I had an old man who was like, 'Are you from suicidegirls.com?' He was really shy—it was cute. He tipped me well, too."

Just as SG's left-field countercultural move has become coffee-table-bound, indeed an acceptable topic for water-cooler chatter, it also has spawned controversy in the neo-punk scene, where opinion on the SG experience typically pinballs between two extremes. "They're welcome in the punk scene as far as I'm concerned—I think those chicks are punk as fuck," says Bryan Kienlen of Bouncing Souls. "Think about it: punk should still be a place for everyone who lives outside society's regulations that wants to be there. It's not yours or my job to censor people or run this community home. Instead, make room for all types of people."

Others reflect how, in some viewpoints, what suicidegirls.com is doing remains taboo, even in punk's supposedly open-minded collective consciousness. "If may be mistaken, but Suicide Girls is 'punk porn,' right?"

says Dropkick Murphys' Matt Kelly. "Most of us are guilty of having viewed porn now and again, but I think it goes against some of the basic precepts that punk tends to hold. It objectifies women." And some have called out Suicide Girls for exploitation, even from among the SG ranks. Every exodus of SGs leads to rants by former Suicide Girls on message boards and on suicidegirls.com itself on how the site has sold out its ideals, and especially the girls who bare all as SG-branded models. (Rae, whom I interviewed for this book, is no longer a Suicide Girl, for example.) "A group of angry ex-models is bashing the SuicideGirls alt-porn empire, saying its embrace of the tattoo and nipple-ring set hides a world of exploitation and male domination. The women are spreading their allegations through the blogosphere, raising the hackles of the SuicideGirls company, which has until now enjoyed a reputation as porn even feminists can love," stated a September 28, 2005, wired.com article headlined "SuicideGirls Gone AWOL."

Elsewhere, SG-related items in alternative weeklies like the *Boston Phoenix* focused on the problematic fact that suicidegirls.com was co-founded and co-owned by a man, Sean Suhl, better known as "Spooky" to SG denizens. Articles by Kate Sullivan in the *LA Weekly* repeatedly take suicidegirls.com to task as well. In a piece from November 3, 2005, Sullivan chides SGs for "stripping for peanuts while SG's owners rake in the cash (just Google 'suicide girls' and 'exploitation' for details)." Had the "punk porn" backlash begun?

Art Versus Porn? The Great Neo-Punk Debate

" 'What's the difference between art and pornography?' It's one of my favorite questions," Missy Suicide groans sarcastically; she hates that people put what she does into the porn category. Indeed, while there is full frontal nudity on suicidegirls.com, some of it very silly, some of it including multiple partners, there is no actual penetration on display. But Suicide Girls acknowledges its legacy to mainstream adult entertainment in its official marketing manifesto: "In the same way *Playboy* magazine became a beacon and guide to the swinging bachelor of the 1960s, Suicide-Girls is at the forefront of a generation of young men and women whose ideals about sexuality do not conform with what the mainstream media is reporting."

For Missy Suicide, the most important distinction between what SG does and porn is that her SG army is educated in its choices: they can make all their own choices about how they look, how much skin they show, what they write, and who they fuck and when. Still, the porn tag—and subsequent taboo—still lingers; most SGs have come to accept it. "I've heard people say that Suicide Girls is straight-out porn," Rae says. "I know it's porn, but it's not, like, *hardcore*; it's punk erotica. It's a Web site full of different, strong women defining themselves and their personality through *their* photographs."

For others on the site, the whole "Is punk porn legit?" argument ultimately proves irrelevant. "There's a million kids looking at it, and I don't care if they're masturbating to it or actually looking at it as some kind of art," Bee claims. "The guy at the grocery store who puts my food in the bag might think I'm hot and masturbate to me, or vice versa, so what's the difference? It's the same process. It's about getting into that part of people's brains that's about *acceptance*."

"There's a classic argument in feminism, you know, are these women empowered, or are they victims of abuse?," Brett Gurewitz says. "On some level, there's probably a little of both in there; I don't think there's any black and white. But for some of them, I think it's empowering to just be naked, like, 'Hey, look at my body and what I'm gonna do with it.'"

There is a consequence to letting both your ideology and your genitalia hang out on the Internet, as various SGs have learned. "My mom wasn't angry about me doing suicidegirls.com, but I don't think she was thrilled about it," Bee says. "She was like, 'I don't want to hear about it, but it's great that you're doing it.'" "I would let my kids do suicidegirls," Rae says, "but I wouldn't let them get a tattoo until they're eighteen. I wouldn't want them to get mad at me when they're like nineteen. I would let them get piercings, though—my mom came with me to get my naval piercing, which was my first piercing other than my ears."

Mypunk.com: Communicating with the Community

There's an aspect of what Suicide Girls does that connects with punk's fanzine culture. Fanzines have been the lifeblood of punk's intercultural communication, from England's seminal 1977-era fan-driven publication *Sniffin' Glue* to trail-blazing U.S. titles like Bay Area–based *Maximum Rocknroll* and the late, lamented SoCal punk bible, *Flipside*. "*Maximum Rocknroll* and the political/cultural ethos that they put forth really dominated the Northern California punk scene," explained Lawrence Livermore, "while *MRR* and that ideology was considered almost kind of a joke in SoCal."

"So much is happening on so many different levels all over the world, doorways into this huge world still exist though zines like *Maximum*

Rocknroll, Profane Existence, Slug, and *Lettuce,*" says Bouncing Souls'
Bryan Kienlen. "These 'zines have been around as long as I have been hanging out, and they're still going. They've survived the ebb and flow of punk's
popularity because they're based on something more real, having been born
in an era before punk was just the latest style on MTV. 'Zine culture is still
here, but most people are only aware of what they're spoon-fed on TV."

Still, fanzines can tend toward the elitist and policing, especially old
warhorses like *Maximum Rocknroll,* which per policy will not cover any
punk music that is aimed in any way toward the mainstream. Some feel
that this has made this institution a little tired, straining vainly against the
inevitable pull of pop culture.

"Punk rock is also an anti-authoritarian culture, right?" queries Brett
Gurewitz. "But once you get people enforcing the rules of that culture,
then they kind of police themselves out of it, too, you know. *Maximum
Rocknroll* becomes to the punk police what the Offspring had become to
underground punk: they've edged themselves out of their unique spot. It
doesn't really matter in the end because they both have important parts in
the history of this culture—really what it is is a *popular cultural* movement, you know."

Fanzines, of course, have translated to the online world, with sites like
punknews.org proving to be the hub of like-minded punk aficionados internationally. And while suicidegirls.com gets all the publicity ink from
the adult portion of the Web site's content, Suicide claims that the majority of site visitors come for what she calls SG's "community" aspect: chat
rooms and discussion boards on any number of topics (from music to politics), news (which members help keep constantly updated), original site-
generated content (with interviews with everyone from Alkaline Trio to
Ewan McGregor through Woody Allen), and a dating interlink à la My-
space.com or Friendster—think "Punkster.com" and you're getting somewhere. As such, it's no surprise that suicidegirls.com and myspace.com
grew into Internet social phenomena around roughly the same time.

"A lot of the writers on suicidegirls.com have their own fanzines; it
kind of serves as a collective fanzine," Missy Suicide says. "It's like all the
aspects of a fanzine, and the members and girls put it together. People
write reviews and opinion pieces; people dedicate their journal to one
band, group, topic, or aspect of their life. People can be fanatical about
anything on SG and share it with the world; they know it's reaching an
appreciative audience."

It sounds a bit disingenuous, too good to be true, just as "I read *Playboy*
for the articles" always did. Still, SG's marketing numbers back up Suicide's
claims of the site's nonerotica appeal: "20 percent of traffic is the unique
pin-up photography, 80 percent is the dynamic growing community."

"When I got into Suicide Girls, it felt like a part of my life was finally complete," Bee claims. "Whenever I hang out with the other girls, even if I never met them before, we're all on the same page—like, 'Dude, where have you been all my life?' "

Much of this appeal comes down to the fact that all the members of suicidegirls.com have personal journals. "Some use it to be their own rock critic and review all the new CDs that come out on Tuesdays. People write poetry in them, about what's going on in their lives, their sexual exploits, their dogs," Missy Suicide explains. "There's also regional groups from every major city in the world, vegan and meat-eater groups, sexual deviants and cooking fans, along with every subgenre of music and culture conceivable. No one really mocks the other side; if you can find the group, you can find people you relate to. Everybody can be themselves and be appreciated—nobody's going to mock you for being too . . . *metal*."

"You go online and check everyone and everything out," Bee explains. "It's like going to a bar every Friday and getting to know each and every one of those people, but figuring them out first. I've discovered cool local bands on SG that I would never know about otherwise—and if they have a show coming up, I would go to their shows. That's what I like about Suicide Girls—it's great to have different opinions, and to hear them. You might learn something."

There's a political, countercultural component undercurrent to SG's entire presentation, even when it's not implicit. "We're very political, especially when the election was going on, although I wouldn't say we take one stance or the other," Bee says. "By keeping it completely open, it gets different points of view out." SG has also become a place for relations and issues between men and women to play out. "The girls are very open—they'll be writing about how they are on their period, like, 'I'm fuckin' bleeding right now,' " Bee says. "The men are very nice; sometimes they're weird, but if they are rude or mean, they're kicked off immediately. I have at least five or six fans who keep up with my life and e-mail me personally. There's a member called Sothers8—I don't know his real name, I've never seen a picture of him, I don't know how old he is. But if I'm having a bad day, he'll send me something to brighten me up, and it does. They're not looking at you to be perverted, but because they think you're beautiful."

Bee also claims that SG helped her "understand men more." "The kind of man who's not going to come up and talk to you, the shy man, they can hide behind their computer and say 'I think you're pretty,' " she says. "It helps them to be open about those kind of things. I can definitely say I wouldn't be with my boyfriend today if I didn't understand the men on the site."

In the Eye of the Beholder: Punk, Savior, Warrior, Madonna, Whore . . .

Suicide Girls came about on some level at a time when an interesting shift was going on in pop culture's ideal, or *ideals,* of beauty, sexuality, and power. Newer-generation performers like Brody Dalle, Peaches, and Karen O of the Yeah Yeah Yeahs along with more established names like Gwen Stefani, Courtney Love, and Garbage's Shirley Manson all began presenting more complicated personas of femininity in a pop context. These are sex symbols, yes, but strong women fitting no easy stereotype: the sex part may be easy on your eyes, yes, but it's surely on *their* terms.

These women represent a new kind of rock star, one that builds on the more dimensional, bohemian example of someone like New York's original punk goddess, Patti Smith. Smith is defiantly independent; she's claimed many times over the years how the icons that shaped her sexuality and influenced her as an artist often were male—edgy, gripping performers like Iggy Pop, Mick Jagger, and Jim Morrison, rock's androgyne agents provocateurs, or tragic poets like Rimbaud. But unlike early feminists who wore power suits, thinking that putting on the uniform would impart some of the power, Smith makes her appropriation of male sexual power her own. "To be that powerful in a sexual iconic way—it's used to be just male figures like Mick Jagger and Steven Tyler," says SG Bee. "Females can do that now and still be respected."

Indeed, Brody Dalle and others are part of music's uncompromising female legion for whom any talk of "women in rock" is most likely a snooze. Missy Suicide notes artists like Pixies/Breeders front woman Kim Deal and Sonic Youth's Kim Gordon as trail-blazers of unconventional, hard-to-pigeonhole women in rock, along with Siouxsie Sioux, the titular head of Siouxsie and the Banshees (and one of the original punks on the 1977 London scene). Over the years, Siouxsie has become a Goth icon due to her extremely innovative personal style and mystical persona; Karen O of the Yeah Yeah Yeahs definitely gets her Siouxsie on vocally, for sure. As well, someone like Courtney Love has made it her mission to do everything in her own eccentric style: her persona encompasses being a mother, a junkie, a rock star, a wife, and a lover all at once. These contradictions make up who Love is, so that they're no contradiction at all. "Siouxsie was definitely in the scene when most girls weren't allowed," Missy Suicide says. "Wendy O. Williams from the Plasmatics, Courtney Love—these are these great icons of punk rock, women that weren't ashamed of who they were, and that included every aspect of who they were."

"I think Penelope Houston with the Avengers was one of the greatest punk rock singers ever," says Lawrence Livermore. "And while maybe Blondie wasn't strictly punk, Deborah Harry had a totally punk attitude when it came to her vocals. The female or female-fronted bands that I like are ones where the woman or women involved don't seem to be stressing so much about gender identity issues, but are just themselves."

Brody Dalle recognizes how being stuck with female responsibility affects how she expresses herself; it becomes clear when she discusses her birth father, who abandoned her and her mother shortly after she was born. "He was just the sperm donor, you know," Dalle says. "Totally irresponsible, just spraying his sperm all over the world and creating these lives and then having nothing to do with them. I can't imagine doing that: I'm sorry, but it's not something that's intrinsically female. That's a male thing—women don't pop babies out after carrying them for nine months and then fuck off, you know."

According to Missy Suicide, artists like Brody Dalle and Courtney Love have "found a way to have all the aspects of their particular brand of femininity exist within one person." This is enhanced by the legacy of Yoko Ono that is placed on both Love and Dalle by the media—the idea that they are powerful enough to have destroyed the powerful men seen as their mentors. "They have all the contradictions and aspects of the female qualities—motherhood, the virgin/whore dichotomy," Missy Suicide explains. "They're savior, artist, and warrior all wrapped into one. Nobody says you have to stick to just one thing."

Dalle and Love have also created their own more individual ideal of beauty in opposition to that of the mainstream. "Brody and Courtney are not what you'd call the model of the skinny blonde," Suicide says. "That's a great thing—each person is different, so when you see them at least it doesn't make you feel bad if you don't look like the girls in *Vogue* magazine." The sexual appeal of Brody Dalle, in fact, stems from her embrace of who she is, not who someone else wants her to be. "I love the way her body looks—it looks *real!* When I first saw Brody, I was like, 'Oh, she's beautiful! She's got fucked-up makeup on, and she doesn't care if it gets everywhere!' " Rae says. "It's not about looking perfect, it's about looking how you feel. Sometimes how you feel is fucked up and pissed off."

A crucial icon to both Suicide Girls and punk's ideal of beauty is Bettie Page. Page was a pin-up icon of the 1950s who proved highly controversial: her sexuality was as blunt as her bangs and as oversized as her breasts, all of which proved threatening to stiff McCarthy-era America. More than anything, the appeal of Bettie Page rested on her realness; she was so fleshy, she threatened to ripple off the page. Page posed for early issues of *Playboy*, when that magazine was still somewhat dangerous, waging a war on conventional sexual mores of the time. But Page wasn't like *Playboy*'s typical girl-next-door subject. Even in images designed for male enjoyment, Page seemed in charge: if she was posing, the viewer suspected, it was for her enjoyment.

Bettie Page was in a way an underground Mae West: on a mission to open minds via her oversized sexuality, an image of empowerment despite a successful career as an ultimate object of heterosexual desire. Not surprisingly, Page has also served as the unwitting source model for any number of female underground-comic characters, as she served as a role model to a nation of alienated girls and boys in search of their sexuality.

"I was always the kid that never fit in, the kid people made fun of," Bee says. "I worshipped David Bowie and Cyndi Lauper. Every Friday I had Cyndi Lauper day where I'd wear what I want to—I even made a stupid papier-mâché tutu like the one she wore. I wore it to school, and unfortunately it happened to have rained that day, and it fell apart. It was quite embarrassing." Bee found herself in Bettie Page, however. "In high school, the first time I dyed my hair black and had bangs, people kept saying 'You look like Bettie Page,' " Bee explains. "I had no idea who Bettie Page was, so I went and got a book on her." Bee read it four times: "She was amazing to me—here was this woman that expressed herself when it was looked down on. Once she got arrested for indecent exposure. She told the policemen, 'I don't feel like I'm indecent—I shouldn't be arrested. I think I'm beautiful.' "

Missy Suicide sees Bettie Page's influence across all types. "One of the girls on the site, Bettina, is the biggest throwback to old-school pinup glamour ever," Suicide says, "but she's also very very much into the straight-edge scene. The politics of straight-edge you'd think are the antithesis to bombshell sexuality, so there's a lot of dichotomies there. But that's part of the fun of punk rock—that you can be so punk rock by not being so punk rock."

"Bettie Page got me started thinking about it," says Bee. "I realized a woman's body isn't indecent at all. The female body has developed so many associations: it's erotic, sexual, motherly—it can mean *creation*. A woman represents so many different things that men don't. Bettie Page was letting that out in sexuality even back then, and I felt it was necessary to carry it on."

All the elements of SG style, in fact, are laden with significance of some sort beyond the decorative. Like tattoos. "It's an art you bring with you everywhere," says Rae Suicide, who has skulls, colorful birds, and gorgeous Tim Burton–style line drawings adorning what part of her flesh isn't already pierced. "People wear jewelry; I wear tattoos. It's like a decorated art that's part of me. I try to express myself through my tattoos. Back in the day, women didn't have tattoos; they were just supposed to look pretty. With Suicide Girls and people like Brody—now it's like we have power."

"We should be photographed," adds Bee. "We have more art to look at on our bodies." Art that for Bee has to mean something significant: "I have my wrist tattooed with the words 'trust time' as a reminder I went through a really bad traumatic childhood. When I was nine, I wrote a poem about feeling unable to see the light at the end of the tunnel and wanting just to give up. I promised myself when I was old enough, I would get the words 'trust time' on my wrist so I could read them when I was going through something hard."

"My job is about shifting the ideal of beauty into realism and acceptance," Missy Suicide explains. "Beauty is something I feel very passionate about. People went to the extreme trying to be this blonde bombshell, silicone-enhanced, plastic surgery. It's still happening today: I think suicidegirls.com is the antithesis of TV 'reality' like *The Swan* and *Extreme Makeover*." For Suicide, that means includes accepting models on her site who don't fit what have become SG tropes. "There are Suicide Girls that have no piercings, no tattoos, that wear their natural hair color—and they're more punk rock than the girl with head-to-toe tats," she explains. "Through their stature, they come across as being punk, even without the visual cues."

Missy Suicide remembers the moment when the underground alternative culture she followed burst out of the cult and became youth culture lingua franca to everyone—even those who had shunned her previously. This was the moment when the SG phenomenon first became possible. "I remember distinctly in eighth grade, I had this outsider thing and all the preps wouldn't talk to me," Suicide recalls. "When I went into ninth grade, *Nevermind* came out, and it totally changed everything—and Green Day was a year or two later. Suddenly, it was cool to be punk rock or alternative, and all the prep girls that didn't want to give me the time of day before suddenly wanted to know what CDs I was listening to. Suddenly Billie Joe Armstrong is cute; there's no denying it. That was the changing point: not being accepted was how you claimed your identity—but suddenly you were accepted and had to evolve and change!"

Society seems to be evolving and changing, too, finding room in our conservative moment for the bohemian mores of the SGs. "People are more accepting little by little of the tattoos, the Mohawks, people looking different," Rae says. "I also dance [nude at strip clubs] and I'm the only one who looks like this at my work. Customers tell me, 'We like you because we're different—it's something we want to learn about.' People aren't as close-minded as they were. Being punk was taboo before, and while it's not accepted by everybody, it's cool to be punk now. It's going to be more and more like that."

Playboy's embrace of Suicide Girls seems like the ultimate proof that even shifting ideals of beauty are tilting toward greater mass acceptance of punk style—but is it to the point where little of genre's original "outsider thing" is present? "*Playboy* has always been about showing beautiful pictures of beautiful women—whether it's my particular aesthetic, there's no denying the women are beautiful," Suicide says. "Definitely *Playboy*'s early stuff influenced me—the Marilyn Monroe, the early pinup photos of girls on a bearskin rug. It's beautiful and sexy—there's something classy about it."

The Hardest Core

Not surprisingly, in the wake of the success of suicidegirls.com, more "punk porn" is being rushed to market. Just as *Hustler* upped the hardcore ante to stand apart from *Playboy*'s "tasteful" nudes, the new generation of punk-associated adult entertainers are offering up an even harder, dirtier, raunchier product than Suicide's pinups. Hilariously, one punk porn auteur has named himself "Eon McKai" as his directing pseudonym for raw romps like *Art-School Sluts*, an arch homage to father-of-all-straight-edge Ian MacKaye. Not all of the punk-porn *arrivistes* come packing the SG's message of female empowerment, either, but regardless, the point has been made: Internet porn is—you guessed it—the new punk.

Even though porn is an industry worth billions, sex and nudity still carry a transgressive kick that most neo-punk simply lacks these days. "Porn is more punk than most punk music," Joanna Angel, proprietress of the hardcore punk-porn Web site burningangel.com, told *The New York Times* in a May 2005 feature on punk porn.

Missy Suicide's not worried about the competition in her area of body-modified alternative eros. If anything, it shows there's a market for what she's doing. It also indicates unrest: that there's demand for such ideologically charged erotica shows that something is happening, that forces are mobilizing to shake up society and its dusty mores.

There's nowhere better to start than in the minefield of sex and gender. Ultimately, Missy Suicide sees that, despite advances, such sex and gender issues remain as complex and unresolved as ever in punk rock culture—and the culture at large. She's frustrated that it's still "unexpected in society today that a woman would be in control and in charge and doing what she wants to do"—like Brody, the Suicide Girls, and other femmes paving the way today for the Tsunami Bombs and Go Betty Gos of the future.

"Having the guys in the Distillers following Brody as leader plays into a kind of 'Red Sonja,' female Amazon warrior fantasy," Suicide explains. "As time progresses, the erotic part of that will taper away, as more and more women will do what they want to, and men will follow."

Suicide has faith that the egalitarian punk utopia of the future will happen. "Sometimes men will be in charge, but more and more bands will be fronted by women," Suicide explains. "More and more companies will have women CEOs. The stigma or oddity of women leading will disappear."

As well, punk porn just may be getting its closeup: it appears to be going "pop" just as punk music did. Joanna Angel is now a popular media figure, with her own (short-lived) column in *SPIN*. As these are times where a hardcore porn actor like Jenna Jameson can become a media superstar, have a bestselling book, and guest on *Oprah*, one can only imagine the possibilities. A Bettie Page biopic film, *The Notorious Bettie Page*, opened to some critical acclaim, strongish box office, and a healthy amount of media notoriety; as well, the film starred a conventional Hollywood starlet, Gretchen Mol, in the titular title role. This is that moment . . . a moment of deep confusion about just who owns what sexuality means in punk rock culture today.

Death Sex: Sexuality in Punk Rock

Part of the decadent thrill of blogging in general, and reading SGs' journals on suicidegirls.com, is its erotic-confessional aspect. "They're sexual creatures and they're not afraid to talk about their sexuality or sexual conquests," Missy Suicide says of her Web site charges. "Sex is fun and it's nothing to be ashamed of."

Except in the neo-punk community, of course. Sexuality in the neo-punk scene in no way resembles the twisted eros of the original punk scene, where the underground sex symbols were Malcolm McLaren's protégée Jordan. Jordan was an S&M nymphet who managed to be simultaneously androgynous, confrontational, subversively attractive, and hard to pin down as gay or straight. "That early punk rock had a lot of sexuality, especially if you look at someone like Jordan," Brett Gurewitz says. "The Sex Pistols talked about S&M on 'Submission,' and there's a dark sexuality to even the early groups like Throbbing Gristle. Meanwhile, early West Coast punk rock groups like Screamers and the Germs had this dangerous homosexual undercurrent. But then what ended up happening is the second wave of punk rock—the Adolescents and all that stuff—came in from the suburbs."

And along with them, suburban ideas about sex—the very kind the urbane McLaren was trying to shock out of the system with the Pistols' transgressive ethos (Sid Vicious was notorious for wearing a T-shirt featuring two well-hung cowboys jerking each other off). Ian MacKaye's straight-edge mantra of "don't drink, don't smoke, don't fuck" became a smokescreen for garden-variety, suburban-style emotional repression. Putting the straight-edge "X" on the hand often ended up taking the sex out of the neo-punk equation entirely. "I think maybe people need to lighten up a little about sex," says Bouncing Souls' Bryan Kienlen. "It seems backward for punk to be repressed and uptight about this subject."

For Gurewitz, punk rock's current state of sexlessness comes from its roots in the male psyche. "Rock and roll has a lot to do with sexuality," Gurewitz explains. "If you look at a typical punk-rock audience, it is mostly teenage boys. Punk rock, being a very extremely desperate form of music, maybe expresses the desperate sexuality of teenage boys."

As a result, Gurewitz says, current punk is all about sex—but expresses that in its absence. "Emo is all about sex, but it's more a '50s idea of it," he explains. "Maybe it's more like the '70s idea where you want to get laid but you can't, so the last thing you can ever do is say that you're interested in sex—like it has to be about your mantra or something. The fuckin' hate and pain and violence of straight-edge is about fear of sexuality, and the pain of celibacy. Let's face it, these kids' bodies are exploding with hormones." And along with the incendiary hormonal disturbance, they're also bringing in juvenile ideas of power about romantic relationships—especially in the punk rock subdivision that is emo. Keleefa Sanneh explores this topic in a March 16, 2006, essay in *The New York Times* entitled "The Glamour (Sigh, Whine) of Heartbreak." Sanneh writes that "in an influential essay called 'Emo: Where the Girls Aren't,' Jessica Hopper reduced the genre to its brutal archetype. 'Girls in emo songs today do not have names,' she wrote, adding, 'We leave bruises on boy-hearts but make no other mark.' She called the genre 'a high-stakes game of control—of "winning" or "losing" possession of the girl.'" That "high-stakes game of control" gets played out incessantly in emo anthems, as song titles like Fall Out Boy's "I Slept with Someone in Fall Out Boy, and All I Got Was This Stupid Song" make clear.

On the other hand, Gurewitz also notes that sexuality is "part of the Distillers' appeal for sure." As such, chances are that the nonfemale punk bands on Warped didn't have to endure comments like "We like it because Brody's hot," as says a *Stuff* magazine review of Distillers' *Coral Fang*; similarly typical is a *Razorcake* review of *Sing Sing Death House*, where the reviewer notes that Brody "happens to be one of the hottest girls in punk. I felt like a teenager in heat when I saw them live. I think I have a crush. Anyways, they actually sound great too."

Then again, Brody Dalle understands the power sex—and being a sex symbol—brings. "Baby, you make my heart beat faster," she scream-croons on *Coral Fang*'s "Beat Your Heart Out"; on the same album's "The Hunger," Dalle is thinking presumably about Josh Homme when she sings, "Holy eyes, I never knew I'd beg down at your feet . . . /Open sky, the wave of pain, the scent of you is bliss." But Dalle kills the whole sex conversation cold once and for all on "Death Sex." "I came so hard, I'd do it and do it again/Shoot your gun, baby, I come undone," she rasps on the "Death Sex" chorus. No, Brody Dalle and the Distillers are not your mother's emo.

Gender-Bending in Punk Rock: Glad to Be Gay? Or Is the Queen Dead?

From its earliest days, some aspect of punk rock's transgressive nature reflected an interest in alternative sexuality. In *Passion Is a Fashion: The Real Story of the Clash*, Clash guitarist Mick Jones recalls Morrissey (later of The Smiths) calling from Manchester about trying out to be the singer of the then-forming Clash (the more macho, hetero Joe Strummer ultimately got the gig). Jones didn't pay Morrissey any mind, alas: imagine the possibilities of a Morrissey-fronted Clash—it definitely wouldn't have been the Clash as we knew them!

For all we know, in fact, the Clash may have been better with Morrissey. Later in *Passion . . .* , Gilbert asks *London's Burning* writer Jon Savage about the particular allure of punk's latent early homoeroticism. "One of the things I liked about punk was that it wasn't like the old machismo and, obviously, being a gay bloke, I was not interested in that," Savage tells Gilbert. "I liked punk's sexuality, I liked the hopeless boys and dominating women . . . Johnny Rotten was quite an androgynous figure in a funny kind of way . . . he wasn't standard-issue sexuality. But then nor were the Clash in the early days. They were like hurt, scared boys and I find that a very attractive idea in rock 'n' roll."

Emo of late has made an industry out of "hurt, scared boys"; indeed, while '77-era U.K. punk outfits weren't afraid to wear their pro-gay politics on their sleeves in anthems like "Glad to Be Gay," Missy Suicide points out that there's a homoeroticism to neo-punk that those involved may not entirely be aware of. "Oh, definitely," Suicide asserts. "Frat-punks will take their shirt offs, bump into and jump on top of each other, grabbing and holding onto each other. The pit can be a very . . . *pagan* sort of ritual."

However, there are those in neo-punk who both understand homo-eroticism and accept it—even the kings of pop punk, Green Day. "I think

I've always been bisexual," Billie Joe Armstrong told the gay-themed magazine *The Advocate* in 1995. "I mean, it's something that I've always been interested in. I think everybody kind of fantasizes about the same sex. I think people are born bisexual, and it's just that our parents and society kind of veer us off into this feeling of, Oh, I can't. They say it's taboo. It's ingrained in our heads that it's bad, when it's not bad at all. It's a very beautiful thing."

When asked in *The Advocate* interview about whether he's acted on his bisexual desires, Armstrong admits "mostly it's been kept in my head . . . I've never really had a relationship with another man. But it is something that comes up as a struggle in me. It especially came up when I was about sixteen or seventeen. In high school, people think you have to be so macho. People get attacked just because someone insinuates something about their sexuality. I think that's gruesome."

Armstrong's commitment to alternative sexuality is no bandwagon-jumping: he had a beloved gay uncle who died of AIDS, and wrote one of *Dookie*'s most meaningful songs, "Coming Clean," concerning a gay teen's identity struggles. "I've gotten letters because I wrote 'Coming Clean' about coming out," Armstrong told *The Advocate*. Echoing sentiments that would come up later in "American Idiot's" talk of "faggot America," in 1995 Armstrong talked of the importance of touring with openly gay punk bands like Pansy Division in keeping the mind of the American punk open. "I think Pansy Division is the kind of band that saves people's lives," Armstrong says matter-of-factly. "They're catchy, and they're really educational. They're honest about their sexuality, and that saves lives."

Alternative sexuality is not limited to neo-punk's boys' club, either. "I'm sure Brody's had experience with a woman," Missy Suicide explains. "I don't know any girls under thirty that haven't had some sort of experience with a woman—and I don't think they identify as bisexual necessarily."

"There's a new paradigm of female sexuality: females who don't identify necessarily with being gay, or being straight, or being bisexual for that matter," Bee says. "It's neither dominant nor submissive—totally off gender. It's so far detached from mainstream beauty right now, and so am I."

There is a certain electric sexual charge in Brody Dalle's friendship with Peaches, the arch Sapphic art-punk rapper with a filthier mouth than 2 Live Crew's Luther Campbell. A joint interview cover story featuring both Dalle and Peaches in U.K. heavy-music magazine *Kerrang!* describes how "within five minutes [Peaches] has her face pressed into Brody's chest, enviously sighing that she wishes she had breasts like that."

"I liked the Peaches record when it came out," Brody laughs. "I was like, 'This is cool, this crazy chick with weird sex-rhyme shit.' We played shows with her and it was incredible. She was the right girl."

The Distillers' fans don't always necessarily fit the gender of sexuality stereotypes of neo-punk, either. The traditional male punk fan is definitely represented in the crowd at Distillers shows, but there's space for those usually oppressed, beat up, or just left on the fringes. One of the Distillers' biggest fans who travels to all their concerts is a cross-dressing boy with a fondness for hot-pink fishnets. At a 2004 concert for the Distillers' *Coral Fang* tour at Los Angeles's Henry Fonda Theater, I met a young "drag king"—a lesbian impersonating the look and style of a male—who insisted on being called "Wolfgang" and spoke in an exaggeratedly deep voice.

"It's about being fiercely independent, nonconformity, and being who you are and not apologizing for it," Missy Suicide says. "That message appeals to all types, especially those who are not easily compartmentalized. There are a lot of gay boys on suicidegirls.com for that reason. People are disenfranchised everywhere, be it sexuality or socioeconomically. Even the cheerleader that feels different can be accepted and find a place on suicidegirls, and find something in a Brody song, in the same way a transgender person or gay male or lesbian could. It's all inclusive."

The Great "Women in (Punk) Rock" Debate

Even as suicidegirls.com works inclusively to open minds, the great "women in (punk) rock debate" still lingers on in the parts of the neo-punk community that aren't so open-minded. "A lot of people say, 'Oh, it's a female singer?' They don't want to hear them sing," Rae says. "It's funny—it's kinda still like that, which is ridiculous. If a girl can sing, she can sing; if a girl can play drums, she can play drums."

Lawrence Livermore admits that his Lookout! label wasn't renowned initially for its gender-inclusiveness, chalking that up to punk's Darwinist market forces. "The Go-Gos were one of my favorite bands of all time, and one of my regrets with Lookout! was that I wasn't able to sign more female bands," he explains. "Still, I wasn't going to run some sort of affirmative action program just for the sake of evening up the numbers. Spitboy were an exciting band, but they kind of ran counter to my rule about not making an ideology of one's gender, which might be why they ended up making their album at a more 'p.c.' label than Lookout! Actually, some of the most negative reactions I saw were to the Donnas.

I think that might at least be in part because they kind of pandered to the dirty-old-men-in-raincoats types. The young punk rock kids took umbrage at that, and sometimes slagged off the Donnas for going after that kind of attention."

It's a conflict of feeling one way but knowing that it's wrong: as such, some in the male-dominated punk scene practice a sort of Dutch tolerance about female punks. "I don't think there's a question whether or not they should—of course they should be able to, and be welcome to do so," says Matt Kelly. "Some people are equal opportunity, some people prefer dudes on the mic. . . . I think it's a matter of taste and preference; I don't particularly dig female vocals in punk, but I have my exceptions. Bands like X, Klasse Kriminale, Deadline, NY Rel-X, the Violators, Siouxsie and the Banshees, and X-ray Spex are great."

The Distillers' first lineup was an estrogen-powered triple threat—a true oddity in the neo-punk world with three powerful female punks up front leading the band: Brody, bassist/vocalist Kim Chi, and spitfire guitarist Rose Casper. "Kim was just the best chick: she had a really nice voice, and her and Brody sang really well together," Tony Bevilacqua recalls. "I liked that stage of the Distillers the most. It was weird having the front lineup be all girls, you know—it was cool to see that. But every night the audience would yell shit. We don't hear that anymore from the crowd, though."

Other female-driven bands making an impact in the neo-punk world are Tsunami Bomb and Go Betty Go. "Agent M and Tsunami Bomb's impact is just starting now," Kevin Lyman says. "When they played Warped, the kids *flocked* to Go Betty Go. I think they're going to grow into women that have an influence." Lyman noted that Brody and the Distillers had a similar effect on Warped audiences—particularly the young women in the crowd starved for role models to identify with on Warped's stages. "Young girls were pulled to Brody à la Courtney or Gwen," Kevin Lyman recalls. "They were pulled to her when she used to walk out onstage. She got out in the crowd a lot, too."

There's hope for the future, however. Missy Suicide sees the Karen Os and Brody Dalles of the world as representing a new, more dimensional rock persona for women—one that doesn't conform to stereotypes, punk, rock, pop, or otherwise. "Brody and Karen O are the same kind of deal— totally creative," Suicide says. "They write amazing songs that just spoke to everybody, touching on these moments that you have no idea are universally applicable." Suicide wasn't surprised when she heard the Distillers cover Patti Smith's "Ask the Angels," either; she sees Brody as a like-hearted soul to Smith's punk-poet siren, on a similar search for transcendence. "Brody has a very bohemian Patti Smith vibe," Suicide says. "It's about taking the best parts of something and making it apply to life. I have angel wings tattooed on my back, but I'm in no way religious."

In the absence of options, the few females allowed to rise through the neo-punk scene are scavenged immediately as role models. Whether that's fair or not, Brody Dalle certainly fit the part. "She's a girl out there kicking ass, playing guitar and singing, do you know what I mean?" says Tony Bevilacqua. "The coolest thing about the Distillers for me is when I think about what the music means to the fans: they just get stoked that there's this girl out there like them doing this fucking crazy music. It's the feminine quality: there are always tons of little girls in the audience when we play. It's cool that some little girl out there in the middle of the country started to play guitar because of Brody. It's going to spawn something."

What feminism has spawned within punk and alternative culture is still a matter of some debate, however. "I came of age in Portland when Nirvana was just coming out," Missy Suicide recalls. "It was that riot grrl, Pacific Northwest, going-to-Bikini-Kill-shows-at-roller-rinks kind of thing. Those girls had a lot more 'fuck you' attitude, were a lot more independent, and even had a bit more power than the boys did in that sort of a scene, because women were proclaiming their independence so fiercely."

Not all under neo-punk's umbrella feel such a great debt to feminism—even those in all-female bands. "I'm not a fan of all-girl bands, even though I'm in one, but this is no gimmick," says Aixa Vilar of Go Betty Go in the band's official bio. "We don't fit into the stereotype of screaming, angry girls. And we're not feminists, either. We just want to be accepted on our own terms. We'll play to a Spanish rock crowd one night and a regular punk audience the next."

Brody Dalle is no stranger to feminism. "On my debating team, I was the only person on my side actually who was pro-choice, because I grew up in a very political family," Dalle recalls. "My mom was a very outspoken, politically motivated woman in society; feminism was like at the top of her list." Dalle, however, has been disappointed by the actions of those supposedly holding the feminist torch for her generation; as a result, she's just not sure if she wants to be linked solely to one perspective of looking at the world. "Bikini Kill started all these beliefs," Brody says, "but they are just catty bitches. We played together once at a festival. They watched my old band Sourpuss play our whole set, but in the two days I spent around them, not once did they come up and talk to me, or even comment on it. This was something I just could not even fathom; I was so disappointed. It wasn't about women really doing something different: it was about power and ego for those women—it was judgmental, and I'd already moved beyond that."

It's no shock that Brody and Go Betty Go's Aixa Vilar feel limited and conflicted by feminism as artists. They feel their world is bigger than feminism, even if they've taken the road the movement's trailblazers paved back in the 1970s (and earlier). "Feminism can be so limiting sometimes," Missy Suicide explains. "What's so admirable about Brody and Karen O is that they're trying to forward any movement—or capitalizing on one—to gain success. They're not doing it just to appeal to the feminists. They're artists and can be whoever they want to be; they don't have to fit into a category. There's so many varied aspects of being a woman, and as a feminist you can be empowered by different parts of that experience."

Representing those different parts are Brody Dalle's songs, which encompass issues affecting women without didacticism. In her hands, they're gender-specific but universal in their plain human drama. "Seneca Falls" is a powerful ode to women's suffrage, name-checking icons of female empowerment like Susan B. Anthony and Elizabeth Cady Stanton. "Gypsy Rose Lee" uses the woman allmovie.com calls America's "intellectual stripper" as a symbol in this warm-hearted coming-of-age anthem about two girls. In songs like "Young Girl" and "The Blackest Years," Brody uses a literary device, a recurring character named "Gertie Rouge." Dalle claims Gertie Rouge is a fictional persona who stands in to represent all the struggle and abuse, self-inflicted and otherwise, young women go through, from promiscuity to the pathological self-mutilation known as "cutting" that particularly afflicts young women.

Brody's lyrics about Gertie seem so vivid they could be autobiographical, but Dalle claims Gertie is based on a friend from Australia. Still, Dalle has claimed to have "cut" in the past to the media (as has Dalle buddy Shirley Manson). As a result, her lyrics connect with those who can tell they're coming from a real place. "My best friend, when she was in high school, she cut 'love' into her arm; it was for Courtney Love. I remember I made fun of her—I was like, 'What the fuck is your problem? Why do you want to mutilate yourself?'" says Suicide Girl Bee. "At that point, that's when I realized it wasn't a bad thing, because she wasn't an unstable person. She was reaching out to find what's real. The way she explained it, when she sees her body bleeding, then she knows she's real. I think it's more about understanding your own power, and how you can affect yourself completely."

Bee feels that Dalle's gender is the reason the Distillers' music proves more universal and passionate than most neo-punk. "The Distillers' music has more of an embrace of the human condition than your more generic punk band," Bee says. "and it's probably because the band is headed by a woman. Instinctually, women are concerned with the effect their work has more so than others."

Indeed, that Brody is seen as a survivor contributes to her charismatic appeal to both sexes. "People definitely identify with that," Tony Bevilacqua says. "When someone speaks from the heart and talking about personal issues, people always identify way more on that then anything else."

"I hope I can give something back," Dalle says. "Music was my salvation. If I hadn't discovered music, God forbid."

So, are you ready to be liberated?

9

Punk was not a musical genre; it was a moment in time that took shape as a language anticipating its own destruction . . .

—Greil Marcus, *Lipstick Traces:*
A Secret History of the Twentieth Century

Its pretty standard that all things, especially all things punk rock, come to an end.

—Matt Skiba, Alkaline Trio

Will punk ever die? Is punk dead? I believe it was the political philosopher Rousseau who said the state of nature was disrupted almost instantly the moment someone said "mine" and the idea of property came into existence. These questions of punk's health are like that. Ever since punk was called into existence, its death has been foretold. U.K. anarcho-crusty innovators Crass titled a song "Punk Is Dead" in 1978. Others thought punk died the moment they saw Good Charlotte on MTV. Before that, Green Day was the band that killed punk. From punk's birth, whoever felt entitled to an opinion said "mine."

In 2005, punk rock is everywhere. Even in those places where those in power don't want it to be. As an October 2004 Associated Press article on the Singapore punk scene noted, "Even in famously disciplinarian, squeaky-clean Singapore, underground punk rock is belting out its anti-establishment message." Singapore is famed for its censorious tendencies:

any method of public communication, be it music, television, radio, and the press, is tightly controlled by the state. Even here, punk has found its grass roots. The AP article goes on to quote Francis Leong, a.k.a. Francis Frightful, lead singer of Singapore-based punk band Opposition Party. "When I first became a fan of punk music," Frightful/Leong says, "there were only a handful of kids interested in it. Now there are thousands."

More like millions. Across the world, around the corner, or near the minefield. "In the war-torn areas of the world, such as the Middle East, Eastern Europe, Malaysia, Indonesia, and even places like China, punk's original values still exist and mean something," says Matt Kelly of the Dropkick Murphys. "These are places where the young are in constant danger, and being a punk or skinhead is grounds for a beating or jailtime. Those kids are living the shit."

All over America, meanwhile, punk scenes continue to marinate in suburban basements, backyards, garages, public parks—anywhere they can. A 2004 article in the *Boston Phoenix* by Camille Dodero describes the "basement rock" phenomenon:

> If legendary punk club CBGB had a baby brother, it might look something like the three-month-old basement venue Bloodstains Across Somerville. Spray painted phrases drip from every visible surface: CLASS WAR, warns an overhead air vent; CLEAN KIDS GET SICK AND DIE, prophesies a stairwell wall; SPEED KILLS, screams Styrofoam insulation, quoting a lyric from Agent Orange's 'Bloodstains,' an underground punk anthem that helped inspire the cellar's nickname. The room resembles an alley. . . . Feathers made sticky [when used as] props in a fetish film shot here recently—flutter in dark corners.
>
> Bloodstains is one of a handful of rental-house basements in the area that moonlight as live-music venues. Some of the rawest rock shows in town are performed in DIY places like this, beside dusty furnaces, cylindrical water heaters, and laundry hampers. They are accessible only through crawlspaces and creaky back doors . . . The best, most frenetic, in-your-face shows sometimes happen quite literally underground . . . in craggy, walled, cramped dingy cellars situated in cheap-rent districts . . . .

Most likely, there are ramshackle venues like Bloodstains Across Somerville in the town you live in, whether it's in Southern Illinois, Southeast Asia, or the Southern Hemisphere. Their proprietors—often either a collective of like-minded scene followers or a single, passionate fan turned under-the-radar club manager via a sheer obsession to hear music—know these are not ideal circumstances. "Few people really want to deal with these headaches," Dodero writes in the *Boston Phoenix* article. "It's just that they don't have many other options."

Not having options can sometimes be a good thing. For one, it means that if the people involved in hearing and making music are willing to do so anywhere and anyhow, there's a passion inherent that's crucial to any music culture's survival. This passion is resistant to market and mainstream trends—if anything, it's typically an indicator of trends that will crop up on, say, MTV long after its originators have moved on to something else.

In the United States, a lack of options mixed with a lot of punk ingenuity has produced some of the most genuine music and communities to come out since the genre's most vital moments in the 1970s and 1980s. The Gilman St. collective encompassing the East Bay comes to mind, as does the East Coast-based emo scene that produced bands like My Chemical Romance, Thursday, and Taking Back Sunday. Those East Coast bands bubbled on the outskirts of pop culture consciousness in veterans' halls and college basements. When they finally were ready to take on the mainstream—or not—they already had fans passionate enough about them to sing every word.

It's easy to understand why both authorities in Singapore and parents in America don't know what to do as the punk phenomenon grows with every year. Even in its most commercialized state, punk rock still retains a kernel of the rebellion that started the whole fuss in the first place. It's easy to forget in our age of disposable culture, but this is revolution music, remember? And the revolution just may be televised on MTV.

Remember the gateway drug analogy: if you start a kid on Blink-182, he or she might progress to (gasp!), the Clash, and Black Flag, and then Dead Kennedys, and then, most dangerous of all, the selected musical accomplishments of Steve Albini. Most likely, he or she may choose to stay in the comfort zone of the mall punk, with the familiarity of its Hot Topic clothes and MTV bands. But maybe, just maybe, punk rock will open the mind of this youth the way it opened mine.

Most of the kids I've encountered through punk rock are some of the most motivated and well-read I've ever met, with their own ideas about politics, aesthetics, and society. Even those with whom I disagree, or don't find compelling, there's a shared sensibility, a mutual desire to question the status quo. Are Pennywise meatheads? Yes, definitely. But I'd rather hang out with a politicized meathead who questions authority in a somewhat intelligent manner than one from a social group that unquestionably accepts blindly every tenet of the Establishment. Punk gives you the option of choosing just what kind of American idiot you want to be.

The neo-punk generation may discard this moment of rebellion over the years, just as the baby boomers of hippie yesteryear became the George W. Bushes of today; many will work for the Man, just like their parents, and undoubtedly become parents themselves. But I doubt they'll forget those sweaty afternoons at the Warped Tour. In many cases, they'll learn from the various ideas they've been exposed to and maintain a healthy skepticism, even if they've entered the corporate world and seemingly shunned their outer punk exterior. Hopefully, even as younger and younger generations outgrow their spiked hair and Green Day T-shirts, they'll take some of punk's egalitarian, questioning stance into their jobs as corporate leaders, politicians, mechanics, or whatever. Inevitably, there will be a President of the United States with embarrassing pictures of a wayward Mohawked youth.

When Joe Strummer sang, "Back in the garage with my bullshit detector" with the '77-era Clash, he was giving those with open ears and open minds a gift. A lot of people have garages, but only a few got the bullshit detector. Punk gave me *my* bullshit detector. It wasn't always accurate, but after punk It could generally tell if something had soul—if it had the suss.

Many Catholics joke about how it wasn't hard to stand out as a rebel in Catholic school. We live in such a conservative moment that something that seems even slightly real—that aspires to any concept of putting authenticity above all else—is rebellion enough, even if it happens to make itself known on MTV. And for so many kids (and adults) today, *Dookie* remains their *The Catcher in the Rye*.

In a moment that's so conservative, any voice of opposition is more discouraged than most, even if it's compromised. And punk rock has been compromised—even those involved in its day-to-day creation and maintenance know it's true. "The future of punk will not be too good . . . ," states Tsunami Bomb's Agent M. "I think it will become unpopular and maybe even disappear for a while before reemerging in some other form." Others in the scene, however, feel hope brewing in the new generations bubbling under. Lawrence Livermore finds that "there are still many punk rock record labels motivated primarily by love for the music as opposed to lust for commercial success."

Still, nobody can even agree on what punk *is*. Even today, punk holds many forms, all in dispute. I asked a great punk icon to be interviewed for this book, and he refused, claiming, "I don't think what I think is punk rock is what anyone else considers 'punk.'" A famous quote from artist Barbara Kruger comes to mind: for Kruger, there is not one feminism but "feminisms." And there are many "punkisms." That's why, most likely, Bad Religion singer Greg Graffin titled his landmark attempt to define punk in essay form "A Punk Manifesto" instead of "*The* Punk Manifesto." Everyone has their own version of what punk rock is to them: I've surely missed a few. There are too many bands, too many movements, too many subgenres (to this end, I've included a blank page at the end of the book for the reader to scrawl the names of any bands, individuals, albums, or scenes I may have inadvertently left out).

At this point in history, while there may be some very good books on the topic, there can be no complete, utterly definitive history of this genre. But there are themes that continue to resonate through every punk era— themes regarding maintaining integrity versus selling out, regarding appropriate musical and political stances, regarding even if having a female vocalist is "real" punk. More than anything, this book is about searching for the soul of punk rock after it cataclysmically evolved into big business— when the pop in pop punk actually meant "popular" and not just "catchy." When, after looking at the massive success of bands that *look and feel just like you*, being in MTV's idea of a punk band seems like a potentially more fun alternative to law school. Punk just might give you, as Green Day sings, the time of your life.

Punk is a great national treasure gone international, a distinctly American art form that has evolved into the world's loud, fast lingua franca. Behind jazz, blues, and rock and roll, punk rock is one of America's great contributions to culture everywhere. And if the Offsprings and Green Days and Good Charlottes stop existing, punk will do what it has always done before: go underground and find its edge. Punk remains a tabula rasa whose marking depends on who's holding the paper: on it, either the orthodoxy of the past or the innovation of the future will be written. "No one saw any of the musical explosions happening before they happened," says Tony Bevilacqua. "Things have been rehashed so much, it's weird. But something has to come out."

"Warning: Contents Under Pressure," indeed. In the great teen rebellion film *Over the Edge,* disaffected kids in a planned community lock their parents in the high school and try to burn it down when their precious recreation center is closed and a student (played by Matt Dillon in his acting debut) is shot by a cop. Punk is that now: those unwitting churches and rec centers used as venues are actually a release valve, sacred places for teenage expression, from hardcore rage to emo cry-on-your-shouler sensitivity. Those feelings will always find their way into poetic expression, even of the most mundane variety. The youth need a place to say what's on their mind, even if what they have to say isn't very interesting.

"We are all to some degree 'outcasts in the high school of society,' " says Bouncing Souls' Bryan Kienlen. "Punk can still be one place for people to feel at home to find themselves. One good result of all this 'punk expansion' was that many of these new people, once exposed to this scene, found their home and have since added something positive."

Maybe a future CEO will be a kinder, gentler one after being exposed to the more collective-oriented, yet still capitalist, efforts of punk entrepreneurs like Kevin Lyman, Brett Gurewitz, and Ian MacKaye. Maybe a young racist skinhead will have second thoughts about burning a cross in someone's yard after encountering different ideas and views in the mosh pit. Maybe a great band will come out of a basement or a garage clutching ragged, worn bullshit detectors and make us put someone new into the punk hall of fame alongside the Sex Pistols, the Ramones, and the Clash. Maybe it'll be Green Day, who may have already earned their spot. Maybe it'll be a ferocious new band like the Bronx, the one band who just might be tough enough to tame a major label. Indeed, the Bronx's 2006 major label debut (on Island/Def Jam) was produced by Michael Beinhorn, an industry veteran known for smoothing out the raw likes of Soul Asylum, Soundgarden, and Courtney Love in the studio—but it still sounds like the Bronx's trademark raw powerage, just times ten. "We are pushing ourselves to the limit so our limit can expand and grow," the Bronx's Matt Caughthran exclaims. "The new record will destroy you."

Maybe it won't be a band like the Bronx, or even a man, but a woman like Brody Dalle who saves punk. Or maybe it will actually be Brody, or someone inspired by her as a role model. Brody's example shows that punk means being whoever you want to be and staying true to her ideals. For Dalle, whatever kills her makes her stronger. Fans are inspired by her survivor persona—she's punk regardless of the sounds she chooses to make, or even if the punk scene turns against her. Maybe she's more punk *because* that punk scene turned against her.

As well, punk proves to be as mutable a creature as ever when it comes to survival. The latest pop punk success story, Fall Out Boy, hail—surprise, surprise!—yet again from the emo world. They have the entire package for saturation identification: a cute, motley crew of suburban misfits from John Hughes central casting, a cred-building spell toiling in the indie trenches, and witty song titles ("Our Lawyer Made Us Change the Name of This Song So We Wouldn't Get Sued," "Champagne for My Real Friends, Real Pain for My Sham Friends," an obscure reference to the film *The 25th Hour*) that elaborately mask the bald, earnest lyrical confessionals that make girls cry and boys ball their fists. As well, Fall Out Boy—named for a character from *The Simpsons*—archly comprehend their place in pop culture: another F.O.B. song is titled "A Little Less Sixteen Candles, A Little More 'Touch Me.'" Of late, other burgeoning factions in the pop-punk world are also artfully manipulating the nostalgia factor. With a great name that could've been a lost Smiths song, the Fall Out Boy–endorsed Panic! at The Disco are combining emo/pop-punk sensibilities with the retro-hip '80s electro-synth revivalism of bands like the Killers, the Faint, and the Postal Service. And from the U.K., Towers of London have been making waves with a Pistolian sound and show that deliberately mimics the rock and roll self-destruction wing of the 1977 generation (with a soupçon of smeared blood and Guns N' Roses' debauched glam added to crank it up a notch). Hey, to paraphrase Neil Young on Johnny Rotten, it's better to flame out brightly than it is to rust—even if it's canned heat.

Ah, the nostalgia for a future generation of misspent youth. . . . from my calculations, I predict the next wave of punk nostalgia will occur somewhere between 2020 and 2025. Only time will tell what challenge to culture will erupt next out of punk's incubator, and who will be leading the charge. Then again, life won't wait, either. "There are always gonna be new kids who live in squats or play in garages, which means punk rock will always be around," Rancid's Tim Armstrong told *Guitar World* in 1998. "As long as America is the way it is, punk is never gonna die. Kids are always going to be going through shit, and will be using guitars as vehicles to express how fucked up they feel."

"Music is freedom of expression," explains Greg Attonitoi of Bouncing Souls. "When you start classifying it into genres, it starts to lose the fun. Fuck punk, fuck rap, whatever—if it feels good to you, if it hits you and moves you, it's a *revolution!* Anybody with a laptop in their garage can now digitize their magic moment and make it available to all of us to download to our brains. It could be anybody."

"I think the best message you can deliver is that a kid in the front row could be onstage with a guitar in his hands five years from now," says Fall Out Boy's Pete Wentz.

Meet the new punk.

Chances are it looks a lot like . . . *you.*

BIBLIOGRAPHY

Books/Essays

Azerrad, Michael. *Our Band Could Be Your Life: Scenes from the American Indie Underground 1981–1991*. Boston: Back Bay, 2002.

Bangs, Lester. *Psychotic Reactions and Carburetor Dung: The Work of a Legendary Critic: Rock 'N' Roll as Literature and Literature as Rock 'N' Roll*. New York: Vintage, 1988.

Blush, Stephen. *American Hardcore: A Tribal History*. Los Angeles: Feral House, 2001.

Cuda, Heidi Siegmund, and Chris Gallipoli. *Warped Book: Tales of Freedom & Psychotic Ambition*. 4 Fini, 2002.

Dannen, Frederic. *Hit Men: Power Brokers and Fast Money Inside the Music Business*. New York: Vintage, 1991.

Gilbert, Pat. *Passion Is a Fashion: The Real Story of The Clash*. Cambridge: Da Capo Press, 2005.

Graffin, Greg. "A Punk Manifesto." www.badreligion.com, 1998.

Greenwald, Andy. *Nothing Feels Good: Punk Rock, Teenagers, and Emo*. New York: St. Martin's Griffin, 2003.

Hebdige, Dick. *Subculture: The Meaning of Style*. New York: Routledge, 1981.

Marcus, Greil. *In the Fascist Bathroom: Punk in Pop Music, 1977–1992*. Cambridge: Harvard University Press, 1999.

———. *Lipstick Traces: A Secret History of the 20th Century*. Cambridge: Harvard University Press, 1990.

McNeil, Legs, and Gillian McCain. *Please Kill Me: The Uncensored Oral History of Punk*. New York: Penguin, 1997.

Pierson, John. *Spike, Mike, Slackers, & Dykes: A Guided Tour Across a Decade of Independent Cinema*. New York: Miramax Books, 1997.

Savage, Jon. *England's Dreaming: Anarchy, Sex Pistols, Punk Rock and Beyond*. New York: St. Martin's Griffin, 2002.

Sinker, Daniel (editor). *We Owe You Nothing, Punk Planet: The Collected Interviews*. New York: Akashic Books, 2001.

Spitz, Marc, and Brendan Mullen. *We Got the Neutron Bomb: The Untold Story of L.A. Punk*. New York: Three Rivers Press, 2001.

Wolf, Naomi. *The Beauty Myth: How Images of Beauty Are Used Against Women*. New York: HarperPerennial, 2002.

Magazines/Publications

The Advocate
Alternative Press
Albuquerque Journal
Americore
Arikona Daily Star
Big Takeover
Billboard
Blender
Chord
City Pages
Creem
East Bay Express
Entertainment Weekly
The Face
Flagpole

Flipside
Guitar World
Interview
L.A. Weekly
Las Vegas Weekly
Last Rites
Matter
Maximum Rocknroll
Modern Fix
Mojo
Morning Call
New Music Monthly
The New Yorker
The New York Times
Playboy
Punk Planet
Razorcake
Rolling Stone
SF Weekly
Spin
The Stranger
Stuff
Threat
Under the Volcano
Ventura County Reporter
VIBE
While You Were Sleeping

Web sites

www.absolutepunk.net
www.allmusic.com
www.badreligion.com
www.burningangel.com
www.conservativepunk.com
www.downloadpunk.com
www.emotionalpunk.com
www.epitaph.com
www.fatwreck.com
www.greenday.com
www.lookoutrecords.com
www.maximumrocknroll.com
www.msopr.com
www.mtv.com

www.myspace.com
www.nme.com
www.pastepunk.com
www.pitchforkmedia.com
www.punkbands.com
www.punkhardcore.com
www.punkinformationdirectory.com
www.punklist.com
www.punkmagazine.com
www.punknetwork.com
www.punknews.org
www.punkrock.org
www.punkrockacademy.com
www.punkrocks.net
www.punkvoter.com
www.rebelwaltz.com
www.sideonedummy.com
www.smartpunk.com
www.suicidegirls.com
www.thedistillers.com
www.victoryrecords.com
www.warpedtour.com

Films

1991: The Year Punk Broke (1992)
Dance Craze (1981)
The Decline of Western Civilization (1981)
The Decline of Western Civilization Part III (1998)
The Epitaph Story (2003)

INDEX